Transformative Worship in Islam

Transformative Worship in Islam

EXPERIENCING PERFECTION

Shaykh Fadhlalla Haeri
with
Muna H. Bilgrami

Zahra Publications

Zahra Publications

First published in 2013 by Zahra Publications

Distributed & Republished in 2018
Publisher: Zahra Publications
www.sfhfoundation.com
www.zahrapublications.com

All rights reserved. Except for brief quotations in critical articles or reviews, no part of this book may be reproduced in any manner without prior written permission from Zahra Publications.

Copying and redistribution of this Book is strictly prohibited.

Designed and typeset in South Africa by Quintessence Publishing
Cover Design by Quintessence Publishing

Set in 11 point on 15 point, Palatino Linotype
Printed and bound by Lightning Source

ISBN (Printed Version); Paperback: 978-1-919826-7-69

Table of Contents

Book Description ix
About the Author xi
Acknowledgment xii
Preface xiii
Introduction xv

CHAPTER 1: Creation and its Direction 1
   1.1 Cycles of Life and the Arrow of Time 1
   1.2 Knowledge, Consciousness & Intelligence 5
   1.3 Rationality, Inspiration & Revelation 11
   1.4 States & Stages of Development 18
      The Purified Heart and the Light of Soul 19
   1.5 Oneness, Dualities & Universal Connectedness 23
   1.6 The Return to Origin – *Ma`ād* 29

CHAPTER 2: Roots & Foundations of Truth 33
   2.1 The Desire to Believe & Worship 33
      Prescriptions for the Spiritual Wayfarer 37
      Historical Evolvement 40
   2.2 Traditional Foundations of Faith 42
   2.3 Unity (*tawhīd*) 45
   2.4 Justice (`*adl*) 52
   2.5 Prophethood (*nubuwwah, imāmah & wilāyah*) 59
      Layers of Understanding Prophethood 59
      Imamate and Wilayah 61
      The Connection between Imamah and Wilayah 63
   2.6 The Return (*al-ma`ād*) 65
      Spiritual and Physical Resurrection 66

CHAPTER 3: Preliminary Keys to Effective Worship 77
3.1 Rituals, Intention, Attention & Appropriate Action 77
3.2 Ritual Purification (*taharah*) 80
3.3 Outer and Inner Ablution (*wudu'*) 82
    The Significance of wudu' 82
    Ritual Ablution According to Revealed Law 83
    Meanings of Ritual Ablution 84
    Higher Meanings of Ritual Ablution 86
    Additional Recommended Actions of Ritual Ablution .91
    Invalidations of Ritual Ablution 92
3.4 Ritual Bathing (*ghusl*) 94
3.5 Dry Ablution (*tayammum*) & the Meaning of Water 100
    Invalidations of Tayammum 101
    The Meaning of Water & Dust 102
3.6 Supplicatory Prayer (*du`a*) 109

CHAPTER 4: Traditional & Transformative Acts of Worship 119
4.1 The Branches of Faith or Acts of Worship 122
    Prescribed Behavior 125
4.2 Formal Prayer (*salāt*) 129
    Timings 132
    Preparations for Acts of Devotion and the Presence of the Heart 133
    Preface to Prayer and the Meaning of Various Acts ...114
    Obligatory Actions and Conditions 139
    Intention (*niyyah*) 141
    The Standing Position (*qiyām*) 143
    The Initial Takbīr (*takbīr al-ihrām*) 143
    Bowing from the waist (*ruku`*) 144
    The Prostration (*sajdah*) 146

Other Obligatory Actions 148
Further Obligatory Actions of Prayer 150
Additional Requirements 155
Disliked (makruh) Actions During Prayer 163
Meaning and States in Prayers 168
4.3 Fasting (*sawm*) 184
Fasting in History 184
The Islamic Fast 186
Meaning and Benefits of Fasting 190
Making Up or Expiation 191
The Feast of Fast-Breaking (`Id al-fitr) 203
4.4 The Pilgrimage (*hajj*) 205
The Pillars of the Pilgrimage 208
1. Al-Ihrām 207
2. The Walking Around the Ka`bah (tawāf) 208
3. Hastening between the Stations of
Pilgrimage (sa`y) 209
4. The Pause on `Arafah (wuqūf) 212
Other Obligatory Actions 214
The Lesser Pilgrimage or `Umrah & the Ka`bah 216
The Ka`bah 217
The Levels of the Pilgrimage 218
4.5 Obligatory Wealth Tax (*zakāt* and *khums*) 232
Basic Legal Foundation and Purpose 234
Types of Tax and their Significance 238
Khums 248
Those Deserving of Spiritual Donations 248
4.6 Striving in the Way of God (*jihād*) 255
4.7 Commanding Goodness & Forbidding Evil
(*amr bi'l-ma`rūf wa'n-nahi `an al-munkar*) 260

CHAPTER 5: Appropriate Conduct 265
   5.1 Islam & Reforming the Lower Self (self/soul dynamics) 265
      The Remedy for Grooming the Self 266
      Self-Knowledge and Its Refinement 268
   5.2 Transformation through Self Accountability & Reflection (vices & virtues) 273
   5.3 The Relationship between Mind, Brain & Conduct (emotions & rationality) 276
   5.4 Relationships 274
   5.5 The Necessity of Living Teachers & Guides to Realize Oneness 282

CHAPTER 6: Transformed Beings 285
   6.1 Return to the Beginning 285
   6.2 Maps & Boundaries & Life's Topography 289
   6.3 Transition to Infinite Boundlessness 291
   6.4 The Complete Person – Mulla Sadra's Journey 292
   6.5 No one but ONE 298

Conclusion 301
Glossary 309
Bibliography 319

Book Description

'*Transformative Worship in Islam – Experiencing Perfection*' uniquely bridges the traditional practices and beliefs, culture and language of Islam with the transformative spiritual states described by the Sufis and Gnostics. In this collection of teachings on how the worship of Islam can transform insight and perception of Reality, Shaykh Fadhlalla Haeri presents profound guidance for those who journey through the path of Islamic belief and practice. He draws from the Noble Qur'an, the Prophet's traditions, narrations from the *Ahl al-Bayt* and seminal works from Sufi masters and scholars.

Transformative Worship in Islam – Experiencing Perfection will inspire the serious seeker of spiritual knowledge to make the connections between intention, attention and direction. Describing in detail the stages of spiritual evolvement, the author highlights the need for grooming the self, refining its lower tendencies, practicing self-accountability, and guiding it towards the higher virtues of the soul, through the regular discipline of a worship which brings one into Divine Presence. The seeker will be taken to the stages of self-realization where all dualities meet and unify within the human soul. The purified heart is a precondition for this awakening, while enlightenment is the natural outcome after dispelling all causes of egotistic confusion and concern for personal survival. This book reveals how the soul is forever embedded in sustainable joy and contentment and awakening to this condition is not only our birth-right but the very purpose of our existence.

About the Author

Shaykh Fadhlalla Haeri is a spiritual philosopher and writer whose role as a teacher grew naturally out of his own quest for self-fulfillment. Since childhood he has been attracted to scientific investigation and intellectual pursuit. He was born in Karbala, Iraq, and is a descendant of several generations of well-known and revered spiritual leaders.

After a stint in industry and consulting, he embarked on teaching, writing and meditating.

His awareness of global realpolitik compelled him to seek a truth that would reconcile the past with the present, the East and West. His discovery affirms that One Cosmic Reality is the source behind all known and unknown states.

Shaykh Haeri's unifying perspective emphasizes practical, actionable knowledge of self-transformation. It provides a natural bridge between different approaches to spirituality, offering common ground of higher knowledge for various religions, sects and secular outlooks.

His main work has been to make traditional Islamic teachings more comprehensible and widely available to the modern seeker through courses and publications. Shaykh Fadhlalla Haeri is currently engaged in lecturing and writing books and commentaries on the Holy Qur'an and related subjects, with particular emphasis on ethics, self-development and gnosis (*'irfan*).

Acknowledgment

The author and co-author thank the sincere and invaluable help of Anjum Jaleel, Yaqub Moosa, Shafia Mohamed, Leyya Kalla and others who have facilitated this production.

Preface

As a child growing up in Karbala, Iraq, I often wondered about the practical and personal benefits of Islamic practices and rituals. I was taught that *salāt* (prayer), *sawm* (fasting) and other key practices help to bring about desirable personal habits, discipline and thus success in life. It was not until much later that I began to realize the transformative effects of practicing Islam as a *Dīn* – way of life. This understanding was mainly due to my exposure to the rich heritage of *'irfan* (gnosis or inner knowledge) from the school of Ahl al-Bayt and the great Sufi Masters of Asia, Africa, and elsewhere, from different schools of thought. Personal conduct and outlook on life will no doubt change when a sincere Muslim absorbs and lives the *Dīn*.

Islam is the pathway to the realization of Allah's perfect grace, dominance, presence, and control over the universe – seen and unseen. All states and manifestations, physical and the spiritual, what is in time and eternal, are all emanations from the original Single Divine Source and Essence – Allah. The *Dīn* is a life map that can take the committed seeker to the desired destiny through knowledge of reality and the experience of sacred presence – self-realization of eternal truth.

Our present time is dominated by rationalization, material power and ambitions to the detriment of inner health and spiritual delights. This state of global imbalance between outer wealth and lack of spiritual well-beingness may also be a driving force to rediscover the *Dīn* and prophetically prescribed practices. Personal illumination, understanding and wisdom are essential foundations for a healthy society and its stability and justice.

Originally gathered mostly from Arabic sources which have influenced and inspired me over several decades, this book is an attempt to share with the spiritual seeker (especially Muslims), the keys to inner transformation and awareness of the One God. The book may also be of interest to the general public interested in the wisdom of the prophetic teachings. Allah's light illumines the known and the unknown, the inner and the outer, and this life and the next. There is no light except His and He is the All-Encompassing Power and Truth. Light upon light.

Shaykh Fadhlalla Haeri
February 2013

Introduction

Life is a practice to understand how and why experiences come about in order for us to maintain wellbeing and happiness. Most religions present descriptions of earthly realities and provide prescriptions for human contentment and the stability of society. Sets of defined behavioral patterns, rituals and religious practices are hallmarks of most human cultures.

Islam provides details of numerous 'necessary' or obligatory practices and rituals for individuals and communities. The Qur'an and the Islamic way of life provide the spiritual path, maps and codes which may unlock the durable common purpose and meaning of life on earth. The Qur'an addresses numerous facets of existence, all encapsulated within the mysterious Divine Unity that encompasses all. The Makkan *āyāt* of the Qur'an are mostly to do with Truth, which is absolute and permeates the whole of creation. Many of the Madinan verses relate to community, society, relationships, justice and other important aspects of governance. The life of the Prophet (S[1]) exemplified the most complete and dynamic way of living in the moment without denial of the passage of time. For many centuries before the life of Muhammad (S) all true prophets had lived this appropriate way, according to their time and communities.

---

1   *Sallā Allāhu `alayhi wa-ālihi wa-sallam*: Allah's salutations and peace be upon him and his family. This invocation is implied every time the Prophet's name is mentioned.

All acts of worship begin with self-awareness and a desire for higher knowledge. The preparation for worship is the declaration of intent and the hope to be focused, attentive and engaged in the process of a deepening one's state of awareness. A point may arrive when the worshiper loses concerns with worldly mundane matters and begins to experience subtler levels of awareness which are deeper than the normal day to day variety. The ultimate purpose of worship and prayer is to experientially realize a state that is not subject to earthly or mental limitations. This may be variously identified as the sacred void, inner bliss, pure peace, or ultimate or higher consciousness. From ancient times, Shamans and priests led circles of people in attaining this 'transcendent' experience.

The metaphor of the heavenly creation of Adam and the subsequent descent to earth describes how the human being is made from elements of earth, water, fire and air, and is imbued with special knowledges through the sacred soul. The difference between Adam and other creations in the 'Heavens', such as angels, *jinns* and satans, was that Adam had the capacity and ability to exercise some independent will. This 'will' could either cause damage and destruction or speed up insights and enlightenment. The desire and love of worship is the enactment of the hope of transcending the limitations of the physical and material side of our make-up, and attain the metaphysical, boundless and timeless zone, which is where we can experience liberation from all mental limitation.

Human beings are the only creatures who have a full sense of awareness of their awareness. When you look in the mirror and see yourself, you know that the image is of your own self. It is thus natural for human beings to anthropomorphize God and in that way try to bring that idea of Divinity closer to us in form. All creative acts emanate and overflow from Allah, according to innate and subtle patterns. There is a great danger in reducing the mystery which pervades the universe and permeates it all into an entity or idea which we label as 'God'. Allah is not an entity. Allah is *The Reality* from which all realities emanate and by which they are sustained. It is safer and more appropriate to characterize this as sacred light, rather than a defined entity. Religious people can fall prey to the pitfall of personalizing God, as is evident in the phrase, 'God is most kind,' or, 'He is generous to me'. All energies, matter, Attributes and essences are simply shadows of this sacred light. Sweetness is not honey, but simply one attribute of honey.

Worship in Islam is based on the prophetic realization of the pervading unity of the original force and power in life (*tawhīd*). The prescribed acts of worship are part of a culture that grooms and brings up its children to develop outer and inner references regarding appropriate conduct. Islam acknowledges the forces of nature and prescribes appropriate ways to work along natural paths and patterns towards a higher level of spiritual realization. Islam does not deny personal identity or the quest for success and achievement, but rather it highlights the need to transcend whatever is experienced within the created dimensions of space and time so as to awaken into the zone of eternal presence – Allah. In Islam the *sajdah*, or prostration in prayer, symbolizes the act of annihilation of the self-identified individual into the original 'no-thingness', where only Truth, or Allah, is present.

Traditionally Muslims have emphasized fear of suffering or fear of the unknown in order to change the behavior of the seeker. Teachers adopted strict methods of upbringing and ādāb (courtesy and comportment) in order to influence behavior and mind-sets. The oral culture of the years gone by, the rural communities and their socio-economic and religious connections, were very helpful in reducing natural egotistic tendencies and deviations. In our present day, however, most educated young people can be more incentivized by the love for self-improvement and expanding awareness into higher levels of consciousness than by fear of punishment or eternal fire. The way of the Sufi gnostics was to give a taste (*dhawq*) of the inner joy to the new seeker in order for the individual to accept the need for personal discipline and restrictions and to focus upon the 'higher'. In this way they attuned the seeker's ability to glean insights from the heart, the locus of gnosis, and soul.

The culture and religion of Islam is founded on the Qur'an and the way of the Prophet (S). The Qur'an reveals that the essence of the foundation of creation is Allah's light (Verse of Light, 24:35). That light permeates whatever is known and unknown in the heavens and on the earth. Āyat ul-Kursi (Verse of the Throne, 2:255) which is very frequently recited by Muslims declares that it is Allah Who governs the universe, that His signs are evident throughout existence and whatever is in the heavens and earth belongs to that Reality. The Āyat ul-Kursi declares that whatever manifests in the universe is transient and dependent upon Allah – the Constant, Eternal, Ever-Present.

Just as acts of worship are prescribed in the Qur'an, human development is described by numerous verses, such as, 'O mankind, you are constantly struggling towards your Lord until you will come to meet [know] Him' [84:6]. Adamic consciousness has within it the seeds of supreme reality; thus we cannot stop until that is realized.

INTRODUCTION

Transformative worship begins with sincere hope and trust and ends in realizing that in truth the whole universe is in adoration and worship of its sustaining original Light. The fully realized being knows that in truth there is none other than the One and everything else is a shadow of that truth.

All human endeavors that increase knowledge, ability, efficiency and wholesomeness imply a journey towards higher consciousness. Life begins with basic sentiency and ends with spontaneous awareness of awareness. The arrow of time moves from the 'no-thingness' towards the absolute Oneness. Worship can be regarded as an evolutionary spiritual exercise to transcend the mind and come into unison with the divine soul within. Ultimate liberation and enlightenment implies taking constant reference from the immutable soul. In a sacred tradition Allah declares that, 'The Heavens and Earth do not contain Me but the heart of he who believes contains Me.' Every heart contains a soul and the potential to realize that truth is open to all.

This book attempts to bridge the traditional cultures and language of theologians with the transformative spiritual states described by the Sufis. In a way these two voices are, in essence, complementary. One relates to the basic foundation of prophetic practices and Islam for everyone. The other voice emphasizes the spiritual states and transformational purpose of outer practices and disciplines. This voice appeals to all human beings interested in higher consciousness, or spiritual awakening and enlightenment.

As my intention is to give the modern reader ease of access to spiritual development along the path of Islam, I have chosen to minimize or avoid certain traditional or technical terms as far as possible and substitute them with ones that feel lighter and easier to the contemporary reader, so that the focus is on one of ontology rather than morphology, on meaning rather than linguistic form. Specifically, terms like 'basic', 'intermediate' and 'advanced', or variations thereof, have been preferred, so as to reflect the increase in depth from outer form to deeper meaning when looking at foundational beliefs and practices of worship prescribed by Islam. Traditionally, these levels would have been most commonly categorized respectively as *shari`ah, tariqah* and *haqiqah* (cf. Chapter 1, 1.2 for detailed explanation). In this way I hope to give pliancy to these categories, for they reflect different stages in knowing. It is, after all, the light of these states and stations which we hope to share.

While such tools of division are useful to distinguish and denote different stages in awareness, implicit within them is the temptation to see them as a linear progression. While no doubt our progression from childhood to youth to adult is chronological in our understanding, and the growth in our layers of awareness is tied to that process, all are in fact part of a multi-dimensional whole. There is as much lateral movement as vertical and, indeed, at other subtler planes of cognizance, insight, and gnosis. Without the outer, the inner finds no means of expression, and without the inner, the outer can become a mere shell – often used against the path of awakening to higher consciousness, rather than to facilitate it. In the pursuit of higher, transformational knowledge, it is wise to see these tools of identification for what they are, and not as the thing itself.

Excessive categorization and labeling may also induce complacency or self-congratulation about 'attainment' along life's journey. If the goal is to live a life of transformative worship, then none of these 'levels' can

INTRODUCTION

be considered separately or neglected. They are merely indicators of a spectrum. No two people go through exactly the same duration of time or intensity in any spiritual path.

I prefer to bring forth the seamlessness of the *zāhir* (outer, manifest) in relation to the *bātin* (inner, hidden). In truth they are always connected. For the purpose of didactic teaching such categorizations or labeling are helpful. My interest, however, is in the transformative impact, particularly for the mature and advanced practitioner who is less concerned about distinction and differentiation and is entering the zone of personal experience which transcends all of these barriers.

A few words are in order about some of the terms used in this book. The term 'emanation' implies that the origin is non-discernible, unseen, pure energy, coming into more discernible energy and form. 'Evolvement' is the same as evolution, i.e. a growth process involving change in response to time and circumstance.

In the Qur'an the word *nafs* is used to indicate the lower self, the high self or soul or heart, or the entire being; it is the full verse that makes clear which particular aspect of the human being is being addressed. This is why the Qur'an can be confusing for the uninitiated, particularly when read only in translation. The following two verses are good examples: 'And the Self (*wa nafsin*) and how He made it, and inspired it to know] its…' – here it is talking about *insān*, how mankind has been made, with lower and higher aspects; another e.g. is 'And We created you from one soul (*nafsin wahidatin*)'. To distinguish the lower self from the higher, I use 'soul' or 'spirit'. The human reality is that of a soul or spirit which is inseparable from the cosmic Soul, or God, and gives rise to connectedness to the world of matter, through mind, brain and senses. The 'self' is that individuation of the soul deriving its life from it, but having particular qualities and characteristics which are changing and evolving all the time.

Generally speaking the first third of a person's growth and development is when the lower self, or the ego, is shaped and given its own character. In the second third the individual begins to question their authenticity, independence, seeking their origin and the light which is the soul. In the last third, generally, the *nafs* and all the layers of ego and personality begin to be discarded and the reference to the soul, or living by it, starts to become dominant. So the movement is from creating an entity to shedding everything in a conscious return to its original cause and reality. A helpful metaphor for this is light understood as either a particle or a wave. Light is, of course, both wave and particle. The photon is a 'personality' and dies. The wave never dies. When the two combine you get the full spectrum of the human being – from the lowest end nothing other than decadence and disruption, yet at the higher end noble and divine. The full being contains the interplay between the human and divine. The emphasis is different that an ordinary human being sees through the lens of *insān*, through humanity, the fully evolved, or enlightened being looks at everything through the lens of oneness. In Imam `Ali's words, 'I did not see anything unless I saw Allah before it, in it and after it.'

Qur'anic extracts are introduced by the (sun) symbol while quotations (*hadith* or otherwise) are introduced with the ~ symbol. Other than in a few places references have not been given but a bibliography is supplied.

The material in this book is a natural extension of original Islam. It also does not elaborate on the intricate details of practice and application; that is left to the

INTRODUCTION

specialized books on *fiqh*, jurisprudence, according to the different schools of thought. The hope and intention of this work is to benefit all practicing Muslims (and other seekers) by raising their level of consciousness. That is the real purpose of all human endeavors, struggles and aspirations.

CHAPTER I

Creation and its Direction

1.1 Cycles of Life and the Arrow of Time

The beginning of creation is a mystery, described in the Qur'an as originating in a sacred command: '*Kun*' or 'Be' [2:117, 3:47]. From utter unity and apparent nothingness, an explosive cosmic expansion and diversity came about. Countless stars and galaxies vibrate, circulate and orbit in an extraordinary dynamic and interactive way. A similar, amazing, invisible world exists within the atoms. Early on in creation splitting and dispersion was the dominant force in bringing about our known and unknown universe to us. The Qur'an describes the beginning as well as the end of time and the collapse of the universe back to its original nothingness with signs and allegories. Solid mountains will move like clouds and return to dust and all of creation will discover the truth of absolute Oneness.

The most constant force that drives human beings is to explore, discover and understand the multiple levels of connections in the world around us, and the origin and end of things and life. We now know that matter and energy are totally linked and that whatever we consider as solid matter is a temporary freeze of some energy, which will be released in time. Light is composed of photons which are particles flowing as waves; so is the rest of the universe. Stars, galaxies and creations have qualitative and quantitative Attributes and, are thus defined entities. Each also has a beginning and an end. In the case of humans, we are also composed of physical matter and other forms of energy such as the electromagnetic waves that drive our muscles, as well as neurons, and a mysterious entity called soul or spirit, which we consider to be the source of personal, individuated life. Thus we are both heavenly and earthly – made up of matter and light.

Life on earth started a few hundred million years ago when chemicals and molecules in tidal pools interacted in a special fashion due to the incessant energy given to them by light and heat. Early original life was simple in form and function. Early complexity appears as reproduction, growth and then other specializations occur. Then multitudes of realities appear as opposites as well as complementarities, such as gender pairs. Matter is accompanied by anti-matter as well as dark matter. Bright stars have their total opposite in black holes and so on. Light and consciousness seem to have a very special relationship. Visible light constitutes a very small portion of the electromagnetic wave spectrum. Normal consciousness also seems to be only part of a much wider spectrum of consciousness, which includes sleep, dreams, the sub-conscious, and many other subtler states like intuition and other psychic phenomena.

In creation we observe countless dualities, pluralities and complementarities, all of which seem to be moving in time towards finality. Within this mysterious movement of time, from the beginning (such as the Big Bang, or God's command of 'Be') to the end of the universe, there are countless beginnings and endings. Each entity has a destiny and in the case of humans we can influence our destiny by will, within limitations that pertain to time and space.

1. CREATION AND ITS DIRECTION

The arrow of time seems to begin from nothingness moving towards a very complex expanding universe, with infinite interlinked creations and finite realties. For human beings there is a clear arc of consciousness or an arrow of time that we experience which begins with conception in the womb, moves to a new stage of consciousness after birth, and continues to rise until the brain is fully developed and the healthy mind fully functional (between the ages of 30-40). For a physicist, in theory, time can be reversed. But in actual experience we know that today is the product of yesterday and will only give rise to tomorrow and not the reverse. Also, we know that whatever is born is also on its way to its end or death. Entropy increases and, therefore, from an experiential point of view, there is no reversal of time.

The human drive to acquire knowledge and understanding results in ever-increasing degrees of complexity in both individual and social behavior. Human knowledge and collective understanding have been accelerating during the past few centuries and especially during the past few decades. We are now reaching a point where knowledge is potentially available to all human beings.

Islam addresses our material, mental and spiritual needs at all levels – personal or communal. Islam's path is based on the fundamental realization that truth, higher consciousness, or the 'Absolute,' permeates all the universes and realities, seen and unseen, and that the direction of the life-force in human beings is towards experiencing and realizing the mysterious grace of Sacred Presence. If there is a purpose in life it is to know that life is eternal and intrinsically utterly perfect, irrespective of short term human perception. The prophetic revelations emphasize the need for human beings to accept responsibility for intentions and actions and to willfully desire higher levels of consciousness and insight, i.e. knowledge of God. All acts of worship and religious prescriptions are intended to reduce the veils and background noise in the human psyche or ego, so that the innate light within the heart (soul) shines and elevates the individual to God consciousness without denial of earthly limitations.

1. CREATION AND ITS DIRECTION

1.2 Knowledge, Consciousness & Intelligence

There is a natural, innate human drive towards a metaphysical understanding, knowledge of, and experience of a reality that is beyond rational and mental limitation, that is, God or Allah. Archaeological discoveries of earliest burial sites indicate a deep primal force within the human soul that drives us towards a higher level of consciousness or transcendence. Some of these burial sites are over 100,000 years old and contain stone pillars representing focal points for ritual worship. The rational mind and the material world seem insufficient to contain the natural human drive to 'know all'. Furthermore, we seek a certainty that is not subject to changes in space or time.

Islam is God-centric and is based on descriptions of Allah as pervading the fabric of the universe – He 'is closer to you than your jugular vein,' [50:16] and, 'Wherever you turn there is the face of Allah' [2:115]. The ultimate challenge in life is to realize this spiritual fact. People will experience various stages of this mystery. Real personal development of this knowledge relates directly to sincerity, trust and certainty of this truth. The result is conscious awareness of Allah at all times and circumstances.

Knowledge affects us in two ways. One is practical, factual, empirical and rational, what the sound mind accepts and uses, e.g. if you go out in the rain without protection you will get wet. The other is metaphysical, subtler, interactive, intuitive, spiritual and transformative – e.g. your relationship with other people improves if you are kind and compassionate towards them. We human beings are like 'living mirrors' which absorb and reflect some of the information or impact made upon them.

Human consciousness has two levels or spheres of awareness:
- the personal, local or conditioned consciousness.
- the boundless, pure consciousness that enables us to go beyond the limitations of local awareness.

The 'fall' of Adam from paradise can be regarded as the force that propels his offspring to seek eternal perfection through higher consciousness. The Qur'an's description of human life as a gift, or 'loaned trust' implies a pure consciousness that is boundless and eternal, a sacred realization or presence.

Like others before them, Muslims have tried to chart the layers, different levels and subtleties of knowledge and conscious awareness. Various terms and descriptions have been used by Muslim scholars and realized Masters to indicate the stations and degrees which people have attained in this knowledge. Terms like *shari`ah*, *tariqah* and *haqiqah* will be familiar to readers who have sought higher knowledge through the path of Islam.

One important description states that *shari`ah* is the name applied to a divinely revealed system of laws consisting of basic tenets, or roots or foundations (*usūl*) and their various branches of knowledge (*furu`*); and that *tariqah* consists of adhering to them in a careful and consistent manner; while *haqiqah* is the confirmation of the ultimate Truth behind existence by way of illumination and witnessing, or through attaining certain spiritual states.[2]

In this classical paradigm, the 'people of *shari`ah*' (those who abide by the revealed laws) are those who have attained a degree of knowledge in Islamic jurisprudence

---

2   Sayyid Haydar al`Amuli (d. 1385 CE / 719 AH), *Asrār alSharī`ah wa Atwār alTarīqah wa Anwār alHaqīqah* (The Secrets of the *Shari`ah*, the Stages of *Tariqah* and the Illuminations of *Haqiqah*).

1. CREATION AND ITS DIRECTION

(*fiqh*) as represented by the *faqih* and others of that caliber. The 'people of *tariqah*' (those on a defined path) are those who possess knowledge and wisdom, represented by the `ālim (scholar) and the *hakim* (judge). The 'people of *haqiqah*' (those seeking the ultimate truth) possess an inner knowledge based upon their own witnessing, represented by the enlightened Master (`ārif).

~ The *shari`ah* is a river and *haqiqah* a sea: thus the *faqih* makes his way through the river and the *hakim* dives into the sea for pearls, but the `ārif moves along [the sea] aboard the ship of salvation. ~ Imam `Ali

In this same vein the Prophet is reported to have said:

~ The *shari`ah* is my words, *tariqah* my actions, and *haqiqah* my state. Understanding is my capital, reason (`aql) the basis of my way of life (*dīn*), and love my foundation; longing is my mount, fear my companion, and knowledge my weapon; forbearance is my master, trust in Allah my helper, and contentment my treasure; truthfulness is my stopping place, certainty my shelter, poverty my pride, and by it I am honored over all Prophets and Messengers.

Other triadic descriptive terms have often been used to describe the reality of different levels of people's knowledge of Allah, such as:

- ◈ the Common People (*al-`ām*) – this term refers to the general class of believers who adhere to the *shari`ah* of Islam and whose understanding of the Islamic way of life is centered around it;
- ◈ the Elect (*al-khās*) – these are the learned men (*al`ulamā'*), the men of wisdom (*alhukamā'*), and the

ones with the knowledge which enables them to make legal decisions;

- ◈ the Chosen Few of the Elect (*khās al-khawās*) refers to those who possess a deeper knowledge, i.e. the Master (`ārif*) or gnostic who has awakened to the all-encompassing Divine Unity and knowledge.

Using this same approach when looking at the act of worship known as prayer, it has been said that prayer (*salāt*) as prescribed by the *shari`ah* consists of:

- ◈ service – i.e. serving yourself by lessening your ego;
- ◈ nearness – i.e. nearer by being less caught in dualities;
- ◈ and the reunion of lovers – Truth is ONE.

Regarding foundational beliefs, yet another Master[3] had divided the stages of the knowledge of the unity or Oneness of Allah (*tawhīd*) into three divisions:

- ◈ Unity of the Common People;
- ◈ Unity of the Elect;
- ◈ Unity of the Chosen Few among the Elect.

Ibn `Ajiba wrote that the lights of *shari`ah* lead to the rulings of outer conduct, which then guide the lights of *tariqah*, which are the rulings of inner conduct. And the lights of *tariqah* lead to the lights of *haqiqah*, which illumine the entire universe.

By way of cautioning the reader, as stated in the introduction, the use of certain terms or categorizations

---

3   Khwajah `Abdullah Ansari (d. 1088 CE / 481 AH), author of the books: *Tafsīr alQur'ān alMajīd* (Commentary of the Qur'an) and *Manāzil alSā›irīn* (Stations of the Wayfarers).

1. CREATION AND ITS DIRECTION

have been minimized, as the intention is to give the contemporary Muslim easy access to spiritual development along the path of Islam. As far as possible I have substituted them with ones that are more user-friendly and hope, thereby, to mitigate excessive structure and avoid the pitfall of complacency and vanity about 'progress' on the path. Specifically, when looking at foundational beliefs and practices of worship prescribed by Islam terms like 'basic', 'intermediate' and 'advanced', or variations thereof, are used to reflect the increase in depth from outer form to deeper meaning. Progress is in the sense of journeying, and this can be as much lateral as vertical, or indeed, multidimensional. None of these 'levels' can be taken separately or neglected if one seeks to become transformed through one's worship. These categories merely indicate a spectrum of consciousness, for no two people experience anything exactly the same in any spiritual path.

Human beings are driven to higher consciousness by prayer, meditation and a host of creative pursuits such as the arts, music and other transcendental activities, reflecting our yearning to return to a blissful state of contented happiness – paradise. It is ultimately supreme consciousness that we all desire, here and now. The objective is not prayers or rituals per se, but a sustained state of well-being and happiness.

Human perception and experience begins with rudimentary self-awareness. The baby looks at her hands and wonders about the movement of her arm. Self-awareness develops into egotistical identities and the illusion of individuality and separation from creation. Nature has programmed us to care for personal survival as a foundation to subsequent evolvement and growth. Consciousness begins with conception and birth and grows into wider and deeper levels of awareness until maturity, at which time intelligent people begin to question the purpose, meaning of life and subsequent experiences like death and the hereafter. The arc of consciousness leads to higher levels and what religious and spiritual people call transcendence. While there are countless levels of consciousness, such as non-REM sleep and REM sleep, states of hypnosis, transcendence implies a radical shift into another zone which is the essence and root of life. In religion it is called God-consciousness, or *taqwa*, and in Islam the emphasis on attaining this is through *dhikr*, remembrance and awareness of this primary and ultimate light within us, the source of self-awareness. The purpose of life, therefore, is to be in constant reference to this Supreme Consciousness which enables us to put into perspective all other changing states that we experience in life. Self-realization or enlightenment implies this natural awakening.

1. CREATION AND ITS DIRECTION

1.3 Rationality, Inspiration & Revelation

Islam regards the physical world as only a part of the vastness of reality, the greater portion of which is unseen. Life is based on the two zones of the 'rational/causal' and the 'Unseen' and they are seamlessly connected. The evolution and development of life proceeds from the material, visible, and tangible, towards the subtler zones of feelings, emotions, intuitions, insights and the vast domain of the Unseen. Revelation refers to what 'descends' from the Unseen towards the more discernible human understanding. It therefore gives greater clarity to the direction and purpose of movement and change in life, from the physical to the metaphysical, from the personal to the universal, and from the short duration of life on earth to the infinite domain of life itself.

It is said that reasoning (`aql) will never be guided except by the *shari`ah* and that the *shari`ah* will never be clearly understood except by reasoning. The verbal root of `aql means to comprehend, envelop and contain. `Aql is the faculty by which we are able to exercise reason and analysis and its related intellectual disciplines. The *shari`ah* and reasoning need each other in the same way as the soul and the body need each other. The *shari`ah* may be thought of as a building with reasoning as its foundation: one is useless without the other.

It is also said that reasoning is like eyesight and that the *shari`ah* is like 'beams of light'. Eyesight is useless unless it comes into contact with these external beams. Likewise, these beams are useless if they cannot be utilized to give sight. One of the interpretations of Allah's words '...light upon light...' [24:35] is that they refer to the light of the *shari`ah* upon the light of reasoning, because reasoning will not be illuminated except by the light of the *shari`ah*. If a speck of dust of this world falls upon the pupil of a man's eye his vision will be marred. What clarity can there then be if one is attached to the entire world and therefore be veiled by it?

The traveler upon this path who possesses reasoning will be guided by it to adhere to *shari`ah* and thereby progress towards realization of truth. This can only be achieved by harnessing the natural physical and spiritual forces within so as to experience transformation.

Reasoning and rationality show us causal connections. Yet there are also situations which are counter-intuitive that do not follow the norm of reasoning, e.g. emotions and feelings, or the 'sixth sense', and insight supersede basic reasoning in our behavior. Beyond the mind's limitation there is a subtler causality. For example, prayer (*salāt*) is considered to be the most important of the acts of worship and yet the Prophetic teaching rules that a woman does not have to make up the prayers missed during her menstrual cycle, whereas she is required to make-up her missed fasts and this would seem to imply that fasting was more important!

Human beings may be considered as the people of the 'middle way'. One of the meanings of 'middle' is the half-way point between the visible and material realm on the one hand, and the metaphysical unseen realm on the other. Potentially we contain the essence of these two domains. The journey in this life is about realizing the connectedness between:

- ❖ the relative and the absolute
- ❖ conditioned/personal life and boundless/eternal life
- ❖ humanity and divinity

1. CREATION AND ITS DIRECTION

The evolvement and development of human life involves personal will and effort to experience the relationship between personal limitation and the vastness of what the soul contains – a reflection of God's light. All acts of worship are to facilitate this unification.

Revelation differs from inspiration. True inspirations are reflections of the Prophetic revelations. Those who follow in the footsteps of the Prophets and seek insights and inward inspirations must maintain outward precaution and acceptance of the revealed laws of Islam. The world of the unseen opens up to those who live in harmony with the material and unseen world. This can happen when the primal and natural codes are adhered to – that is, the *Dīn*.

The word *wahy*, translated as 'revelation', literally means 'a writing, a mission, an inspiration, or words which are hidden and which originate from other than man himself'. Used as a verb, *waha* means 'to reveal to someone', or 'to show, indicate or speak to someone by utterances which are hidden from others'. The word *ilhām*, which we translate as 'inspiration,' has the tri-literal Arabic root of *lahima*, meaning 'to swallow or devour something'. The fourth form of the verb, which is the corresponding verbal form of the verbal noun, *ilhām*, carries the meaning that something is placed within the heart (soul or spirit) of man by Allah. The means used for conveying an inspiration or *ilhām* is an angelic force which brings spiritual knowledge and what is praiseworthy for the soul, without the interference of lower desires.

Inspiration must be distinguished from what is traditionally understood to be the 'whispering' of negative thoughts. In Arabic *waswās* refers to thoughts, ideas or concepts which confuse the heart, causing misfortune, grief or other negative effects. This whispering is the root of false notions and fears, including baseless fears regarding ill health, poverty, or the fear of imagined disasters. Whispering is considered to be a satanic voice that is able to afflict the self due to inattentiveness or distraction.

The way inspirations and other illuminations which spring from them (during sleep or when most relaxed, or during prayers) become manifest are subtle and often not very clear. Occasionally inspirations do occur during waking consciousness when, due to Allah's grace, wonders from the realm of the unseen illuminate the heart like a sudden flash of lightning.

Revelation differs from inspiration, in the strength of its clarity and the fact that the means of transmission (the angelic medium) is also witnessed.

> ✧ It is not for any human being that God should address him except through inspiration (*wahy*) or from behind a veil or by way of a Messenger whom He sends. [42:51]

The point here is that knowledge and insight come upon the heart in various ways, by way of revelation and inspiration, by way of signs, Messengers and teachers. Revelation, in particular, is transmitted by the angels, or 'angelic' agency. The source of higher consciousness is the universal governance that emanates from supreme consciousness and the way higher consciousness reaches us is through different streams or packages with varying intensities. Revelation is of the highest; intuition, inspiration and insights are of lower degrees.

It is related from the Imams that revelations were received by Messengers (*rusūl*) while in a waking state and that the remainder of the Prophets (*anbiya'*) received them while asleep.

1. CREATION AND ITS DIRECTION

The direct and inward receiving of knowledge without the existence of any external agent is due to the capacity of man's soul to perceive the nature of phenomena, as well as its original root and essence of phenomena. This essence is usually veiled due to man's lack of preparation to accept these illuminations and knowledge.

When this veil becomes thin or is lifted altogether insight becomes clear. In Arabic, this insight is referred to as *basirah*. It is by means of this inner vision that the soul witnesses what is inscribed upon the 'Preserved' or 'Well-guarded Tablet' [85:22]. The ease by which the veil is lifted is proportionate to the degree of the soul's readiness and its submission, the purity of the heart, and the evolvement of intellectual reason.

Some religious scholars and theologians may be primarily concerned with acquiring formal information and knowledge without due regard for the states of the heart, for eliminating reprehensible qualities, or for grooming the self by replacing vices with virtues. Throughout the history of Islam we generally detect clear differences in divine knowledge between the religious scholar and the spiritual Master. Scholars and theologians are generally most concerned with the application of religious injunctions and laws. The seekers of gnosis, on the other hand, are concerned with severing attachments to creation in order to gain insights and subtle knowledges relating to the soul and Allah's lights. This is the path of liberation and enlightenment which ignited the hearts of the early Muslims and the Sufis.

The balanced approach to acquiring knowledge is through the study of and the struggle against the self, as well as the purification of the heart. The seeker will take from the Master and follow in the footsteps of the Prophets and the people of gnosis and realization. It is related in a divinely revealed tradition (*hadith qudsi*) from the Prophet (S) that Allah said:

> ~ My servant does not draw near to Me with anything more beloved than by way of the obligations which I have ordained for him. He may draw near to Me with additional actions (*nawāfil*) if I love him. If I love him I become his hearing by which he hears and the sight by which he sees. I become the tongue by which he speaks and his hand with which he grasps. If he asks Me in prayer I will answer him, and if he beseeches Me I will grant it to him.

The state of the spiritual Master is described as:

> ~ His body is within creation and his heart is with Allah. If his heart should become distracted from Allah for one instant it would perish because of its longing for Him. The Master (`ārif*) is the guardian of Allah's Trust, the treasure-house of His Secrets, the mine of His Light, the guide to His Mercy over His creation, the storehouse of His Knowledge, and the scales of His Abundance and Justice. The *ārif* has become annihilated from the creation, from desire, and from the world and has no companion but Allah, no speech, no signs of indications, no self except in Allah, for Allah, from Allah, with Allah. ~ Imam Ja`far alSadiq[4]

There are two verses in the Qur'an which, on the face of it, seem to describe the Prophets differently. One says: 'And We do not differentiate between them' [2:136], meaning that their inner state and knowledge of the sacred

---

4 *Misbāh al-Sharī`ah*, 'The Lantern of the Path'.

1. CREATION AND ITS DIRECTION

domain is the same (i.e. they have all awakened to the prevailing truth). However, another verse tells us: 'Some of them we have favored over others' [17:55], implying that their impact on the society and culture at the time in which they appear differs in extent and durability. Some of them produced radical changes in their people, others were much less well known and their outer impact was minimal. The extent of laws and regulations given to them also differs. The true message is always the same however: creation is an emanation from an eternal light that permeates the entire creation and to which it ultimately returns. The purpose of human spiritual growth and development is to enable humanity to realize its root of divinity. Prophets and Messengers were people who experienced that unity, and revealed it in their times. They were wholesome and modest human beings imbued with divine qualities, heavenly beings on earth.

1.4 States & Stages of Development

The evolvement of human consciousness resembles the growth of a seed into a mature plant with the fruit as its final product. The ultimate fruit of human life is the realization of Allah's utter and perfect presence and universal dominance. All created entities undergo cycles in their growth and development, and this is true of mankind not only in biological growth but also in emotional and spiritual dimensions. Sincere, diligent and conscious practice leads to the transformation that is the goal of the *Dīn* of Islam.

The original meaning and purpose in life is engrained within the human soul and is enacted through the dual nature of human consciousness. Biological evolution and the love of survival and growth is the foundation upon which spiritual evolution takes place. First the ego develops, and then it has to surrender to the soul which is its source and essence. The limited, conditioned consciousness of the lower self can naturally lead to higher consciousness and enlightenment. Our mind is the connecting point between the inner and the outer world, enabling us to maintain a balanced life.

Every sentient creature on earth grows and evolves towards a higher state of consciousness or self-awareness. Although life on earth seems to have evolved in a random fashion, the directionality of the desire for the highest possible state of consciousness is clear in more evolved animals – especially man.

The soul within the heart draws its power directly from the Omnipresent. For outer direction we take counsel from others, and for the inner direction we simply need to turn to the heart and the sacred light therein. All actions and all desirable Attributes have their essence in Allah and – they

1. CREATION AND ITS DIRECTION

belong to God and emanate from Him. That original sacred light is the beacon towards which everything is directed.

Terms like god-consciousness, soul consciousness, or self-realization, all indicate states or situations more evolved than that of ego consciousness and its limitation to issues of survival, personal identity, and dominance.

The Purified Heart and the Light of Soul

The physical heart is a major organ of the human body. The metaphorical heart is where the soul inhabits and emits its life force. It is this heart that is often referred to as the most important factor in spiritual progress. There can be numerous diseases of this heart, which range from being sick, jealous, mean or tarnished, to being attached and numerous other ailments. The metaphorical or inner-heart needs to be purified so that the connection between the earthly world and the sacred soul within this heart becomes clear.

Generally, it is easier to reign in the ego and the lower self through improved behavior, and accountability, through tutelage of mind and conduct. However, to purify the heart and render it wholesome, the inner heart requires different disciplines and tutelage than mind and conduct. The human love for meditation, peace or even monastic life, are signs that we want to purify the heart from all outer tarnishes. A purified heart has no lust, anger or attachments within it; therefore the light of God will shine through it. The ultimate test is the willingness to give away whatever one loves to keep.

When the heart is pure the soul will bring about the realization that life is ever-perfect and is forever. The truly awakened heart has no concern about personal death, for it knows that the soul is eternal. Respect for life on earth can be genuine and real due to the realization of the sacredness of the soul within the heart. Through reverence of the soul, we also tolerate or respect other aspects of human life.

It is the wholesome heart that enables us to pick up signals from the unseen, past, present, or future, and endows us with intuitive, spontaneous insights. The purified heart allows the light of the soul to shine through whatever Allah wills, in His infinite generosity.

The glow or energy of a purified heart, freed from the shadows and veils of 'otherness', is called 'presence'. Much has been written about polishing the heart and cleansing off the tarnish that prevents it from reflecting the Light of Allah. Beyond the ritually prescribed acts, practices like meditation and invocation, or *dhikr*, have been practiced in varying forms so as to strengthen this process.

The purpose of verbal confirmation by invocation and remembrance (*dhikr*) is to awaken the heart. As one repeats with the tongue, gradually the heart will 'take over' and the meaning of what is invoked takes over one's consciousness. Likewise, the remembrance of Allah in the heart will, in turn, spur the tongue on to *dhikr*. Thus the outer aids the inner and the inner enhances the outer.

A high degree of pure consciousness may be attained during deep meditation and when the heart is in a state of complete stillness and the mind, thoughtless. Enlightened Masters have categorized four levels or stations of worshippers:

- *The first group*: They understand the manner of performing the physical / mechanical aspects of prayer, and they may even understand the meanings of the words they utter. The inner state, as far as they are concerned, is to pay attention (i.e. have presence of mind) during the actual recitations

1. CREATION AND ITS DIRECTION

and to conceptualize them in their heart while they are actually in prayer. This group equates the inner truths with the traditional meanings only.

- *The second group*: They understand the inner truths and meanings of the various forms of acts of devotion and remembrance, both intellectually and conceptually. They know that everything which is praiseworthy is attributable only to Allah. Presence of the Heart for them is when their hearts are focused on the remembrance of these qualities or Attributes.
- *The third group*: They perceive these truths conceptually and intellectually and realize them within their own hearts. They have realized a deep and profound knowledge of these truths. There is a great difference between the degree of faith one attains in the heart and the mere perception of it by reasoning. Often man has an intellectual understanding of something, which is confirmed by empirical evidence, yet his belief in it has not reached or affected his heart.
- *The fourth group*: They have combined these truths and experience them within their heart and thus have reached the station of serenity and contentment – a wholesome realization of truth. They now know that acts of devotion resonate within the heart, making clear the foundation of unity (*tawhīd*).

The great metaphysician, Sadr alDīn alShirazi, otherwise known as Mulla Sadra, divides men according to the levels of discipline of the self (*nafs*)[5]:

---

5   *Al-Asfār al-Arba`ah* (The Four Journeys), d.ca 1637 CE / 1050 AH.

- *The first division*: Those who discipline themselves outwardly by way of the revealed laws, the *shari`ah*, and by performing the night prayers, fasting, giving alms in charity, making sacrifices, observing religious celebrations and various congregational activities, and so forth.
- *The second division*: Those who discipline the heart and purify it of impurities.
- *The third division*: Those whose state absorbs divine Attributes and who unify with them.
- *The fourth division*: Those whose self has vanished and whose very being has been annihilated, whose wandering has finished and whose sights are fixed only on the light of Allah and nothing else.

1. CREATION AND ITS DIRECTION

1.5 Oneness, Dualities & Universal Connectedness

To Allah belongs whatever is in the heavens and earth. He is the Source, the Cause, the Sustainer and the Governor. All creations exist within the confines of space and time and are fashioned according to intricate patterns which trace their future destiny. Allah is not definable, measurable or tangible, yet His Attributes and qualities are most desired by all of creation. He witnesses everything known and unknown. He is the Creator and Sustainer of everything. Thus our senses are derived from His Attributes. He is above all, within all and after all, and His signs are there wherever you turn. Allah is the One, Unique, incomparable Reality from which all transient, contingent realities derive their power and characteristics.

The path to understanding the Truth and the Real begins by admittance of personal inadequacy, needs and reliance on the source of mercy and generosity – Allah. Through love of Allah's Attributes and qualities the process of evolvement of consciousness begins. When we shift our focus and attention from the tangible, discernible world to the subtle world of essence, a personal bridge is established between the soul and the self. Our consciousness will link what is conditioned and limited (self), with pure consciousness (soul). Practicing Muslims punctuate their prayers by declaring *'Allahu Akbar'* – Allah is greater than any description. From the unseen, we experience the seen. These two realms are seamlessly connected and emanate from Allah.

The lights emerging from the One Essence spread out throughout the universe to reveal countless qualities and multiple shadows, forms and shapes. There is a wide range of hardness and softness in the tangible world. The same variations can be seen in all other matters of senses and feelings. Creation appears in pairs and symmetries that show different degrees of opposite qualities as well as complementarities.

It is a constant human quest to discover the roots, origin and the relationships between these diversities and dualities. We also look for causalities and correlation in the endeavor of reaching a conclusion that is secure and holds true. In the outer world, there is no permanent stability as everything is naturally subject to change in time and space. What is a poison for a certain condition is a cure for another, and what is desirable now can be despised later. The children of Adam have to battle on earth under the shadows of the tree of discord and dispersion. Only by transcendence do we start on the desirable journey of ascendance back to the sacred realm of true security – the sacred light within the heart.

Most worldly quests are like chasing after a mirage that only appears to be water, but cannot quench thirst. It disappears only to reappear in another illusion. Those who follow a religious or spiritual path, with demarcated outer boundaries and limitations, and practice constant reflection and self-correction are struggling to transcend the confusions of lower consciousness so as to attain the delights of higher consciousness and Oneness.

From this source of absolute gatheredness, separation began with the emanation of movement and energy and then patterns emerged, all of which generated the archetypes of all that exists in creation. Further down this arc of creation, energy, matter and form interlinked. At yet a further stage in this process, separation took place when the opposites in creation, such as day and night, hot and

1. CREATION AND ITS DIRECTION

cold, and wet and dry, became clearly distinguishable one from the other. The fabric of our experience is woven from inner and outer aspects, from gatheredness and separation, from the heavenly and the earthly, from meaning and form. These patterns exist in dynamic tension with each other and every other dimension, seen and unseen in existence.

As we know, every human being is biologically different from another, although there is a common genetic connection going back through time. Even in our personal experiences, deep down, we can all discern a shared sense of sameness in what matters most in our lives. Our form or color may differ but we all unite in our desire for contentment and happiness. We are the ultimate example of how difference, or separation, meets in sameness or gatheredness.

With regard to the outer world, then, we are compelled to connect with and relate to the thread of unity that permeates all existence. At the very instant that separation occurs (i.e. the cosmic Big Bang or human inception), what comes into being is the seeking of its gatheredness or original unity. The source of our desire for gatheredness is the soul within us, which replicates the original primal gatheredness and unity. The self, which is shadow to the light of the soul, drifts away to experience separation, insecurity, restlessness and all the opposite qualities beamed out from the soul, such as tranquility, contentment, joy and bliss. The shadow/self imagines that by acquiring wealth and worldly reputation, for example, it may increase its status and honor. The self imagines this because the acquisition of wealth and reputation is a small reflection of what the soul already has, which is being totally honored and loved by its Creator. The self in its waywardness spends a lifetime trying to imitate the soul by striving to acquire fame, wealth, knowledge, security, and so on, with a modicum of success that is always short-lived and never ultimately satisfying. When and if the self truly surrenders to the soul, it realizes the folly of its years of being the prodigal child. It sees that while people may reject us, our soul or our Creator never does.

We return to the divinely revealed tradition already mentioned:

> ~ My servant does not draw near to Me with anything more beloved than by way of the obligations which I have ordained for him. He may draw near to Me with additional actions (*nawāfil*) if I love him. If I love him I become his hearing by which he hears and the sight by which he sees. I become the tongue by which he speaks and his hand with which he grasps. If he asks Me in prayer I will answer him, and if he beseeches Me I will grant it to him.

The language of distance is metaphorical, for Allah is not subject to place or time, for He pervades the universe and beyond – *Allahu Akbar*. If the decree of *tawhīd* or unity prevails, the being far or being near is merely a function of the individual's perceptual framework, the state of which is itself modulated by the degree of higher consciousness. Since, however, our experience of life is moderated by patterns of duality along a spectrum of extremes, the idea of being close or far can be helpful in distinguishing levels of awareness.

Drawing 'near' to Allah is always preceded by withdrawal from all else. Preeminent among the things which one turns to other than Allah is the self itself and its various spheres of influence, which are:

1. CREATION AND ITS DIRECTION

1. The sphere of the senses, that is, the connection with the material realm of nature.
2. The sphere of emotions and the realms of allegory and symbolism.
3. The sphere of reason and intellect's true essence; this realm is void of matter and form.

The serious worshipper, in his prostration, passes by these three spheres as he withdraws from this world and enters into a sacred state beyond the mind:

> ✲ And remember the name of your Lord and devote yourself to Him completely. [73:8]

When Imam Ja`far alSadiq was asked which was the best action that enhances awareness of Allah, he replied:

> ~ I know of nothing after gnostic knowledge (ma`rifah) which is better than salāt. Have you not seen that the righteous servant (of Allah), `Isa bin Maryam, said (in the Qur'an): "He charged me with prayer and almsgiving as long as I remain alive." [19:31]

Being with people, serving them, and putting up with their difficulties is balanced by the act of withdrawal, seclusion, and reflection. Prophet Muhammad (S) regularly spent time in the cave called Hira outside Makkah for several days at a time. It was at the culmination of such periods that revelation occurred. The Qur'an describes the 40 days Moses spent in seeking his Lord, before he was given the 'tablets'. The tradition of 40 days of seclusion (khalwah or chillah, from chehel, forty in Persian) was taken by Sufi Masters to be a rite of passage, a serious emptying out (khalwah derives from khāliya, to empty out) – 'And when you are free [of worldly concerns] ...then turn your desire to your Lord' [94:7-8].

Smaller periods of time are also practiced regularly. The smallest period is ultimately symbolized by the *salāt* which punctuates the day five times, giving us the chance to reconnect in awareness with the underlying reality that grounds our existence. This is useful until a time comes when the fourth journey which Mulla Sadra noted (for further elucidation cf. Chapter 6, 6.4), becomes established, that is, when you are with people but your inner state prevails. What is frowned upon is being extreme in anything and in this case, being monastic is not prescribed. Islam advocates the middle way.

Islam is founded upon experiential *tawhīd*. The whole universe has emanated from one source and appears in infinite levels and layers of dualities, diversities, complementarities, competitions, cooperation and other forces. All these dualities reflect an aspect of a higher attribute which includes the names of Allah. With spiritual progress we realize that all actions emanate from the One essential source of all energies – Allah. All Attributes, ideas, and qualities also emanate from Allah's qualities. The ultimate realization and inner peace is attained when one realizes that there is only one essential essence that pervades the whole universe – the essence of Allah. That is the deep meaning of *Lā ilāha illa'Llāh*.

1. CREATION AND ITS DIRECTION

1.6 The Return to Origin – *Ma`ād*

Adam descended to earth to be challenged by all the limitations and diverse interactions. The metaphorical descent is completed by the yearning to return to the bliss of paradise. After death, comes the mystery of the hereafter. The consciousness of a deceased person may need some time to adjust to the new state where personal will and the ability to act are lost. All of our human experiences on earth are limited by the speed of light and the hereafter beyond that. There may well be some deep subconscious memory of the original nothingness or pre-creation. The soul however, will carry with it the trace of earthly exposure, desires, attachments, actions and the states of mind and heart.

It is in the hereafter that every self will fully experience and realize the effects of its earthly intentions and actions, down to the smallest events. 'Permanent' hell or paradise, as referred to in reference to the afterlife, means that durations in that realm are radically different to our earthly notions of time and space. If during our life we were illumined by higher consciousness, then the passage through resurrection will be with ease. Otherwise, processes of purification (chastisements) will be experienced before the soul carries along its final journey. Every soul will be given its just due in the hereafter.

Immediately after death, the 'soul-self' energy entity that is the individual undergoes adjustments due to the loss of the body, mind, and will to act. Both the light of the soul that occupies the higher end of the spectrum of consciousness that resides in the individual as well as the individuated self, or ego, that resides at the lower end of this spectrum, experience a profound change in state of being. It is during this intermediate state, it is thought, that the deceased experiences bewilderment and confusion.

Whatever is born will die. Individual entities and creations, as well as celestial bodies and galaxies, all have beginnings and ends. Whatever is on this earth has its roots and origins in the heavens. All the materials on earth were originally stardust and gases. Every entity that is within the limitations of space and time has emerged from beyond the boundaries of any place or time.

Death is the end of earthly realms and resurrection is the return to origin, with an earthly color or tag representing our overall state of evolved-consciousness. Whatever has emanated from the heavens onto earth will return to the heavens with an additional earthly trace of biography and colors superimposed upon the original pure soul-energy. Human experiences on earth are like preludes, samples and preparations to witnessing 'other worldly' states of new dimensions beyond mental grasp and reason.

Life on earth has evolved over millennia culminating in human consciousness. Earthly existence occurs within the womb of space and time; whereas the afterlife is a new realm and comes about instantly after death. Resurrection is beyond all limits and ideas. It is a great mystery that awaits us all. The final material death of the universe triggers off a new re-emergence of a different life – that of souls and spirits. The new life will witness Truth in Divine Presence.

The rise of the Adamic consciousness with its complex brain and mental processes (producing a sense of separation, identity and inquisitiveness) necessitated the descent to the earthly domain of experience. In this dynamic environment there are all kinds of dualities and forces and dynamics that did not exist before. This new cradle of mankind is based upon earthly trials, tests and

1. CREATION AND ITS DIRECTION

struggles in order to return to the inner state of peace and bliss as known by the soul before its imprisonment within body and mind.

The physical nature of man is from earth, water, air and fire, whereas the spiritual essence is beyond imagination. Every human being goes through a physical process of growing from a cell, to a clot, to a fetus, which matures within the womb and later outside of it for a few more months before further growth and maturity occurs. The cycle of human creation begins with birth, followed by the subsequent evolvement of the self and its complexities, which presents challenges and mysteries in relation to behavior, conduct and desirable states of contentment, stability and knowledge. The creation of Adam in paradise is a great metaphor of how, from Allah's will, all kinds of creations emanate, the pinnacle of which (man) yearns to return to the original state of perfection and happiness in the eternal garden.

The cycles of birth and death are echoed in the descent of Adam and the ascent through passionate worship back to pure consciousness. The living emanates from the dead and the dead from the living – a paradox that cannot be resolved rationally. The paradox may disappear through insight and illumination, whose keys are faith in God and transcendence to the truth of Oneness.

CHAPTER 2

Roots & Foundations of Truth

2.1 The Desire to Believe & Worship

Through archaeology and anthropology (and the traces of pre-historical evidence) we now know that the earliest structures on earth (huge monolithic stones arranged in specific formations) were places for communal worship. Trance experiences and other 'non-earthly' insights were early examples of altered states of consciousness sought by man. The desire to know the mysteries behind existence and the rites and rituals of worshiping the power inherent in or behind phenomenal existence is as ancient as man himself.

Transformative 'faith and practice' is the key to enlightened existence. It begins with questioning the meaning and purpose of life. The ever-changing experiences of life lead us to seek a knowledge that will always be reliable and to find a consistent voice of real authority, where 'authority' means the voice of true wisdom and knowledge, not power. It is the voice of deep knowingness or certainty, not the office of command, which is what we often associate with this term. To listen to God is to be aware of the light of the soul within the heart. This light can shine when 'the egotistic shadows are least' and when the heart is purified from the confusion of dualities and 'otherness'. The higher self (soul) will then illumine and override the lower self (ego).

Faith begins as trust and can lead to an experientially transformed state. The requirements of this journey are sincerity, commitment, perseverance and total reliance upon the higher state of consciousness which encompasses all life forms. With increased awareness 'living faith' unifies the seen and unseen. The outcome is a new outlook on all aspects of life on earth.

The efforts of the Prophets, the Imams and the Masters, in their instruction to people, were directed at perfecting intention, knowledge and action. Among Muslims this became known as knowledge of the fundamentals or 'Roots' (*usūl*)[6] and the 'Branches' of faith (*furu`*).[7] It has been said that all of Allah's commandments and prohibitions are contained within two phrases of the Prophet's:

~... Reverence for Allah's command and compassion for Allah's creation....

The role and responsibility of the Prophets, and the Messengers are immense. Allah said (to His Prophet):

✡ So, be steadfast as you have been commanded. [11:112]

With regards to this the Prophet commented:

~ Surah Hud [chapter 11 of the Qur'an] has caused my hair to turn grey.

---

6   *Usul alDīn*: unity (*tawhīd*), justice (`*adl*), prophethood (*nubuwwah*), imāmate (*imāmah*), and judgment that takes place at the return (*al-ma`ād*).

7   *Furu` aldīn*: prayer (*salāt*), fasting (*sawm*), pilgrimage (*hajj*), obligatory wealth-tax (*zakāt*), striving in the way of Allah (*jihād*) and enjoining good and forbidding evil (*amr bi'l ma'ruf wa'n-nahy `an al-munkar*).

2. ROOTS & FOUNDATIONS OF TRUTH

All creatures and existing beings (be they high or low in intelligence or evolvement) are searching for perfection and for attaining the highest potential possible for them.

☼ There is no creature that crawls on the face of the earth, nor any bird that flies on its two wings, but that they are nations like you; We have not neglected any matter from the Book; then they will be gathered together unto their Lord. [6:38]

As for acts of devotion or worship, Allah says:

☼ I have not created the *Jinn* or Humankind except that they worship [Me]. [51:56]

Worship is the final stage of passionate adoration. One likes, loves and adores that which one knows is most desirable. Allah's Attributes, such as Power, Knowledge, Wealth etc., are most desirable qualities. When the entire being (body, mind and heart) is united in its focus, then worship is an act of recharging the human being. With such worship a person will be thrilled by the Creator's presence and prevalence.

☼ Surely if you would ask them who created the heavens and the earth, their reply would be "Allah". [31:25]

Everything remembers and affirms Allah's divinity and His Oneness in its own way:

☼ There is nothing that does not glorify His praises. [17:44]

Because our main concerns on earth relate to the physical, material and mental dimensions of life we do not comprehend their special way of glorification.

Just as physically a child grows to become an adult, so too spiritually we grow along a ladder of knowledge, insights and worship, by starting with the basics of rituals. In time the limbs and organs, including the sense perceptions, begin to orientate towards the higher zone of consciousness. With maturity in spiritual practice, subtler awareness and sensing begins to take place until such time as it becomes easy and normal to depart from the normal state of consciousness to a higher state. The union between the lower self and higher self or soul now becomes natural and constant. A stage may be reached which is described in the Qur'an as 'those perpetually steadfast in prayer (*salāt*)' [70:23].

With spiritual wisdom and maturity we realize that existence is one cycle revolving between the lover and the Beloved, between the knower and the Known, the seeker and the Sought. Original sacred love is what unifies that which appears diverse or different in our minds.

☼ Thus Allah will bring forth a people whom He loves and who love Him. [5:54]

Likewise, in a *hadith qudsi*, Allah says:

~ I was a hidden treasure and I loved to become known, therefore I created so that I could be known.

Love is Allah's power that holds the universe along its journey. The True Beloved is Allah and created beings are the lovers. Each created entity has a unique direction in its journey to His Presence. The goal of all is the Eternal One, free of any multiplicity. In truth:

~ Allah is not loved but by Allah, Allah is not known but by Allah, Allah is not remembered but by Allah, and there is nothing true in existence but Allah,

2. ROOTS & FOUNDATIONS OF TRUTH

His names, His Attributes and His works. Thus, everything is Him, by Him, from Him, and to Him.

As He says:

✧ He is the First, the Last, the Apparent, the Hidden and He is the Knower of all things. [57:3]

Prescriptions for the Spiritual Wayfarer

The human quest for a path in life that leads to sustainable contentment is relentless. We all seek knowledge of the root and origin of our lives so that we can arrive at living wholesomely and enjoyably in all situations. The Prophets present the Truth and prescriptions which deal with matters concerning the worldly existence of man and his journey towards his final destiny. Allah has said the following concerning this:

✧ ...as We have sent among you a Messenger to recite Our signs to you and to purify you and to instruct you in the Book and in wisdom and to instruct you in what you do not know. [2:151]

✧ Do you not see that to Allah prostrates whoever is in the heavens and whoever is on the earth and the sun, the moon, the stars, the mountains, the trees, the animals, and many of the people...? [22:18]

✧ There is nothing that does not glorify His praise but you do not understand their glorification. [17:44]

These verses indicate that all creation follows paths that acknowledge aspects of Allah's qualities. The Qur'an refers to man as `abd, which means slave, servant or worshiper. Being a slave in this context indicates man's fundamental state of dependence upon the greater reality, which is beyond the merely physical and visible, i.e. man's permanent state of need to be connected to his Source, Allah. The term 'slave' (God-servant or bondsman) derives from the term `abd, which indicates the human state as a complement to Allah's attribute of *Rabb*, Sustainer or Lord. Similarly, included within this is the glorification (*tasbih*). The reference here is not to what is commonly thought of as glorification, because Allah said, '...but you do not understand their glorification (*tasbih*)' [17:44]. However, every creature's prayer and prostration before Him is what is most suitable for its station, as He says:

✡ Say: Each person acts according to what befits (knowledge and state) him. [17:84]

Just as there are always two aspects to every created thing, there are also dual aspects to the rules and prescriptions or code of conduct, i.e. an outward act and an inward meaning, one which is perceived through the senses and one which relates to the heart and soul. Rationality and reason are necessary entry points to subtler inner knowledges.

~ Allah does not allow anything to exist without a reason: thus He made a reason for everything and He made an explanation for every reason; He gave a knowledge for every explanation and He made a door for every knowledge. Those who know this know it, and those who are ignorant of this are ignorant of it. The Messenger of Allah and the Imams are doors which speak and relate this knowledge. ~ Imam Ja`far asSadiq

2. ROOTS & FOUNDATIONS OF TRUTH

The task of correct guidance and sound leadership lies with the men of knowledge who are the heirs to the Prophets in exemplary conduct and wholesomeness. Some of the Imams taught the following:

~ Whoever does not have a wise man to guide him correctly will perish. ~ Imam Zayn al`Abidin

~ Whoever acts without insight is like the one who chases after a mirage in the desert: his haste will only increase him in distance. ~ Imam Ja`far alSadiq

~ Whoever acts without knowledge is like the one who travels off the path: the distance he travels away from the path will only increase his distance from the goal. ~ Imam `Ali, *Nahj ul-Balagha*.

In a supplication Imam `Ali says:

~ O Allah! Illuminate my exterior with my obedience to You, my interior with Your love, my heart with the witnessing of You, my soul with the most profound knowledge of You, and my innermost essence with the contemplation of Your divine presence, O You Who are the Possessor of glory and noble generosity!

The Islamic way of life is founded upon observance and restrictions within the various branches of the faith (*furu` aldīn*). It encompasses the pathways of the heart and the internal state of the believer so that the remedy for the self (*nafs*) can be applied, and so that both the sensory and subtler veils may be removed. The Prophet said:

~ And I arrived at the veils of my Lord, the veils of might and power, of splendor and graciousness, of greatness and magnificence, of light and darkness, of reverence and perfection... until I reached the veil of glory.⁸

In respect of which Abu Nasr alFarabi said:

~ You possess a veil originating from yourself which covers you from yourself in addition to the clothing which covers your body; so attempt to lift that veil and you will then witness and no longer enquire about what you are. If you witness affliction then misery will be upon you and if you are at peace then blessed are you. You will see that yourself; and you are located within your body as if you were not actually there within your physical body but, rather, as if you were in the most subtle and divine regions, and you will see what no eye has seen and hear what no ear has heard and witness what has not occurred to the heart of any mortal.⁹

The traveler of this path is responsible, by his or her innate nature, by reasoning and by actions, to know the nature of the self/soul dynamic in order to attain the goal of the most profound knowledge (*ma`rifah*) of the Lord. This is the path of the Prophets and the Messengers and those who follow their guidance.

Historical Evolvement

Within a few decades from the dawn of Islam, the natural linguistic and cultural differences of the new Muslims who spread out over a large geographical area brought about certain variations in detailed interpretations in the

---

8   Quoted from *Al-Fusūs al-Hikām*.
9   In *al-Mabda' wa al-Mī`ād* (The Beginning and the Return) by Abu Nasr Muhammad ibn Muhammad al-Farabi d. 950 CE/ 339 AH.

2. ROOTS & FOUNDATIONS OF TRUTH

practices of the *Dīn*. Lack of easy communication from the center of political and religious authority and the scarcity of qualified religious instructors brought about different sects and 'schools of thought'. A thousand years ago there were numerous schools of thought and sects, some of which differed considerably in their 'theology' to that of the mainstream. Likewise Sufi brotherhoods and 'secret' societies began to appear and flourish. Yet the Qur'an and patterns of prophetic conduct had always acted as a unifying base of Islam and the path of *tawhīd*.

In our present world where Muslims are now spread throughout the world, with hundreds of different ethnic, linguistic and cultural backgrounds, we again find that the Qur'an and the prophetic way are the main unifying thread. In Turkey, for example, after a period of over seventy years of enforced secular rule and culture, we find a rise in the rediscovery of the Qur'an, the wholesomeness of Islamic morality and accountable conduct taking on a new lease of life and popularity.

The natural human desire to believe in a perfect and constant reality and truth – Allah – and the desire to be exposed to the light of this truth has always accompanied human consciousness and will become more universal and prevalent. We love truth and derive much joy and goodness by our awareness of it.

2.2 Traditional Foundations of Faith

In traditional Islam the separation between fundamentals of faith and its branches were often understood as the method of unifying the outer and inner aspects of human nature. Physical practices and rituals help to refine the self and its conduct, and bring the entire being nearer to the light of Oneness which permeates the universe and to realize the truth of the God-centricity of creation.

As already mentioned, traditional scholarship considered that the two potentials of knowledge and action were represented by the 'Roots' and the 'Branches' of the Faith. Perfecting or fulfilling the 'Roots' of the Faith was understood to be accomplished by the purification of the inward and perfection of faith, while the purpose of the 'Branches' was to purify the outward and bring about the perfection of intentions and actions.

In order to cleanse 'the inner' from impurities it was considered essential to have a sound belief in and knowledge of unity (*tawhīd*), justice (*`adl*), prophethood (*nubuwwah*) and the return to Allah for judgment (*al-ma`ād*). Cleansing the body, mind and self of impurities was likewise not considered possible except by way of what came to be known as the five branches of faith: prayer (*salāt*), fasting (*sawm*), payment of the obligatory wealth tax (*zakāt*), the pilgrimage (*hajj*), and striving in the way of Allah (*jihād*). Followers of the Ja`fari school of law also add to this the enjoining of good and the forbidding of evil (*al-amr bi'l-ma`ruf wa'n-nahi `an al-munkar*), as well as following the appointed Imam (*imāmah*). As Imam `Ali has said:

> ~ Allah has made faith based on knowledge (*imān*) obligatory to cleanse oneself of idolatry, [He has made] prayer to remove pride, and the obligatory

2. ROOTS & FOUNDATIONS OF TRUTH

tax as a source for sustenance. He has made fasting as an affliction to purify men, the pilgrimage to bring one close to the Islamic way of life, and struggle in the way of Allah to strengthen Islam. He has made the command of goodness and the forbidding of evil as something which improves people's conduct and obstructs or reduces foolishness. He established the ties of kinship to increase the numbers, and retaliation to prevent the loss of blood. He has established punishments under the law to destroy what is not permitted, and has decreed the abandonment of drinking intoxicants as a protection for reasoning.

Anyone who desires to purify both the outer and the inner should therefore follow both the roots and the branches, on any of the three levels: the basic (i.e. *shari`ah*), the intermediate (i.e. *tariqah*) and the advanced (*haqiqah*). Whoever possesses true belief and perfected faith must adhere to these foundational pillars, since it is essential to believe in unity in order to be cleansed of seeing other than Allah (*shirk*), and to believe that Allah is Just and Wise.

✿ And your Lord is not unjust to His servants. [41:46]

Belief in unity and Allah's justice are dependent upon the existence of a Prophet and his demonstration of some form of miracle to confirm his authority. Therefore one needs to believe in the Prophet and prophethood, and that Islam will not remain without correct guidance and instruction, as it is expressed in Allah's words:

✿ Obey Allah and obey the Messenger and those set in authority over you. [4:59]

The presence of Prophets and Messengers has been a necessity so as to maintain continuity in the existence of enlightened beings. Everything which proceeds from here is nothing other than an invitation to mankind to return to their Lord and to the correct guidance of the 'Straight Path' on the 'Day of Resurrection', and to remind them of the promise and the promised time.

At its inception, Islam based on the Qur'an and the Prophetic teachings evolved over a period of 23 years. It connected the seen and unseen and the material and physical with its origin of energies and lights. Islam was formative and transformative. Like a torch that illumined the heart of the faithful it brought about a shift in people's perception and conduct.

With its geographical spread and the multi-cultural impact upon Islam and the large number of converts who needed to be taught, it became necessary to establish teaching centers and well defined doctrines. Numerous questions arose, e.g. What was the perfect way of performing ritual ablution? How many people constituted the minimum number for congregational Friday prayers? And scores of other such issues.

Thus, the most acknowledged local theologian was considered as the authority which had to be acceptable to the dynastic rulers of the land. From this process arose dozens of schools of thought which, after some three centuries, were reduced to eight or nine schools of law or 'madhāhib'.

2.3 Unity (*tawhīd*)

Unity (*tawhīd*) is the belief that there is no deity other than Allah, that He is One, without partner in His Godhead and that there is nothing like Him in His essential Attributes and no equal to Him in existence. Allah is utterly incomparable; thus, He possesses knowledge unsurpassed, no one is equal to Him in His creation, and He has no peer.

> ✩ Say, O People of the Book, come to an equitable word between us and you that we will not worship other than Allah and we will not associate anything with Him, and we will not take others among us as Lords in place of Allah. [3:64)]

> ✩ Your god is One God. [2:163]

This *tawhīd* is what the Prophets and Messengers have declared from Adam until our Prophet Muhammad when he said:

> ~ I have been commanded to strive with the people until they say, "There is no deity but Allah."

Scholars of *shari`ah* confirm by reason, evidence and intellectual proof, that if there were in existence two independent gods, each would have been distinct from the other in essence. This Unity is the outward and obvious form of Unity which nullifies the outward form of idolatry. It is perfected by the utterance of the words 'Lā ilāha illa'Llāh' (There is no deity but Allah). Upon doing so one becomes aware of the Oneness of Allah as far as one is outwardly concerned; then one's outward and inward are both cleansed from the impurity of obvious idolatry, as Allah says:

☼ Indeed the people of idolatry are unclean. [9:28]

This type of Unity is also called 'proven unity' or intellectual Unity, because it is Unity which has been confirmed by way of evidence and proof, reasoning and logic.

After Unity at the basic level is absorbed through intellectual evidence (bringing one to the testimony that there is no deity but Allah, the One, the Only, and that there is nothing other than Him in existence) one then turns one's gaze away from the effects and causative factors and begins to witness perfection in Allah's ways in creation. Now one can start to surrender oneself to Him totally and to be contented with Him:

☼ Allah is contented with them and they are contented with Him. [5:119]

Likewise:

☼ And whoever trusts in Allah, He is sufficient for him. [65:3]

The Unity of the Elect, or what we may term the intermediate level, has been described thus:

~ This is the Unity which is confirmed by way of Reality itself. This is when regard for the various outward causes of phenomena is dropped, and one rises above intellectual disputes with their accompanying proofs. This is when one does not look for evidence of *tawhīd*, nor seek a reason for trust, nor a means for salvation. One witnesses only the preponderance of Reality, by way of his judgment, knowledge and ability to discern things in the proper

2. ROOTS & FOUNDATIONS OF TRUTH

order of their significance.[10]

The understanding of Unity at the basic level relates to intellectual knowing and is associated with the general masses. The next level is to witness Unity as the connecting factor in life. Everyone who turns away from the realm of creation and sees the One Whose Existence is absolutely true and permanent will declare that there is nothing in existence but Allah. Thus, both his inner and outer will become cleansed from the impurity of hidden or subtle association, as Allah says:

> ✧ And most of them do not believe in Allah, but, rather, they are people of association. [12:106]

One gnostic Master comments:

> ~ Indeed, purification from obvious association (*shirk*) and idolatry is easier than purification from subtle, hidden association, in the same way as arriving at the Unity of godhead is easier than arriving at the Unity of existence. This is because whoever harbors hidden association considers himself a believer in the Oneness of Allah merely because of his acceptance of the fact that there is no deity but Allah, while he neglects the subtle association which lies concealed within his self and its perceptions and aspirations.

In the same vein, the Messenger of Allah mentioned the following:

> ~ The traces of association (*shirk*) among my people are more hidden than a black ant crawling on a pitch black stone in the midst of a dark night.

---

10   Shaykh Abu Isma'il Abdallah al-Harawi (d. 1087 CE / 481 AH) in the book *Manāzil alSā'irīn*.

The subtle, hidden form of association is relevant to believers and Muslims, and not to unbelievers and hypocrites because Allah has mentioned this subtle association in conjunction with the word 'faith-based-on-knowledge' (*imān*), which applies in Islam. It is impossible to combine outward association with faith based on knowledge. The meaning here, then, could only be that hidden form of association which the Qur'an refers to as '*hawa*', which carries the meanings of whims, desires, lust, or worldly pursuits:

> ✧ Have you not seen him that has taken his desire as his god, and Allah has made him err while having knowledge... [45:23]

It is often 'hidden' desires that lead to hypocrisy and various aspects of '*shirk*'. That is why it is said that the greatest deity worshipped is 'human desire'.

Those who are established at the basic and intermediate levels of *tawhīd* are the ones who witness through the lens of Unity. They are aware of no reality other than Him because they see His Existence is True, while the existence of all else is merely a transient reflection or shadow and therefore subject to change, obliteration and destruction:

> ✧ Everything upon it (the earth) perishes and the Face of your Lord remains, the Possessor of Might and Generosity. [55:26-27]

This is what is meant by the Divine Attribute 'He Who Remains' or 'The Everlasting' (*alBāqi*); that is, He remains within eternity. 'He who perishes' (*alFāni*) means that the one with this attribute will not remain. It is for this reason that one finds that the Master (`ārif*) will say that there is nothing in existence but Allah, His Names, His Attributes

2. ROOTS & FOUNDATIONS OF TRUTH

and His Works; and thus all is Him, by Him, from Him and to Him. Allah indicates this when He says:

> ✧ And wherever you turn, there is the Face of Allah. [2:115]

The word 'Face' refers to Allah's Essence: wherever you turn you will witness His Essence and His Existence because He surrounds all.

> ✧ And Allah encompasses all things. [4:126]

In popular Islamic and Sufi Teachings three degrees of Unity have been described in various ways:
- the Knowledge of Certainty (`Ilm alYaqīn), the Eye of Certainty (`Ayn alYaqīn), and the Truth of Certainty (Haqq alYaqīn);
- the terms 'Islām, Imān, and Ihsān' (surrender, faith and excellent conduct),
- the Companions of the Left Hand, the Companions of the Right Hand, and the Near Ones Who Have Gone Before.

The Prophet referred to these three levels when he said:

~ This world is forbidden to the People of the Hereafter and the Hereafter is forbidden to the People of the World, but they are both forbidden to the People of Allah.

The first group mentioned (*This world is forbidden to the People of the Hereafter*) have reached the station of verification (*tahqīq*), or the level of the inward. They have witnessed Unity and by virtue of this have been counted among the People of the Hereafter. They have gone beyond the outward and arrived at the inward, having witnessed what they sought with their inner eye, or insight (*basirah*).

✪ Say: This is my way, I call to Allah by way of insight, I and those who follow me. [12:108]

The second group (*and the Hereafter is forbidden to the People of the World*) is at the station of emulation (*taqlīd*): they follow someone else endowed with knowledge. This is an outward stage. They are considered to be people of the world because they have not yet gone beyond it by virtue of their attachment to it and their love and desire for it – as the Prophet has said:

~ The love of the world is at the head of every wrong action.

The third group, the enlightened beings (*but they are both forbidden to the People of Allah*) are those who have transcended the lower self and thus are called the 'People of Allah', because they have arrived at the gate of the Ultimate Truth. The people of Allah belong to Allah and not to any identifiable world – hence anything other than Allah is 'forbidden'. They have witnessed Allah's Light with their hearts and thus their tongues proclaim: 'Blessed is the One Who may not be reached except through Him.' Their words concur with those of the Prophet who said:

~ I saw my Lord by my Lord, and I knew my Lord through my Lord.

Salman alFarsi was someone who had attained this station; and the Prophet had said of him: 'Indeed the Garden (Paradise) longs for Salman more than Salman longs for the Garden.' The Garden is a state which the pure heart can experience in this world and the Hereafter. The Prophet said:

~ The good actions of the righteous are on the level of

2. ROOTS & FOUNDATIONS OF TRUTH

the ordinary actions of the near ones.

The Prophet also indicated three types of Unity in his well-known supplication:

> ~ O Allah, I take refuge in Your Forgiveness from Your Chastisement, and I take refuge in Your Contentment from Your Anger, and I take refuge in You from You.

The first reference is to the Unity of Actions (God's acts), the second is to the Unity of Attributes (God's qualities) and the third is to the Unity of Essence (the limitless, unfathomable quiddity of Beingness). There is no station above the Unity of Essence. It is attained only by those who have been granted a mighty portion, as the great Master Ibn al-`Arabi has indicated in his book 'The Bezels of Wisdom':

> ~ If one has tasted this, one has tasted the utmost, and there is nothing loftier to be attained by a created being. So let not your soul desire or long for advancement beyond this degree, for there is nothing beyond it save sheer nonexistence.

The ultimate level of spiritual stations is the realization that there is *only* One and all else are shadows which overflow from the original One.

2.4 Justice (`adl`)

At all times all human beings experience inadequacy and need. Even at a moment of great contentment and wellbeing, the desire to maintain that state persists. Our life on earth hangs in the balance between attracting the good (which can lead to the vice of covetousness) and repulsing the undesirable (which can lead to anger). Justice implies the balance between acting responsibly and appropriately in every situation, with deference to Allah's great qualities of mercy, generosity, forgiveness and perfect governance.

Human efforts to establish justice are a small reflection of Allah's perfect justice. At the social level we are given the opportunity to exercise justice upon ourselves and others (which may not be attainable at all times) in the light of awareness of Allah's supreme justice. Our life on earth is an exercise and training ground for the Hereafter, at which time we will be judged according to our intention, attention and action.

> ✡ Allah has bestowed (goodness) upon the people of faith when He sent to them a Messenger from among themselves who would recite to them His signs and purify them and teach them the Book and Wisdom, even if they had previously been clearly misguided. [3:164]

In a *hadith qudsi* Allah said:

> ~ I was a hidden treasure and I loved to be known so I created.

This process is referred to as 'favor' (*fadl*). It is favor in which the slave finds that the closer he is to obedience and knowledge the further he is from disobedience and ignorance. This process depends upon the faculty of reason

2. ROOTS & FOUNDATIONS OF TRUTH

which is within our *fitrah* (innate nature). The freely chosen actions which one performs are either compatible with one's sense of reason or not. There is no doubt that some of our actions are contrary to reason, e.g. oppression, deceit, foolishness, and corruption; while others are in harmony with it, e.g. gratitude for kindness, returning something with which one had been entrusted, the repayment of a debt, and so on, all of which are quite obvious.

Justice at the basic level is to know that Allah never performs any action which may be considered foul or mean, nor does He neglect or forget anything in creation. He is not an oppressor so this is not conceivable in His decree, nor does He act unjustly in His wisdom. He rewards those who are obedient to His ways and punishes the disobedient. He does not require of His servants that which they do not have the power and ability to do, and He does not punish them with more than what is appropriate. The phenomena of the world which issue forth from Him, even the creation of predatory animals, harmful plants, and deadly poisons – whatever it may be – is considered to be good. All evils like oppression, meanness, and corruption, issue forth from other than Him, as He states:

> ☼ And if they do something vulgar they said we found our ancestors doing it and Allah has commanded us to do it. Say: Indeed Allah does not command indecency, do you attribute to Allah that which you do not know? [7:28]

> ☼ Whatever good befalls you is from Allah and whatever evil befalls you of evil is from yourselves. [4:79]

These two verses show that all good and wrong actions are human Attributes although the source of human energy and knowledge is divine. Justice at the basic level is in accordance with Allah's words:

☼ Whoever does good, it is for his own self, and whoever does evil, it is against it, for your Lord is not unjust to His servants. [41:46]

The subsequent level of Justice is to know that Allah has given each human the means to perfect him or herself, according to natural disposition and instinct. From Allah's absolute generosity flows human kindness, compassion and other virtues that lead to contentment.

☼ And He gave you all you asked Him for. [14:34]

☼ Say: "Nothing will reach us except that which Allah has written for us, He is our Protector," so let the people of faith trust in Allah. [9:51]

Whatever comes from Allah is in accordance with ultimate justice and wisdom. It is incumbent upon us to trust in His will with full confidence and surrender.

☼ Is not Allah sufficient for His servant? [39:36]

And:

☼ And whoever trusts in Allah He is sufficient for him, indeed Allah carries out His commands. For all things Allah has set a measure. [65:3]

This is the station of trust, submission and contentment, which in turn will enable us to experience the ultimate mercy and generosity of Allah.

☼ Indeed, those who have faith and perform acts of

2. ROOTS & FOUNDATIONS OF TRUTH

goodness, they are the best of creation, their reward is with their Lord, gardens under which rivers flow, abiding therein eternally; Allah is content with them and they are content with Him, that is for whoever fears his Lord. [98:7-8]

The *awliyā'* or Friends of Allah (who have attained the station of contentment, submission and trust) neither look to the past nor to the future. Attachment, desire or expectation regarding existence will only bring about insecurity, sadness, fear, sorrow for what has passed and anxiety for what is yet to come. Allah says the following concerning this:

> ✿ Indeed the Friends of Allah will have no fear nor will they grieve. [10:62]

The enlightened ones are those free of anxiety and sorrow.

Imam ʿAli stated the following:

> ~ I have found complete abstention from the world (*zuhd*) in two phrases of the Qur'an: "...in order that you not be saddened over what has passed you by nor rejoice over what He has given you." [57:23]

The Friends of Allah are always content and in balance whether in sadness or happiness. Ibn ʿAbbas relates his experience with the Prophet who told him:

> ~ Be mindful of Allah and He will be mindful of you. Remember Allah and you will find Him before you. Go to Allah in times of wellbeing, and He will come to you in times of difficulties. If you ask of anyone, ask of Allah. If you seek help, seek help from Allah. The ink of the pen has already dried after having

written what will be until the Day of Judgment. If all the creatures of creation wanted to render you some benefit which Allah had not already decreed, they would be incapable of it. If they wanted to harm you in any way, and Allah had not already decreed it, they would be incapable of doing so. Perform your actions for Allah in gratitude and certainty and know that there is much virtue in patience with something which you dislike, that victory comes with patience, and that relief comes from hardship, and with difficulty comes ease.

It is related that Imam Muhammad alBaqir visited the great companion (of the Prophet) Jabir ibn ʿAbdullah alAnsari, who was by then afflicted by old age and lameness in the last years of his life, and inquired of his condition. Jabir replied, 'I am in a state where I welcome old age over youth, sickness over health, and death over life.' The Imam said, 'As for me, if Allah should make me an old man, I would love old age. If He should make me a young man, I would love youth. If He should render me ill, I would love illness. If He should cure me I would love the curing. If He should cause me to die, I would love death. If He should cause me to remain, I would love it also.'

This station is attained through the knowledge that Allah knows one's condition and that Allah is just:

> ✧ Surely Allah does not wrong mankind in any way, but, rather, it is mankind who wrong themselves. [10:44]

The advanced seeker is established in the knowledge that Allah is just in His works and words, and in His giving and withholding. Thus He grants to every being according to whatever is needed. This is true justice as it

2. ROOTS & FOUNDATIONS OF TRUTH

is the ordering of things in their proper sequence in time and space – the opposite of wrongdoing. Allah reveals in the Qur'an:

> ✧ Each acts according to its own state [disposition]. [17:84]

That is, each acts according to its outward form and inner potential and condition. For this reason He has said:

> ✧ Thus Allah possesses the conclusive proof and if He had willed He would have guided you all completely. [6:149]

That is, Allah knows our intentions and actions and thus we experience His justice in our destiny. In this respect the Prophet has said:

> ~ Everyone is journeying to that which has been created for him.

It is said that the Prophet David asked: 'O Lord, why did You create this creation?' Allah replied: 'For what they are,' that is, for what each one possesses of capacity and potential ability. Based upon this there is no room for any complaint, nor can one condemn Allah because He created one in this way or another. Allah would say: 'I have given you your existence only in proportion to your ability and your readiness, based upon your essence and your nature, not just merely from My own whims, because I am the original Actor, the Doer, and you are the receiver of My action.'

> ✧ He (Allah) will not be asked about what He has done while they will be questioned. [21:23]

This indicates that His knowledge and wisdom

supersedes ours and that the All-Knowing, All-Wise, will not be questioned. However, we will be questioned about our intention and effort to realize the truth.

Allah is the All-Knowing, Perfect, and Wise Judge; it is not fitting that He should ever be asked about His actions, because He does nothing which is not in line with His Perfect Wisdom and Knowledge. Nothing, not even an atom in either the earth or in the vast expanse of the universe, is overlooked by Him – hence:

> ✿ The Merciful taught the Qur'an, created man and taught him its explanation. [55:1-4]

> ✿ Recite: And your Lord is the Most Generous, He who taught with the pen, Who taught man what he did not know. [96:3-5]

2.5 Prophethood (*nubuwwah, imāmah & wilāyah*)

Prophethood (*nubuwwah*) occurs when a pure soul witnesses and experiences the truth of Divine Presence. The mission of prophethood is to bring that knowledge and discernment to those people who are their contemporaries or who live within the culture of that Prophet or Messenger.

The position of the Prophet Muhammad is considered most glorious because of the combination of three levels: proximity to Allah (*wilāyah* or friendship), prophethood (*nubuwwah*) and prophetic mission (*risālah*) – all combined and present in him. He was befriended by Allah and was close to Him, he was a Prophet, and finally he had been entrusted with a specific mission – the message of truth.

The Prophets who were referred to as the Possessors of Firm Resolution (*Ulu' al`Azm*) were five in number: Noah, Abraham, Moses, Jesus, and Muhammad. They were sent for all of humanity and to both men and *jinn*. Each brought guidance and regulations (*shari`ah*) which abrogated, restored, or expanded the previous one, and, as their names indicate, they were firm and patient in whatever difficulty and afflictions they encountered.

Layers of Understanding Prophethood

With the rise of humanity and Adamic consciousness it is easy for us to understand that a few people have deeper knowledge of truth and reality than others. These beings are guides to awakening and realization of Allah's light and presence. The distinction between a Messenger and a Prophet is that the former has a clear message or book (*risālah*), while the latter is graced with general apostleship (*nubuwwah*). Sometimes these two functions are combined.

The following are three main criteria for a prophet:
1. A Prophet does not perform actions which oppose sound reason.
2. He calls human beings to the path of Allah and to the acceptance of it (i.e. that which is in harmony with nature), and warns them against denial of human limitation and real needs (i.e. that which is discordant with nature).
3. After proclaiming his prophethood he manifests a miracle which confirms his position and is in harmony with his claim.

The Prophet or Messenger possesses behavior (*akhlāq*), conduct and qualities which are godly and desired by intelligent people. He is purified of all error, and thus other human beings can trust him, believe him and have faith in his prophetic mission. A Prophet is sent to mankind to guide men to their perfection in proportion to the level of and their innate ability and their willingness to change their conduct, intentions and actions.

The Prophet is the complete wholesome person (*insān al-kāmil*) and, as such, represents Adam on earth – a steward of creation. The Prophet knows that all actions and Attributes belong to Allah and the whole universe is held by the unique power and essence of His Grace. The prophetic message is to communicate and demonstrate this reality to the rest of creation. By faith and trust in this message and adherence to the practices and lawful acts of Islam, the lower self yields and submits to its soul and to Allah's unseen forces and patterns that govern creation. Each Prophet is a manifestation of the prophethood of the Universal Soul – Allah. The prophethood of Muhammad is the culmination of previous revelations and manifests the reality of all the Attributes and Names of Allah.

2. ROOTS & FOUNDATIONS OF TRUTH

The Qur'an relates that Allah created man as vicegerent (*khalifah*, 2:30) over the earth to act as His representative, invested with full power and authority, whom He would call 'man' (*insān*) at his highest potential. Adam was given an inward aspect and an exterior form to enable him to move freely in the physical as well as in the spiritual realm. The material and the spiritual realms meet in the heart of man where the soul dwells.

> ✪ And when thy Lord said to the angels, I am going to place a ruler in the earth, they said: Will thou place in it such as make mischief in it and shed blood? And we celebrate your praise and proclaim your holiness. He said: Surely I know what you know not. [2:30]

The essence of mankind's inner being is the Universal Soul, the Primal Intellect being its chief minister, the Universal Self its treasurer, and what may be referred to as the Universal Nature its lieutenant. Humankind's outer form carries the image of the outer universe; the microcosm reflects the macrocosm. This outward form of the universe is replicated in the *insān al-kāmil* (complete, perfected man) and thus enlightened beings refer to the universe as a macrocosm of man. When it is said that man is a microcosm of the universe, reference is being made to the reality of his inner being, and which consists of the sublime soul and the natural evolving self. As for his exterior, it is a copy taken from the universe: within it are the various components of the universe, both subtle and gross.

Imamate and Wilayah

Imamate or successorship (*imāmah*) is the leadership of the Islamic way of life, which involves encouraging people to preserve their spiritual and worldly interests as well as to restrain themselves from actions which would be harmful to these interests. Successorship and continuity is therefore necessary from the standpoint of reason, as well as from that of *shari`ah*, just as Prophethood and Islam are necessary for man by virtue of his very nature.

It is human nature to need a leader (*imām*) who possesses knowledge which prevents him from serious error, who will preserve and apply the laws of the *shari`ah* for them, and who will establish the limits prescribed by the Islamic way of life. This is in the same way that people need a Prophet who brings laws and explains to them what is permitted and what is forbidden. A Prophet is necessary because of his great inner perception and knowledge; likewise is the role of the spiritual leader.

The Qur'an declares:

✲ O you who believe, obey Allah, and obey the Prophet and those set in authority over you. [4:59]

The Muslim is enjoined to obey those in authority, that is, those who are in constant reference to the divine author – Allah. Allah's basic command is obedience to Himself and to the Messenger, and then to those on the same path. If obedience to Him and obedience to His Messenger is obligatory, obedience is similarly required to those who act as responsible stewards.

This verse is interpreted by the Ja`fari school of law as referring to the appointed Imam, a practice that continued for two and half centuries after the Prophet's death until the disappearance of the 12th successor, known as the Mahdi, who went into 'occultation'. Some of the gnostics interpret the Mahdi as a symbol of inner awakening, which will also have a physical manifestation for all mankind. In his absence the most competent of the jurists would be

2. ROOTS & FOUNDATIONS OF TRUTH

considered as the point of reference. The tradition related to the re-emergence of the Mahdi are as numerous in the Sunni collections as in the Shi`a collections. Of significance here is the resonance between meaning and form. If inner awakening is experienced, there will be traces of it in the outer.

The Qur'an describes those who do not seek worldly fortunes or power as potential leaders:

> ✡ We wish to bestow favor upon those held to be weak on earth and to make them guides to mankind and to make them the inheritors. [28:5]

The Connection between Imamah and Wilayah

The Imamate in general represents vice-gerency on earth. Imamate is referred to as the station of authority and nearness to Allah, which is also the inner aspect of prophethood. Just as prophethood is a system consisting of the beings of the Prophets and is perfected in the Muhammadi being, so too is *wilāyah* (nearness to Allah), a process of inner friendship with Allah and perfected by the being of the last Imam (the *Mahdi*) – the seal of *wilāyah*.

Shaykh Ibn `Arabi said:

> ~ *Wilāyah* consists of two parts, one of which is unrestricted and the other which is restricted, or, general and specific, because from the viewpoint that it is a divine attribute it is unrestricted, while from the viewpoint that it may be traced to the Prophets and the Friends of Allah, it is restricted. That which is restricted stands by virtue of that which is unrestricted, while the unrestricted is made manifest by the restricted. Thus the *wilāyah* of the

Prophets and the Friends of Allah is a component of the unrestricted *wilāyah* of Allah. Prophethood is a component of the unrestricted prophethood. The manifestation of this unrestricted *wilāyah* is reserved for his unrestricted heirs, that is, his Ahl al-Bayt, the Pure Imams.[11]

The question of teachers is part of the foundation of the rise of humanity, for mankind is in need of others, i.e. society. Just as a child needs considerable attention in upbringing, the same thing applies to spiritual growth: in the absence of the perfect Master or a Prophet you need to find someone who is better than you and who can mentor you.

---

11   Shaykh Muhyi al-Din ibn `Abdullah ibn `Arabi al-Hatimi, d. 1240 CE / 638 AH, in his book, *'Fusūs al-Hikām'* (Pearls or Bezels of Wisdom).

2. ROOTS & FOUNDATIONS OF TRUTH

2.6 The Return (al-ma`ād)

The return (al-ma`ād) refers to the return of the universe and whatever it contains to where it originated from, in both form and essence. This process occurs in the following three stages of resurrection (qiyāmah): the lesser, the intermediate, and the greater.

Resurrection at its basic level refers to the rejoining of the various parts of the dead body and forming them into what they previously were and returning the soul to it. This is what is referred to as the 'Gathering of Bodies'. Human beings have been given the potential of higher consciousness, knowledge, ability, desire and perception, as well as the will to choose what is appropriate and good. Thus great responsibility is placed upon man, both hidden and clear. While the world is the arena for the fulfillment of these responsibilities, it is also the arena for evolving in higher knowledge and insights. Our short earthly life is an opportunity to transcend the mind's limitations to the state of higher consciousness and divine light. Prophets and Messengers have foretold of the 'Gathering of Bodies' and have described the Garden and the Fire in different ways, according to the understanding of their people and their relevant cultures.

Truth (Haqq) manifests as numerous names or Attributes such as, the Hidden (al-Bātin) and the Last (al-Ākhir), the Just (al-`Ādl), the Life-giver (al-Muhyi), the Giver of Death (al-Mumit). At the beginning of creation the dominant Attributes were the Manifest (al-Zāhir) and the Primal (al-Awwal), along with other names like the Originator (al-Mubdi`), the Giver of Existence (al-Wājid), the Creator (al-Khāliq), the Provider (ar-Razzāq), and so forth.

This world and the Hereafter are the projections of Allah's countless manifestations. Resurrection consists of

changing the outward universe by transforming it, and returning it to its essential inward realm. Our present world consists of the manifestation of the inward in an outward form. Its return is the reverse process. In spite of the existence of countless divine names and Attributes the following four names of Attributes contain all:
- the First (*al-Awwal*) – God is before time
- the Last (*al-Ākhir*) – God is beyond time
- the Manifest (*al-Zāhir*) – All appearances are emanations of God
- the Hidden (*al-Bātin*) – The unseen is simply the other side of what is seen

In any given situation one or more names of Allah become manifest. The Hereafter (*ākhirah*) is the manifestation of the following names: the Subduer (*al-Qāhir*); the Eternal (*al-Samad*); the matchless One (*al-Fard*); the One who Brings about the Return (*al-Mu`id*); the Life-giver (*al-Muhyi*); the Giver of Death (*al-Mumit*) and so on. This world, on the other hand, is the manifestation of the following names: the Manifest (*al-Zāhir*); the Originator (*al-Mubdi'*); the First (*al-Awwal*); the Giver of Existence (*al-Wājid*); and so on.

Ibn `Arabi and other great scholars have traditionally considered the following seven names as the 'mother' of the names. They are *Al-Hayy* (the Living); *Al-Qādir* (the Able); *Al-Murīd* (the Willful); *Al-`Alim* (the Knowing); *Al-Sami`* (the Hearing); *Al-Basir* (the Seeing) and *Al-Mutakallim* (the Communicator).

Spiritual and Physical Resurrection

It has become customary for Muslim scholars to divide the Resurrection into physical and spiritual phases. The

2. ROOTS & FOUNDATIONS OF TRUTH

Resurrection has also been divided into the stages of Lesser, Intermediate and Greater. The Lesser Spiritual Resurrection refers to the awakening and rising after the voluntary death of meaning. This is total silence and peace of mind and heart as a result of perfecting worship, especially *salāt*. It is based upon the sayings of the Prophet:

~ Die before you die.

~ Whoever has died, his own Resurrection has already begun.

A frequent Sufi teaching is that whoever can 'die' voluntarily (i.e. temporarily) will experience the state of eternal life. This death means subduing the desires, attachments, self-concerns, awareness of self-identity and constant human limitations. The lower self is naturally inclined to worldly pleasures, power and desires, and thus is veiled from the light within the heart. When the self is subdued and the heart purified, then the light of the soul will shine upon the self and reduce its egotistic tendency. Experiencing this death is to taste freedom in nothingness; it is to experience the indescribable state of the spaceless, timeless zone of supraconsciousness. This is the death and life which is indicated by Allah when He says:

✻ Is the one who was as if dead and whom We then restored to life, granting him a light with which he walks among men, like one who walks in darkness from which he cannot escape? [6:122]

There is a world of difference between the one who is engulfed in ignorance and darkness and the one who lives by knowledge and light, in perfection, aware of eternal life and divine mercy.

✧ ...So repent before your Creator and kill your (lower) self. That is better for you with your Creator. Then He accepted your repentance. [2:54]

✧ Do not imagine that those who have been killed in the way of Allah are dead, rather they are alive with their Lord sustained and joyous by what Allah has bestowed upon them of His Grace. [3:169-170]

When the Prophet returned from a battle against the enemies of faith he said:

~ We have returned from the lesser *Jihād* to the greater *Jihād*.

When asked what this greater *Jihād* was, he answered:

~ The struggle against the self and opposing its desires.

~ The *mujāhid* is the one who struggles against his own self, because whoever becomes dead to his desires becomes alive in Allah's guidance.

That is, one becomes alive by the light of eternal knowledge and is no longer dead in his ignorance.

The following is attributed to al-Hallaj:

~ Kill me, O pious ones, for in my death is life. My real life is in my death and in my death [of form] lies my real life [of meaning].

The intermediate spiritual resurrection refers to the process of becoming dead to all inappropriate behavior and despicable Attributes. It implies living with constant accountability and awareness of correct behavior and

2. ROOTS & FOUNDATIONS OF TRUTH

noble traits. The Qur'an describes the prophetic model as:

☼ And indeed you are of a character most noble. [68:4]

Or to paraphrase: Indeed your actions are based upon the greatest code of conduct and ethics. The Prophet said:

~ Take on the behavior code of Allah.

~ I was sent in order to complete the most noble code of behavior.

The prophetic code of behavior reflects the divine Attributes and qualities and is thus divinely graced. Therefore, assuming His Attributes is the cause of eternal joy and will bring one to the bliss of Eternal Presence. Allah's commandments to assume this code of behavior and to take on His Attributes are numerous in both the Qur'an and in the words of His Prophet. Among them is this *hadith qudsi*:

~ My Earth and My Heaven cannot contain Me, but the heart of My faithful servant contains Me.

☼ The color of Allah is upon us! And what better dye than that of Allah. It is Him we worship. [2:138]

Thus the path of reaching Allah lies in directing the heart to transmit His Attributes and His decreed perfections. It is for this reason that it is said that the heart of the person of faith is the throne of the Merciful, or the abode of Allah.

The Garden which is attained through this Resurrection is referred to as the 'Spiritual Garden':

☼ The people of faith have succeeded, those who

are humble in their prayer, and those who turn away from foolishness...They are the heirs who inherit the (Spiritual) Garden of Firdaws. They shall abide there eternally. [23:13 & 1011]

The path is to exchange natural egotistic vices for what is virtuous and praiseworthy, and thus emerge from the darkness of confusion to the joy of inner harmony and light. As one takes on the Divine Attributes and qualities, one's outlook on life changes and aspects of the Spiritual Garden are experienced. Thus, one becomes the possessor of two Gardens (material and spiritual – worldly and heavenly) and the Master of two stages, in accordance with Allah's words:

✣ And for whoever fears the station of his Lord there will be two gardens. [55:46]

Personal development and spiritual evolution begin by reducing distractions of the ego and its natural vices of deceit, miserliness, envy, greed, lust, anger and other regrettable tendencies, and by embracing the virtues of knowledge, wisdom, forbearance, humility, generosity, restraint and courage. It is then that one practices appropriate wisdom and durable justice. When the lower self is sufficiently subdued and constant reference is made to the light of the soul, to insights and subtle knowledges the seeker feels encouraged to progress further on the path of *Islām*, *Imān* and *Ihsān*.

The Prophet has said:

~ Indeed, Allah possesses a garden in which there are no Houris, nor honey, nor milk, but rather, Allah manifests Himself there, laughing [with a sacred smile].

2. ROOTS & FOUNDATIONS OF TRUTH

The first garden is experiential (by the senses) and the second one is spiritual (realized at heart); the difference between them is highlighted in the Prophet's words:

~ By the One who has the soul of Muhammad in His hand, the Garden and the Fire are closer to anyone of you than your own shoe-strap.

Imam `Ali has said:

~ Whoever lives by reasoning and has deadened the self of all pride and replaced his grossness with subtleness, illumination and light will show him the way, so he then reaches the Door of Peace and the Lasting Abode.

The greater spiritual resurrection refers to annihilation in Truth (*fan*ā') and ongoingness or subsistence (*baq*ā'). This state is often referred to as Annihilation in Unity and is also called, 'The Nearness of *Nawāfil*' (supererogatory prayers,) because of Allah's words in *hadith qudsi*:

~ As long as the servant continues to draw near to Me with his supererogatory actions I will love him and if I love him I will be his ears, his eyes, his tongue, his hand and his feet. Thus it is as by Me that he hears and by Me that he sees, by Me that he speaks, by Me that he grasps and by Me that he walks.

Whoever realizes this state (of access to the Eternal Divine Presence, after the above mentioned annihilation) has attained the Garden of Witnessing, which is above other gardens. Shaykh Ibn `Arabi refers to it in his book, 'The Makkan Revelations,'[12] when he says:

---

12   *Al-Futūhāt Al-Makkīyyah.*

~ Indeed, there are three Gardens: The Garden of Divine Jurisdiction, this being the one for children who have not yet reached the age of action. The second is the Garden of Inheritance, which is attained by anyone who enters the Garden from those whom we have mentioned and from the people of *imān*. The third is the Garden of Actions in which people ascend according to their good actions.

The people of the Garden are of various categories: the Messengers, the Prophets, the Friends (*awliyā'*, pl. of *wali*), the people of faith based on knowledge who believe in them, and the men with knowledge of Unity, who, through the faculty of reason, have come to know that there is no god but Allah.

Muslims or believers have generally been grouped into three categories.

- The first group are the Prophets, the Messengers, and the heirs who are called the 'friends' of Allah;
- the second group are the people who have knowledge of Allah through unveiling and proof according to their various stages, like the teachers of instruction, the scholars who have delved deeply into belief and the law; and
- the third group are the people of faith and those who have followed by imitation. In other words these consist of the following three levels: the general masses, the elect and the chosen few of the elect. Their station in the Garden is according to spiritual stages they have attained, whether high, low or in between.

After passing through the three resurrections mentioned previously, resurrection for those at the

2. ROOTS & FOUNDATIONS OF TRUTH

advanced level is equivalent to their annihilation in Action, Attributes, and the Unity of Essence, and their remaining within Truth corresponding to their stage within it.

The lesser spiritual resurrection of the advanced level is annihilation in the Unity of Action and arrival at the point of witnessing the actual One Who administers everything. Whoever has had the veils of actions drawn aside by the opening of inner vision will witness the Actions in their absoluteness as only originating from the One Doer and the One Administrator, and he will be freed from seeing anything else, even the acts themselves. He will reach the point of witnessing the acts emanating from the One and only Doer, Allah. When one is firmly established in station of the Unity of Action, one stands on the plane of the lesser resurrection before Allah, like the corpse before the washer of the dead. The signs of this condition are trust, submission, entrusting one's affairs to Allah, and confirming it by one's own actions.

The outcome of this resurrection, after annihilation, is the Garden of Action, which is the first of the Gardens, and its pleasures and joys consist of witnessing the True Doer in every action and event.

The intermediate resurrection at the advanced level refers to annihilation into the Unity of Attributes and the arrival at the point of witnessing the One Attribute which runs through everything. For whomever the veils of Attributes have been lifted, all the veils of witnessing other-than-Him have been completely withdrawn, to the point where in the entire existence he does not witness anything other than One True Attribute running through everything, like the flowing of life itself in the human body. Thus he will have reached the Unity of Attributes, and will be present on the plain of the intermediate spiritual resurrection, free of the confines of seeing other-than-Him, which is true death; and this is confirmed by:

> ✧ We have lifted from you your veils and now your insight is sharp as steel. [50:22]

It is said that Bayazid alBistami was asked, 'How is your day, O Bayazid?' He replied, 'I have no morning and no night. Mornings and nights are for those who are chained to Attributes and for me there is no attribute.' Bayazid was firmly placed within the Unity of Attributes after the Unity of Action, through unveiling and longing. This is what is meant when it is said:

> ~ 'Essence is veiled by Attributes and the Attributes by the Acts, because anyone who has not had the veils of Actions lifted from him will not attain the Unity of Actions; and whoever has not had the veils of Attributes lifted from him will not attain the Unity of Attributes; and whoever has not had the veils of the Essence lifted from him will not attain the Unity of Essence.'

The greater resurrection for those at the advanced level is the witnessing of the Everlasting Quality of the Essence in the Essence of Truth (Allah) after their annihilation within it, which is a spiritual annihilation, not a physical one; as Allah said:

> ✧ Everything upon it will perish and the Face of your Lord will (eternally) remain, the Possessor of Glory and Generosity. [55:26-27]

and His words:

> ✧ Everything will pass away except for His Face, His is the Wisdom and to Him will you return. [28:88]

2. ROOTS & FOUNDATIONS OF TRUTH

This will occur for whoever has the veils of beauty and glory from the Essence of Truth (Allah) lifted from him, and from whom the veils of duality have been lifted completely to the point where he witnesses nothing other than Allah, forever and eternally – which is the meaning of the saying that there is nothing in existence but Allah, His Names, His Attributes, and His Acts. Thus, all is Him, by Him, from Him, and to Him.

Those who have arrived at the Unity of Essence, are present on the plain of the greater resurrection and witness the meaning of Allah's words:

✪ ...and whose is the dominion today? It is Allah's, the One, the Subduer... [40:16]

because their vision of Unity has subdued all other essences by virtue of the truth that there is nothing in existence but Allah. And in the confirmation:

✪ ...Say: Allah, then leave them to indulge in their vain discourses [6:91]

and correspondingly:

✪ ...and take (accept) not any other deity with Allah [17:22]

'Unity of the Essence' is the highest level of all inner states and realizations. As Allah said:

✪ He is the First, the Last, the Manifest and the Hidden and He is Knower of all things. [57:3]

which is an indication of this witnessing.

The outcome of standing upon the plain of this Spiritual Resurrection is 'The Garden of the Essence', which is the highest of all the gardens reserved for the people of Unity who have progressed on the path of Unity:

> ☼ Indeed the cautiously aware are in gardens and rivers in the seat of honor with the most Powerful Sovereign. [54:5455]

because whoever witnesses other than Him in existence is not in Unity, nor is he one who is fearfully aware (*muttaqi*). For this reason Allah says:

> ☼ O you who have faith, be cautiously aware of Allah with the awareness that is due to Him and do not die unless you are in full submission to Him. [3:102]

That is to say, do not die the death of meaning, which in this station is referred to as annihilation, 'unless you are in full submission', that is, *Islām*, which is the Unity of the Essence.

Imam `Ali said:

> ~ I ascribe to Islam something which no one has previously ascribed to it: Islam is surrender, surrender is certainty, certainty is belief, belief is affirmation, affirmation is to execute and carry out, execution and carrying out are good actions.

CHAPTER 3

Preliminary Keys to Effective Worship

3.1 Rituals, Intention, Attention & Appropriate Action

Islam is the path of unity between one's intentions and actions. It begins with a declaration by the tongue, reflecting a sincere heart. A Muslim is someone who professes that there is one God and that Muhammad is the Messenger of that one God. Knowledge of this truth will become clearer in time. Recognition of this condition gives rise to a formal expression of worship for which preparation is required. Our natural needs in life will make us supplicate, invoke and pray for God's power to relieve us from needs, pains and fears. Communal supplications and prayers increase the power of the act.

There are special occasions, times and places, that are auspicious, such as the nights of power during the month of fasting – Ramadan. There are also sacred places where acts of worship are enhanced. The symbolic house of God was established by the Prophet Abraham in Makkah, where people walk around (*tawāf*) the Ka`bah and pray in its precinct. Jerusalem is another major center for prayer and pilgrimage. The practices of regular and formal prayers, fasting, pilgrimage, payment of wealth tax, performing good actions, and exerting outer and inner struggle to reform the self, are part of the essential package of Islam.

Cleanliness of body, mind and heart are essential preconditions to acts of prayer and worship. Equally important is to eat and drink modestly of that which is prescribed as pure and clean. There are clear boundaries and restrictions to be observed on our senses and actions. Outer limitations hint at the limitlessness of the inner. It is important for human beings to realize that we need God's grace and mercy at all times, and that it can be received when we are ready and receptive. Restrictions and shortages are nature's way to limit our egotistic excesses.

The foundation of the *Dīn*, metaphorically and practically, is based upon the mystery of Oneness, which pervades universally. A mature human being can approach this goal after having attained reasonable spiritual confidence within one's own self. If you are not unified within your mind, heart, and intentions then '*tawhīd*' remains a vague idea, rather than a present reality. It is only a unified person who can be at the door of sacred unity.

The success of any action very much depends upon the original intention and preparation. If you start to build an edifice by laying the correct foundation and continue in that disciplined manner you will have a handsome house. But if the building proceeds haphazardly, you will be left with a ramshackle building.

Living faith is about willing submission to the truth of one reality: Allah. The faithful seeker witnesses countless transient realities in this world but his focus is on the never-changing truth behind the changeable. His adoration and worship is preceded by yearning, calling, pleading, praying, and undertaking appropriate action. The best of actions are those that reduce personal desires and earthly attachments.

3. PRELIMINARY KEYS TO EFFECTIVE WORSHIP

As human beings in constant interaction with the world of causalities, we benefit by preparing to disengage from worldly demands in order to be more receptive to the inner world of lights and subtle insights. In doing so, we do not deny the gross reality, but balance the emphasis between the seen and the unseen. The Adamic reality contains an indefinable source of life called the soul/spirit (*rūh*) and a self (*nafs*) that connects the soul with the physical world through senses and limbs. The spiritual path is based upon making the self subservient to the soul which will provide higher guidance through the inner light that shines through a purified heart.

3.2 Ritual Purification (*taharah*)

In Islam the term *taharah* refers to both outer and inner purification (the purification of the self, the sense of reasoning, and the mind). With regards to evacuating impurities, all filth or bodily discharges should be removed and the body thoroughly cleansed. Ritual purification in its entirety consists of ritual ablution (*wudu'*), bathing (*ghusl*), and a process where dust is used in the absence of water (*tayammum*).

- The first stage is the purification of the body and the elimination of its waste to the extent that it is acceptable for acts of devotion. A healthy body and mind are essential for successful meditation and prayer.
- The second stage is the spiritual purification of the self, cleansing it from base behavior and despicable Attributes, and replacing them with praiseworthy and good qualities.
- The third stage is the purification of the sense of reason, which is to cleanse it of misguiding thoughts, doubts (about truth) and egotistic tendencies.
- Finally, purification of the innermost is to cleanse the self from the illusion of seeing other than Allah and from attributing anything to other than Him.

The process of ritual purification is carried out either by means of water or dust. Water is the source of tangible life, and represents 'knowledge'; in its absence dust can represent the same. Dust is the basic material substance from which mankind is made. In Allah's words:

> ✿ And Allah sent water down from the heavens and thus revived the earth after its death. [16:65]

3. PRELIMINARY KEYS TO EFFECTIVE WORSHIP

✺ So if you do not find water then use some clean earth. [4:43]

The purpose of this is so that you will contemplate your own essence and realize who it was that brought you into existence; thus you will be humble before Him and any thoughts of your own greatness will be removed.

The washing of the face has been described as consisting of turning one's outward attention towards Allah, that washing one's hands is to cleanse them from whatever they have come into contact with in this world, and the rubbing of the head is to improve the quality of the mind's thoughts. All of these forms of purification should be performed as a prelude to purifying the heart from all tarnishes that accumulate as a result of desires.[13]

---

13 In *Asrār al-'Ibādah* (Secrets of Worship), by Shaykh Zayn al-Din al-Shahid al-Thani (d.1558CE/965AH).

3.3 Outer and Inner Ablution (*wudu'*)

The Significance of wudu'

Shaykh Qadi Sa'id al-Qummi wrote about the meaning of ritual ablution as follows:

> The certainty and confirmation of both the worlds, seen and unseen, and their rejection, are attained by way of this [ritual] washing. This is accomplished by the washing of both hands and arms while centering one's attention upon the Creator. The face should be washed with a sense of embarrassment before Allah that He should observe you in the act of turning your attention to other than Him when He has forbidden you to do so. Then you wash your hands and arms from the elbow to the fingertips, while observing the means of Allah's creation, which represent the hands of His action. Then rub your head, removing ideas of leadership from it because of its being the highest position upon the body and because of its being the center of thought, thus demonstrating humility and removing pride.[14]

Allah said:

> ✪ There stands the abode of the Hereafter which we have assigned for those who do not seek exaltation and status in the earth nor corruption. [28:83]

The reason behind not rubbing the head in the ritual of *tayammum* is that placing dust upon the head is a symbolic action which represents separation, whereas the purpose of prayer is joining and harmony. Finally, you rub your feet

---

14   In his book 'Secrets of Worship and the Essence of Prayer'.

3. PRELIMINARY KEYS TO EFFECTIVE WORSHIP

and hasten to the mosque in order to confirm your efforts in the two *jihāds*, the lesser and the greater, which are manifested in your swift pace. Walking with a determined gait completes your ritual ablution.

Ritual Ablution According to Revealed Law

The actions of ritual ablution at the foundational level fall into three categories: obligatory, recommended and courteous. The obligatory may be divided into two divisions: acts and stipulations or conditions.

Acts (*alaf āl*) consist of five obligatory actions:
1. Intention (*niyyah*), the inward stating of one's intent.
2. Washing the face.
3. Washing the two hands and forearms.
4. Rubbing the head.
5. Rubbing the feet.

Conditions of Methodology (*kayfiyyah*) including ten obligatory stipulations:
1. That the intention be made at the time of performing the ritual ablution and that it be maintained until the washing is complete.
2. Washing the length of the face from the hairline to the ends of the hair of the beard. The width of the face should be washed the distance between the outstretched thumb and the middle finger.
3. Washing the hands and forearms to the elbow.
4. Rubbing the forward portion of the head.
5. Rubbing the feet.
6. Executing these actions in the proper order, which is to begin with the washing of the face, then the right hand and forearm, followed by the left, then

the rubbing of the head, and finally, the rubbing of the two feet, first right, then left.
7. The various actions of the ritual washing must be executed in the proper sequence of time. This means that each portion of the body should be washed in succession with each part being washed before the one previous to it has dried. The head and feet must be rubbed with the water remaining from the *wudu'* on the hand and face without using additional water. The above is in accordance with the method of the Ahl alBayt. There are some differences in the methods put forward by the various Sunni Schools which can be looked up in the relevant books of law.

Meanings of Ritual Ablution

After one has carried out the process of ablution as prescribed by the *shari`ah*, the self must be purified from all distractions and reprehensible behavior, the mind must be purified of wayward thoughts and doubts, the innermost must be purified from the error of looking to other than Allah and the limbs must be cleansed of the actions which are unacceptable both from the standpoint of reason and of law.

Intention is realized by sincerely and deeply intending to refrain from anything which may displease Allah in any way and that the acts of devotion be purely for Allah, in compliance with Allah's words in the Qur'an:

☼ Surely my prayer, my sacrifice, my life and my death are in the hands of Allah, the Lord of the worlds. He has no partner. Thus have I been commanded and I am the first among the people of

3. PRELIMINARY KEYS TO EFFECTIVE WORSHIP

submission. [6:162163]

Washing the face signifies cleansing the 'face of one's heart' from the impurities of attachment to the world and what is in it. The world is nothing but a fleeting image and those who seek after it can only be disappointed. Imam `Ali has echoed the words of the Prophet:

~ The love of the world is at the head of every error and the abandonment of the world is at the head of every act of worship.

He also said:

~ O World, deceive someone else for I have given you the threefold divorce from which there is no returning.

The washing of the two hands refers to washing them and cleansing them from whatever they have grasped of this world's possessions and human attachments. Their purification cannot truly be realized except through the abandonment of whatever is at their disposal and under their jurisdiction.

The wiping of the head implies purifying the mind and faculty of reason from the love of the world, possessions, position and personal power.

The wiping of the feet signifies the act of preventing them from walking to other than what Allah is pleased with, both outwardly and inwardly. Outwardly the meaning of 'both feet' is obvious. Inwardly they refer to theory and practice, or to the forces of attraction and repulsion (desire and anger). Regarding this ritual the Prophet said:

~ *Wudu'* performed over *wudu'* is light upon light.

That is, the purity of the outward combined with the purity of the inward, or the light of inner vision combined with the light of the *shari`ah* as a result of the combination of both inner and outer purity.

Higher Meanings of Ritual Ablution

This refers to the complete cleansing of the innermost so that one does not witness anything else but Allah, because turning to anything other than Allah is considered to be a hidden association of others with Allah, of which Allah spoke when He said:

> ✧ And most of them do not have faith without also associating [others as partners] with Him. [12:106]

Freedom from seeing other than Allah (*shirk*), either openly or in secret, cannot be attained except through total purification of one's 'face', i.e. the face of meaning. Thus the traveler on this Path sees creation through the unifying light of Allah.

> ✧ ...and wherever you turn there is the Face of Allah. [2:115]

By the tongue of the Prophet Abraham, Allah has also said:

> ✧ I have set my face as a true believer towards the One who created the heavens and the earth and I am not one who associates anything with Allah. [6:79]

Shaykh Ahmad al`Alawi says:

~ Purification should be performed by pure water of the Unseen that pours forth upon the realm of the seen [the world of phenomena]. This is the water

3. PRELIMINARY KEYS TO EFFECTIVE WORSHIP

which is unsullied by change, by which purification must be performed. This water is unadulterated by change; it is eternally the same, nothing is lacking from it nor is anything added to it, nor is it dependent upon anything. Nothing is either above it, or below it. This water is truly unrestricted in contrast to the water of the physical realm and the water of the Spiritual Realm, both of which undergo change and transformation from their original form.[15]

Thus the *tahārah* or purification from the illusion of the existence of other than the One is not achieved except by means of this water. The source of this water is from the hearts of the Masters of gnosis, so it is necessary for those who want purification to go to them and be humble before their doors in order to obtain this water.

Shaykh al-`Alawi also said:

~ The meaning of water which has been transformed by impurity (*najasah*) is that it has been transformed by the existence of the self. Thus, if the self is mixed with this special water, its existence becomes as if it were nonexistent and will become useless for worship or anything else; in fact, the water itself will renounce you. However, if this transformation occurs in one or more of the qualities of this water, then it is suitable for customary obligations but not for acts of devotion. "Customary obligations" refer to prayer, fasting and other such actions. It is not suitable for worship which is the means through which one enters into the Presence (*hadrah*) of Allah and witnesses Him. This *tahārah* then is unattainable without this special water which we have discussed.

---

15 In *Al-Manh al-Quddūsīyyah* (The Bestowal of Holiness) by Shaykh Ahmad al-`Alawi, d. 1934CE/1353 AH in Algeria.

Shaykh al-'Alawi divides water into three categories: impure (*najis*), pure (*tāhir*) and purifying (*tahūr*). Thus, whoever possesses impure water has adulterated his water with the love of the world and inclination towards it. Whoever possesses water that is pure or *tāhir*, but has adulterated it with the love of the Hereafter, would be distanced from the love of its Creator. The possessor of water which is *tahūr*, or purifying, has not adulterated it with anything at all: he witnesses only his Lord and finds no contentment in anything other than Allah and His worship. His acts of devotion are solely for Allah and by Allah.

In 'The Lantern of the Path', Imam Ja'far al-Sadiq said:

~ If you want purification and ritual ablution, then approach the water as you would approach the Mercy of Allah, for indeed Allah has made water the key to His nearness and to your whispered entreaties and He has made it a guide on the carpet of His service. In the way that His Mercy cleanses the wrong actions of His servants, likewise outward impurities are not cleansed by anything other than water.

We are told that:

✧ He it is who sends the winds as good tidings ahead of His Mercy and We have sent down water from the sky as a purifier. [25:48]

And:

✧ We have created every living thing from water. [21:30]

Thus, in the same way that He has bestowed life upon everything of the world, by His Grace and Mercy

3. PRELIMINARY KEYS TO EFFECTIVE WORSHIP

He has made obedience to Him the lifeblood of the heart. Contemplate the purity of water, its fineness, its beauty, its ability to purify, and the blessings it contains. The Prophet expressed it in the following manner:

~ The person of true faith based on knowledge is like water.

Shaykh al-`Alawi said:

~ Let all your acts of obedience to Allah have the same purity as pure rainwater when Allah sends it from the sky with its innate ability to cleanse. Purify your heart with fearful awareness (*taqwā*) and certainty while you cleanse your outer limbs with water. Turn your attention to your inner reality with the water which is sent down from the heavens of absolute Oneness. Purify yourself from the filth of the illusion of multiplicity, because water is the key to reaching the court of the Divine Presence of Allah. Save your outward form by using that which will purify it. Eliminate your laziness and lassitude, with His blessing (*barakah*) upon you. Revive your inward self with the contemplation of the Beginning and the End, with the creation and the Return. Give life to your Innermost by observing the life in the manifestations of His acts, His names and His essence and contemplate the purity of water.

For the people of *haqiqah* washing the hands signifies not being deceived by the worldly provisions which fall into them, like possessions, position, or family, or by the rewards of the Hereafter, like the Garden. Viewing obedience and acts of devotion with the feeling that one is worthy of greatness as a result of them is, from the viewpoint of the men of Allah, disobedience, and one Master says the following about it:

~ And evil which befalls you is better than something good which makes you proud.

Likewise it has been said:

~ The best of actions is a wrongful action which brings about repentance and the worst action is an act of obedience which engenders pride.

It is this which the Prophet indicated when he said:

~ The World is forbidden for the People of the Hereafter and the Hereafter is forbidden for the People of the World and they are both forbidden to the People of Allah.

The wiping of the head is to eradicate the impurity of 'Iness' and 'otherness', and to indicate the sanctity of the inner self which is represented by the head. These impurities act as a veil between oneself and Allah. In connection with this it has been said:

~ Your own illusion of existence is a wrong action incomparable to any other wrong action.

We have previously said that anyone who witnesses other than Him is one who associates others with Allah (*mushrik*), and every *mushrik* is impure and filthy, and that which is impure has no way into the Pure Realm and the Divine Presence:

✧ Allah will not forgive one who associates others with Him and He will grant forgiveness for other than that to whomever He wills. [4:48]

3. PRELIMINARY KEYS TO EFFECTIVE WORSHIP

The wiping (or washing) of the feet implies the human inability to act and the inability to know except by Allah, because these powers are similar to the two feet, for without them movement in the quest for Truth would not be possible. The following verse amplifies this state:

> ۞ ...so remove your sandals, for you are in the Sacred Valley of Tuwa. [20:12]

One meaning of 'sandals' in this verse is this world and the Hereafter. Another meaning is the self and the physical body.

Additional Recommended Actions of Ritual Ablution[16]

- ◈ Using the Name of Allah: before the seeker commences his ritual ablution, he should remember the name of Allah, annihilating himself within it, so that he may then attain annihilation into the Attributes of Allah without great difficulty. While in the state of remembering the name of Allah one must be in inner silence.

- ◈ Using a small amount of water is recommended, because it signifies not diving deeply into *haqiqah* before it comes to you by attempting to hasten its coming or by taking from it what you do not have the strength to bear.

- ◈ Washing two or three times signifies annihilation in the names and in the acts. Annihilation in the Attributes is an obligatory action and therefore

---

[16] This section and the one which follows it are an abridgement of the teachings of Shaykh Ahmad al-`Alawi from his book *al-Manh al-Quddūsīyyah*.

does not fall into this category.

◈ Lining up to the right alongside his brothers signifies the seeker's beginning the journey on the Path so as to give greetings to those on the right path, and to not see himself as greater than any of them, but rather to view each one of them as looking down upon him.

◈ The use of a toothbrush (*miswāk*) is recommended before one begins the remembrance so that the mouth is purified and fragrant.

◈ The recommended, but not obligatory, actions include cleaning various parts of the body from the head, beginning with the eyes, ears, and tongue. There is a deadly poison in beholding with the eyes what Allah has forbidden. These glances are arrows which strike directly at the heart. Thus, if the person of faith averts his glance, holds back his tongue, and shields his hearing, the cleansing of the remaining senses and limbs will become easy for him.

Invalidations of Ritual Ablution

In the eyes of the people of *haqiqah*, ritual ablution is nullified by any impurity which is manifested by the body (e.g. feces), as well as whatever comes from the self. For them ritual ablution is broken by the tongue with lying, gossip, slander, verbal abuse, vilification, ridicule, and sharp words. Among the invalidations of ritual ablution which a person knows of within himself are: the performance of actions merely for the eyes of others, envy, hatred, enmity, cheating, deception, pride and laxity in one's obedience to Allah. Thus, if one discovers any one

3. PRELIMINARY KEYS TO EFFECTIVE WORSHIP

of these qualities within himself, he or she must admit it to his Lord and swiftly purify themselves so that they will not repeat it. Keeping company with those who do not constantly remember Allah and those who love the world and possessions are also considered impurities. Whoever wants to enter into the Presence of Allah must eliminate whatever distractions and impurities present themselves and not allow the self to rule either inwardly or outwardly, because the lowest level of the self (*alnafs alammārah*, the commanding self) is the most vile. One enlightened Master has said:

> ~ O Seeker, do not look to your own qualities at all, abandon everything in order to attain everything.

3.4 Ritual Bathing (*ghusl*)

The rules for the ritual bathing (*ghusl*) at the basic level of *shari`ah* include: obligatory actions (*wājibāt*); authorized nonobligatory actions (*mandubāt*); forbidden actions (*muharramāt*); disliked or reprehensible actions (*makruhāt*).

The obligatory actions are those actions by which ritual bathing is completed in terms of the *shari`ah*. They consist of three actions and three stipulations.

The actions are:

- *istibra'* (which is to cleanse the orifice through which urine and sperm pass),
- intention,
- and finally, washing the entire body from the top of the head to the toes, making sure that water reaches down to the roots of the hair.

The three stipulations which must be met are:

- that the intention be made at the time of the ritual bathing,
- that one remain with that intention throughout the ritual bathing,
- and that the ritual bathing be performed in the proper order.

Do not forget that the term 'state of ritual impurity' (*janābah*) actually means 'remoteness'; thus a true ritual bath will bring the seeker from the state of remoteness into a state of nearness to and awareness of his Lord. The Gnostics consider true *janābah*, as the state of distance or remoteness from Allah, in contrast to the *janābah* which is the physical impurity referred to in *shari`ah*. This true *janābah* is encountered through attachment to the world and its pleasures.

If *janābah* is the state of being remote from Allah then

3. PRELIMINARY KEYS TO EFFECTIVE WORSHIP

everyone who loves and desires this world must be far from Allah. The love for Allah and His nearness and the love for the world and its nearness are two opposites which can never be combined. The Messenger of Allah emphasized this when he said:

> ~ The world is forbidden to the People of the Hereafter and the Hereafter is forbidden to the People of the world and these both are forbidden to the People of Allah.

The People of Allah, as mentioned earlier, belong only to Allah for they see none other than Allah. The Qur'an echoes this:

> ☼ Whoever has wanted the tilling field of the Hereafter, We have increased it for him and whoever has wanted the tilth of the world We have given to him of it and he has no portion in the Hereafter. [42:20]

Imam `Ali also said with regard to this:

> ~ The world and the Hereafter are in mutual opposition; they are two different paths. Thus whoever loves the world and accepts its sovereignty hates the Hereafter and opposes it.

The world and the Hereafter are similar to the East and the West: whoever tries to walk from one to the other will find that the closer he gets to one, the further away he will be from the other. Thus, ritual bathing and purification from this type of remoteness is achieved by abandoning the world, its pleasures and desires, to the point where not the slightest attachment to it remains. Even a slight attachment to the world is still attachment, as it has been said:

~ That which is veiled is veiled, whether by one veil or a thousand.

The order of this 'inner ritual bathing' is that the seeker first washes the head (which signifies the heart) with the water of true knowledge which descends from the Sea of Purity, and then cleanses it from the filth of the various desires connected to the world and to the love of it, which cause one to descend into the Blaze. It is no secret that the source of these desires is the lower self, its animal nature, and the forces of lust and anger. They issue forth from the very nature of man, as Allah has stated:

> ✧ We have created man in the best of stature, then We have reduced him to the lowest of the low. [95:4-5]

That is to say, that by his actions he is brought to the lowest level of the realm of nature.
Then He said:

> ✧ And as for him who fears the station of his Lord and curbs the self and its desires, surely the Garden is the place of his Return. [79:40-41]

This is a warning from the Creator that one should restrain the self from its never-ending desires. Likewise, restraining the self is an enticement to the Garden, which is the true abode of refuge and the original home of the spirit. Beginning the ritual bathing on the right side indicates the purification of the spirit (*rūh*), because the right side expresses the love of lofty and exalted things, referred to in the Qur'an as the 'Companions of the Right Hand'.

> ✧ ...and the Companions of the Right, and what are the Companions of the Right? They are among thornless lote trees, and acacias in clusters, and

3. PRELIMINARY KEYS TO EFFECTIVE WORSHIP

extended shade, and water overflowing... [56:2731]

Likewise:

☼ The heavens will be engulfed within His right hand. [39:67]

The washing of the left side signifies the cleansing of the body as well as the purification of the self. The left side represents the physical realm and the love of anything low or base, and attachments to the world. Water represents abandonment of these things. Thus, the world is specifically for the Companions of the Left Hand, of whom Allah has said:

☼ The Companions of the Left Hand, what are the Companions of the Left Hand, they abide in scorching wind and boiling water and the shade of black smoke... [56:41-43]

Thus, with the attainment of this purification, one becomes worthy of entering the Garden and into the state of nearness to Allah.

The highest level of purification from the true *janābah* implies *'tawhīd'*. *Janābah* means remoteness and distance. Thus, whoever witnesses other than Allah is far from Allah:

☼ Allah bears witness that there is no god but Him and likewise the angels and the possessors of knowledge based upon justice, there is no god but Him, the Mighty, the Wise. [3:18]

The true essence of ritual bathing for the men of Allah is detachment from anything except Allah, to the point where only Allah remains. Before attaining this cleansing it is not permissible for one to enter into the Divine Presence and communion with Truth. This is only permissible when the seeker has cleansed him or herself from the state of impurity brought on by their own illusion of existence and distance from the One Lord. The ritual bathing itself is the abandonment; while the communion with Allah is the adornment. This type of ritual bathing cannot be realized except through the annihilation of the knower into the Known, by the annihilation of the witness into the Witnessed, which is referred to as Unity where nothing is witnessed in existence but One Existence and One Essence; as Allah has revealed:

> ✧ Everything passes away except His Face, His is the judgment and to Him will you return. [28:88]

Allah has also said:

> ✧ Everything upon it will vanish and the Face of your Lord will remain, the Possessor of Glory and Generosity. [55:2627]

> ✧ Indeed this Path of Mine is straight, so follow it and do not follow [other] paths, which will divert you from His Path. He has admonished you in this so that perhaps you might be cautiously aware. [6:153]

True purification occurs when one becomes annihilated from the self into the spiritual existence of the soul and Allah's light. Thus an enlightened one has said:

> ~ I went out at a time after annihilation and from that point I remained without any 'Iness'.

The one in this state realizes the truth and comes to know the One Essence through the veils of infinite variety in Attributes and actions. Thus, he attains inner vision and realizes the meaning of:

3. PRELIMINARY KEYS TO EFFECTIVE WORSHIP

☼ ...and wherever you turn, there is the Face of Allah. [2:115]

The knowledge of Allah is a function of the heart and witnessing Him is the function of the soul. Likewise, the arrival at Him occurs through innermost enlightenment, which is the awakening of the soul. Imam Ja`far al-Sadiq indicates this when he says:

~ O Allah, illuminate my exterior by my obedience to You and my interior by my love for You. Illuminate my heart with knowledge of You, my soul by the witnessing of You and my Innermost Reality by transporting me to the arrival at Your Divine Presence, O Possessor of Glory and Generosity.

After the washing of the head from witnessing otherness – i.e. purifying the mind of all thoughts – comes the washing of both hands. The significance of this is that the hand takes the clean water for purification, and by taking it into the mouth and rinsing the mouth the seeker senses arrival and increase in longing. If he is sincere and real he will hear his heart utter:

~ Purify yourself for indeed you will be one of the pure ones.

So, ritual purification begins by removing that which is false and transient, and is realized by total awareness of Allah, so that nothing is left besides Him. Remembrance is performed continuously by the tongue, the heart and the innermost, until the seeker vanishes within that which is remembered. Then there is only One, as there has always been. *Lā ilāha illa'Llāh.*

3.5 Dry Ablution (*tayammum*) & the Meaning of Water

The *tayammum* at the basic level refers to the ritual purification performed with dust when water is not available, instead of the ritual ablution or ritual bathing. *Tayammum* is only permissible under the following three conditions:

1. Water being unavailable after efforts have been made to find it.
2. The impossibility of reaching it because of the lack of the necessary means for obtaining it, or because of the extreme difficulty in obtaining it, or because of a prohibitively high cost.
3. Fear for one's safety or one's property by using the water.

Tayammum is not valid except when done with earth or what may be referred to as pure earth, that is, dust, or clay, or stone. The manner of performing *tayammum* for ritual ablution and for ritual bathing is the same. You strike the hands twice upon the dust, striking once for the face and once for the hands. *Tayammum* is rendered invalid by the same things which break the *wudu'* and the *ghusl*.

Shaykh Ahmad al`Alawi limits the obligatory actions of *tayammum* to the following eight things:

- *Good earth*: This signifies the substance of a superficial external level of belief. As for the inner deeply rooted belief, it is the knowledge which comes from Allah and which is referred to as 'pure water'. The meaning of 'pure' is that the seeker aspires to a belief devoid of doubt.
- *Intention*: The first action of the one who possesses this belief should be the sincere intention of what

3. PRELIMINARY KEYS TO EFFECTIVE WORSHIP

he believes. The true meaning behind this is that he should make a qualified intention because whoever performs *tayammum* should not intend to persist in this act, but rather, he should intend to perform *tayammum* as long as he lacks water, or is unable to obtain it – in the same way that an ignorant person would not be content to remain veiled so that he lived, died, and was resurrected veiled. Thus every man attains what he intends.

- *The first striking (of the dust)*: Meaning the placing of the hands upon, or grasping of, belief.
- *The wiping of the two hands*: Signifying the utmost in grasping without laxity or lassitude.
- *The wiping of the face*: Signifying complete attention to the belief, both outwardly and inwardly, that is, with both the heart and the tongue.
- *Immediacy*: Meaning one is not slack in confirming his belief.
- *Joining*: That is, to join the belief uttered by the tongue with the heart.
- *Presence*: This signifies that the person who has attained this station is aware of the ever-presence of Allah, as if he actually could see Him and observe Him with his heart and Innermost Secret.

Invalidations of Tayammum

These are the same as whatever invalidates ritual ablution with the addition of one other thing, which is the existence of water. Thus, whoever finds water has found the Truth of Certainty (*haqq alyaqīn*) and invalidates whatever he possessed of the Knowledge of Certainty (*`ilm alyaqīn*). *`Ilm al-yaqīn* is to have knowledge of something with certainty

– say, water. It is the initial stage. Through knowledge one arrives at witnessing: `ayn al-yaqīn (the eye of witnessing) which is to actually see the water. When the witnessing transforms into the drinking of the water, haqq al-yaqīn, or the truth of certainty, is reached.

All these preliminaries are potentized according to the extent of one's inner orientation and intention. The intention of the doer is paramount. The procedure is subservient to the intention.

The Meaning of Water & Dust

The water of purification from the point of view of reason as well as from the standpoint of the traditions is divine knowledge. The explanation of this is that Allah has stated:

> ✪ ...and We have made from water everything living. [21:30]

'Water' in this verse symbolizes knowledge. The perfection of knowledge differs qualitatively and quantitatively. Real knowledge is the knowledge of Allah and His ways in creation and beyond, which Allah confirms in the following words:

> ✪ And there is nothing which does not glorify His praise, but you do not understand their glorification, [17:44]

because the glorification (tasbīh) of something cannot occur until after having knowledge and love of it.

Allah's perfect generosity is described in Qur'an as:

> ✪ He sends down the water from the sky then watercourses flow according to their measure. [13:17]

3. PRELIMINARY KEYS TO EFFECTIVE WORSHIP

'Water' here means 'knowledge', while 'watercourses' signify 'the hearts', and 'according to their measure' means 'according to their readiness and ability to grasp the knowledge'.

✡ And His Throne rests upon the Water. [11:7]

This also bears the same significance because there is no relationship between the Throne of form and the water of form, either from the standpoint of the *shari`ah* or of reason. The word 'throne' must signify knowledge, for there is no true illumined life without knowledge of Essence and the Originator and Sustainer of life – Allah. Thus, the life of everything is dependent upon knowledge.

✡ The All-Merciful sits firmly upon the Throne. [20:5]

To sit firmly (*istawā*) means to exercise power over something. If the Throne is distinguished in this way by Allah, it indicates that the Throne is the greatest thing in the realm of phenomena and the exercising of authority over the greatest and the least. As for the real significance of the word 'dust': in the same way that the word 'water' signifies spiritual knowledge, 'dust' signifies the acquired knowledge in the physical, material realm, as Allah has said in the Qur'an:

✡ Indeed, the like of Jesus with Allah is like Adam; He created him from dust. [3:59]

Dust and all its components are the principal substance in His creation, although other elements also exist within the created form. Thus dust symbolizes the earth and whatever it contains of the various compounds in the creation of Adam. Similarly, the Jinn and Shaytans are created from fire and other related elements.

The source of knowledge and its origin is illumination which is an emanation of divine knowledge, referred to as revelation, inspiration, and unveiling. If the people of *tariqah* do not purify their inner selves with the water of knowledge, it is permissible for them to turn their attention to outward knowledge in order to cleanse their inner self and purify it to the extent of their ability. Outward knowledge, like the *shari`ah*, and inner knowledge, like the *tariqah* or anything above it, are all derived from the knowledge of *haqiqah*, that is, from the divine knowledge already mentioned.

If the pure knowledge of *haqiqah* is not available, one may make use of the dust (outer knowledge) of the physical world, because the purification of the outward will gradually lead to the purification and illumination of the inward. Allah commanded His slaves to purify their inner selves, beginning with the body, by carrying out the duties required by the *shari`ah*. If one is unable to purify the inner self with the help of reasoning, which itself may also be the realm of *haqiqah*, it is permissible to perform, as an initial step, the purification of the outward to help one reach the level of inward purification.

✿ ...and your garment, cleanse it, and shun uncleanliness. [74:4-5]

One profound meaning of this verse is that it refers to the return of the seeker to his original state of pre-consciousness, which is 'dust'. It can also signify 'water', which is also his origin. Thus Allah states:

✿ It is easy for Me, I created you before and you were nothing. [19:9]

3. PRELIMINARY KEYS TO EFFECTIVE WORSHIP

That is, if the seeker is unable to make use of the water of Truth or to obtain it in order to cleanse his inner self then he should return to the basic, lowest substance from which he was created in order that he may attain to the state of humility and poverty (*faqr*) before Allah, which has been well expressed by Ibn `Ata' Allah:

~ When *faqr* (poverty before Allah) is complete, then one beholds Allah.[17]

Shaykh Ibn `Arabi indicates this same thing when he says:

~ When the seeker places himself on the earth, it is because the earth is lowly. This is like the intent of worship and servitude, because servitude is humble and worship springs forth from it, thus the purification of the slave of Allah is by carrying out whatever is obligatory upon him of humble acts of worship and the acknowledgement of his own want and state of need, adhering to the rules set down by his Creator and carrying out His commandments. If one is oblivious to the fact that he has been created from earth, then let him perform *tayammum* by the use of dust because Adam was of dust and we are his sons, and likewise because dust symbolizes poverty and need before Allah. The Arabs have an expression used to describe someone who is poverty stricken which illustrates the connection between dust and poverty. If a man is destitute they say, "The hand of the man has become dusty".[18]

---

17   Ibn `Ata' Allah al-Iskandari (d.709 AH) in his book *al-Hikām*.
18   *Al-Futūhāt al-Makkīyyah*, 'The Makkan Revelations'.

Water signifies knowledge in a spiritual sense because knowledge enlightens the heart. Likewise, water enlivens the body and revives the earth. The same relationship may be observed with regards to the state of one who follows or imitates someone else in the regulations of the *shari`ah* or *haqiqah* in the knowledge of Allah. The follower (*muqallid*) is the one who introduces the theory of the knowledge of Allah to his own intellect and whose thought becomes dominated by this theory. Thus, like one performing *tayammum* who discovers that water is available, his *tayammum* becomes invalid. Similarly, when illumination makes divine knowledge accessible, the domination of the mere theory of this knowledge of Allah over one's reasoning is no longer valid.

In general *tayammum*, in the above mentioned manner, is obligatory in order to advance to the level where one is able to use the pure water described above, the water of *haqiqah*, which will cleanse one's innermost from attachment and love for anything other than Allah.

Then he will wipe his right hand (i.e. his heart) in order to cleanse it from any attachment to the Hereafter and wipe his left hand (i.e. his self) from attachment to this world. The purification of the right side and the left are not complete without abandonment of this world and the next. For this reason it is a stipulation in *tayammum* to wipe the exterior of the right hand with the inner portion (palm) of the left hand and viceversa.

At the advanced level people purify themselves of 'Iness' and whatever remains of it that may lead to 'otherliness' and association (with Allah), according to the teachings of the Prophet when he said:

~ Indeed my heart is overshadowed with worldly concerns so that I seek forgiveness from Him seventy

3. PRELIMINARY KEYS TO EFFECTIVE WORSHIP

times a day.

According to the people of *haqiqah* the 'overshadowing' indicated here signifies returning to the realm of multiplicity, and *tayammum* that of returning to the outward world, the universe of external phenomena, which is in reality 'dust'. Likewise, the universe of the inward is like water. Allah has expressed the concept of '*Mulk*' in many verses of the Qur'an as 'earth' and He has likewise referred to '*Malakūt*' as 'the Heavens'.

According to Shaykh al`Alawi purification with water represents the final stage of closeness to Allah because there remain no veils between the one seeking purification and his goal. The purification which is performed with dust permits one to stand before Allah in spite of the existence of impurities because they cannot be removed except by pure water. If it is not possible to find pure water (i.e. *haqiqah*) the purification of dust may be performed in its place because of certain restrictions, such as fear for one's life, or that other harm will be done to one. This *tayammum* may be performed instead of purification with water in order to adhere to the outward portion of the *shari`ah*. To complete purification the seeker needs a spiritual guide who is acceptable to Allah.

Whoever has no water and does not find someone who will teach him the way to Unity – symbolized by the purification performed with water – may use *tayammum* instead of water until he finds it and pours it over his outward and inward self, so as to gain confirmation which will lead him to discover that which will transport him to the station of witnessing first hand. If one finds the water of the Unseen and limits himself to *tayammum* his prayer will be invalid, because the authorization to use *tayammum* is only given when specific stipulations are met, as Allah has stated:

> ☼ ...thus if you do not find water then wipe your faces and hands [perform *tayammum*] with clean earth. [4:43]

Similarly, the Prophet said:

> ~ Whoever acts upon what he knows will inherit knowledge from Allah which he did not know.

3. PRELIMINARY KEYS TO EFFECTIVE WORSHIP

3.6 Supplicatory Prayer (*du`a*)

Supplication (*du`a*) is distinct from the ritually prescribed prayer of *salāt*. Literally meaning 'calling upon' Allah, it can precede or follow *salāt* and indeed be practiced at any time of the day, on numerous occasions, as a way of directing the will of the supplicant. Muslims are exhorted to call upon Allah for the fulfillment of their needs and desires.

> ✧ And if My servants inquire of you, I am indeed near, I will answer the supplication of one who calls if he calls Me, so let them seek an answer from Me and let them believe in Me so that perhaps they might be rightly guided. [2:186]

The Prophet said:

> ~ Supplication is the weapon of the person of faith.

He also said:

> ~ A supplication is better [for the one in need] than reciting the Qur'an.

Sayyid Tabataba'i said the following in his interpretation of the Qur'an:

> ~ A supplication and a petition turn the attention of the One called upon towards the direction of the caller. The act of beseeching brings about an advantage or benefit by which the need of the petitioner is fulfilled, after this attention is gained. Thus, a petition is the highest form of supplication.[19]

---

19   *AlMīzān fī Tafsīr alQur'ān* ('The Balance in the Interpretation of Qur'an'), by Allamah Muhammad Husayn Tabataba'i (d. 1981 CE / 1402 AH).

It is said that a supplication is the essence of worship and is not actualized without the proper courtesy and the fulfillment of the specific conditions, both outwardly and inwardly. Imam Ja`far alSadiq said:

> ~ Adhere to the courtesy of supplication, acknowledging Whom it is that you are calling to, and how you call Him. You should know the reason you are calling upon Him and realize His Greatness and His Majesty. Be aware in your heart of the knowledge He possesses of what is hidden deeply within you and His perception of your innermost secret and whatever extent of truth or falsehood lies there. Know the ways to your own salvation and destruction so that you will not request something from Allah which will bring about your destruction while you suppose that it will be the cause of your salvation.

Allah says:

> ✧ ...and man supplicates for evil as he prays for goodness, and man is indeed hasty. [17:11]

Think about what you ask for and why you are asking. A supplication is a means used to truly seek an answer from Allah. It is a genuine call of the heart as a result of its actual focusing upon the Lord. It is the abandonment of all preferences and complete submission, outwardly and inwardly, to Allah. The essence of a supplication is connected to what is in the heart and is uttered by the tongue, not what the tongue babbles foolishly and thoughtlessly.

> ✧ Everything within the heavens and earth petitions Him, He is ever engaged upon some matter. [55:29]

3. PRELIMINARY KEYS TO EFFECTIVE WORSHIP

✪ He has granted you all that you have asked Him for. [14:34]

This refers to what is asked of Him by the good nature of man and by the sound heart. These verses indicate that man calls out to Allah through his innate nature by virtue of his connection to the means and medium of supplication. This type of supplication comes through the natural unified state which has existed before any association (of others with Allah) or heedlessness had adulterated it. This supplication and this worship are the original and accepted ones. As for the courtesy of the petitioner, the Qur'an clarifies how:

✪ Call upon your Lord in humility and awe... Call upon Him in fear and longing. [7:5556]

And, as the Prophet Zakariyyah confessed:

✪ I have never been unsuccessful in my prayer to You. [19:4]

Thus humility, longing, fear, perseverance, goodness of action, faith based on knowledge, and calling upon Allah exclusively with total reliance on Him are the various courtesies one should have when petitioning at the door of the Lord, for they are conditions for the acceptance of a supplication. The Prophet said:

~ Allah will not answer a supplication from a heart that is distracted.

There are many reasons why a supplication may not be accepted. The most important of them is the failure to fulfill the above-mentioned conditions. It has been related that the Prophet said:

~ Allah has revealed: "Anyone in creation who takes refuge with someone or something else in creation other than Me, I will cut off the means for him in the heavens and earth. So if he petitions Me I will not grant it to him; if he calls out to Me, I will not answer. Likewise, there is no one in creation who takes refuge with Me exclusively of all others but that the heavens and earth will guarantee their sustenance. Should they call Me, I will answer them. If they petition Me, I will grant it to them. If they seek My forgiveness, I will forgive them."

In 'The Lantern of the Path' we learn that Imam Ja'far alSadiq was asked: 'Why is it we make supplication yet receive no answer?' He replied:

~ Because you call out to One whom you do not know and you petition One whom you do not understand. Need is the essence of the life-transaction (*dīn*). When one is blind to Allah the prayer will bring about disappointment, because whoever is unaware of the lowliness of his self (*nafs*) and is unaware that his heart and innermost secret is under Allah's power, will deem that he may make requests of Allah and he supposes that his request is a supplication. This assumption is insolence before Allah.

The Prophet related the following *hadith qudsi*:

~ Whoever occupies himself with remembrance of Me instead of beseeching Me, I will bestow upon him better than what I will bestow upon those who beseech Me.

3. PRELIMINARY KEYS TO EFFECTIVE WORSHIP

Imam Ja`far alSadiq said:

~ I made a supplication to Allah once and He answered me and I forgot what I needed, because His answer to His servant when he calls Him is greater and more glorious than whatever it was that His servant wanted, even if it was the Garden and its eternal bliss. But only the people of exalted action and knowledge, the victorious, the chosen few of Allah and His Elect, will perceive and understand this.

As for the secrets behind the lack of an immediate answer to a supplication, they include numerous things viz:

a. The **first** among them being: the unacceptability of the supplication. This happens when fulfillment of the conditions and the courtesies mentioned above, among them being sincerity of the heart, humility and courtesy, is absent. Or one may be doubtful and hesitant concerning the acceptance of a supplication, which means doubting Allah's power and generosity. It is related that the Prophet said:

~ Make a supplication to Allah while you are certain of an answer.

In a similar vein Allah said in a *hadith qudsi*:

~ I see what My servant thinks of Me, so let him not think anything but good of Me.

b. **Secondly:** the imagined needs of the petitioner. The ignorant one will ask for something which he thinks he needs but which in reality he does not.

For example, the sick person who has a fever might ask that the fever subside, when the fever might be what is actually curing him. It is the cure he wants but because of his ignorance he asks for something which is actually harmful to him.

c. **Thirdly,** the answer may come to the call of the heart and not merely in reply to the request of his tongue. This is another state in which one imagines that Allah is not answering a supplication when in reality Allah has answered what is in the heart and innermost self of the petitioner, in spite of the fact that this does not concur with the request of his tongue.

d. **Fourthly:** A delay in the answer. The following words are recorded in the will and testament of Imam ʿAli to his son Imam Husayn:

~ Perhaps an answer has been delayed so that it would be greater in terms of the reward for the petitioner and greater in the giving to the hopeful. You might have asked for something and were not given it while you were given something better than it in this world and the next. Perhaps something has been withheld from you for your own good. Many a thing one seeks may prove to be the destruction of one's *Dīn* should it be granted. Let your petitions be for something whose goodness remains, and let its affliction be removed from you. Your possessions will not remain for you, nor will you remain for them.

Delay may mean that whatever is stored up for the petitioner is better than that which has been delayed. As for occasions when one asks that afflictions be withheld and yet Allah sends them, it is perhaps because withholding them

3. PRELIMINARY KEYS TO EFFECTIVE WORSHIP

might have been harmful or destructive for the petitioner.

e. **Fifthly:** the answer comes in the Hereafter or when it is accepted as atonement for some wrong action. The Prophet said to those who make supplication:

~ Hasten to Allah with your needs, take refuge with Him in your affliction, stand in humility before Him and call out to Him. Indeed, supplication is the essence of worship. There is no one in faith who calls out to Allah who does not receive an answer. Either Allah will hasten it to the petitioner in this world or delay it until the Hereafter, or accept it as expiation for some wrong action to whatever the extent of the supplication as long as it is not accompanied by wrongful action.

f. **Sixthly:** Actions which nullify a supplication. Anything which will nullify other acts of worship will likewise nullify a supplication or influence its result and its answer. Imam Ja`far alSadiq said:

~ You must be earnest and not fall into heedlessness for then you would not be worshipping Allah as He should be worshipped.

The Prophet said:

~ A man may live for 60 or 70 years and yet Allah does not accept even one of his prayers. It is like Allah's words: "How many reciters of the Qur'an are there whom the Qur'an curses and how many who fast yet receive nothing from their fast but hunger and thirst."

Also:

~ Allah gives us this world so that we prepare for the Hereafter; He does not give us the Hereafter so that we can labor to gain the world.

Jesus is reported to have said:

~ O disciples, how many lamps have been extinguished by the wind and how many worshippers have been destroyed by pride?

Allah informs his servant in the Torah: Whenever you make a supplication to Me concerning one of My servant's wrongdoing toward you, beware that none of My servants have prayed to Me about you having wronged them; for if I wish I will answer you and answer him and if I so will, I will delay you both until the Last Day.

The Prophet said to Abu Dharr:

~ Remember Allah and He will remember you and you will find Him before you. Know Allah in times of wellbeing and He will know you in times of difficulty.

Imam Ja`far alSadiq reiterates the same teaching:

~ Whoever has offered supplication earlier [in times of ease] will find an answer when affliction befalls him.

It is also the proper courtesy to persevere in your supplications and to repeat them; this persistence acts as a catalyst in removing the pride of the worshipper and in increasing the magnitude of the reply.

Imam Ja`far alSadiq said:

~ There are three categories of people who will not be deprived: Whoever makes a supplication will

3. PRELIMINARY KEYS TO EFFECTIVE WORSHIP

receive an answer, whoever gives thanks will receive increase, and whoever has trust will be granted what will suffice him.

Allah has said in His Book:

✪ And whoever trusts in Allah, then He will suffice him. [65:3]

Also:

✪ If indeed you give thanks I will surely grant you increase. [14:7]

The Qur'an describes the human nature as being always in need, naturally insecure and in doubt. Through expressing one's weakness and need there is relief as well as clarification of intention and hope. Strength and wellbeing always follow weakness and illness. We are born with considerable needs and frailty and grow to recognize Allah's perfections – this is the path of perfect worship.

CHAPTER 4

Traditional & Transformative Acts of Worship

When the seeker has focused with his mind and heart upon worship, then transformation and delight in worship will follow. Once engrossed in the adoration of the Beloved, then all one's actions are for Him. Indeed, one's existence is by Him and unto Him.

In Islam each and every one of our devotional practices opens up new doors to Divine Unity (*tawhīd*). Devotion and remembrance of the Lord help to refine submission, awareness of Allah's might and glory, and commitment to live the prescribed path of Islam. The movements of the outer limbs in prayer (*salāt*) and the abstentions of the fast (*sawm*) and the constant struggles of *jihād*[20] are the battle zones where outer sight and insight are oriented towards the one and only Reality. Everything else in life becomes of secondary importance as it belongs to the created world of duality, opposites, and transient realities.

Each of these acts of worship or *`ibādat* is a *barzakh*, or interspace, between a normal state of consciousness and supra-consciousness. For example, *salāt* is standing up in dialogue, the attempt to connect the seen and unseen – for in standing one expresses praise. In this position one no longer looks ahead but at the earth, from where everything

---

20 The Arabic term *jihād* is derived from the root *jhd* whose primary meaning is to strive or to exert oneself.

has visibly emanated. Prostration is disappearance, going beyond the mind.

Each form of worship has a dual-pronged implication, personal and social. Worship begins as a performance of a duty based on belief and one's religion, and progresses in lifting one's consciousness above all limitations into the ultimate zone of pure consciousness, which is especially symbolized by prostration (where the self totally disappears into the light of the inner soul and into its flight beyond limitations). If performed well, worship leads you to the higher mind, to Adamic consciousness. *Salāt* like other acts of worship symbolizes the rise from our basic level of animality and survival to that zone of spiritual arrival.

In this chapter we will look at those acts of worship that are ritualistic and specified to time, i.e. *salāt, sawm* and *hajj*. The prescribed acts can make a great impact upon the individual person in bringing about heightened awareness and God-consciousness. The ultimate state to which these acts can take a person is enlightenment and transformation. The social impact of these acts has wider implications for the individual as well as the community. Weak members can be strengthened and the stronger ones will be encouraged by seeing the positive effect upon other members of society.

We will also look more closely at the other 'branches' that are not specifically tied to time, like *zakāt*, striving or struggling in the way of Allah (*jihād*) and enjoining good and forbidding evil (*amr bi'l ma`ruf wa'n-nahiy `an al-munkar*). *Zakāt*, for example, is not designated to a specific instance or place, whereas both *salāt* and *sawm* relate to time, while *hajj* is tied to both place and time.

According to prophetic ways there is an optimum way of performing each of these acts of worship. Islam can be

4. TRADITIONAL & TRANSFORMATIVE ACTS OF WORSHIP

lived by anyone in any time and in any place. In *salāt* the Islamic package brings together what appear to be diverse entities such as one's physicality, mind, intention and a special ritual. Each act of worship connects and enhances the others, while each has its specific courtesies and definitions. For example, enjoining the good is required at all times and in every situation and is therefore relative to the particular context in which it is practiced, e.g. it is a good act to stop the pain that a child feels, but it is also inappropriate to over-indulge a child.

The issue of context and relative merits is paramount. After all, all the acts of worship are there to heighten self-awareness, responsibility and accountability, and therefore to bring the self into unison with the soul or God's light. As such, the journey in Islam begins in darkness and ends in Light. It begins with ignorance and confusion and ends up with the knowledge that the whole universe is governed by a One Perfect Reality – Allah. All worship begins in 'professing by the tongue', then acknowledging by the mind that there must be one truth behind all appearances and movements, and ends up with knowing this truth without any need to discuss it. It begins with the tongue but ends up in the heart. It begins with following outer authority and ends up by witnessing the One and only true Authority.

4.1 The Branches of Faith or Acts of Worship

It has been generally agreed among Muslims that the branches of faith or major expressions of prescribed worship are five in number. The reason for limiting them to five is that the actions are either connected to the self alone, like prayer (*salāt*) and fasting (*sawm*), or they deal with wealth, like the obligatory wealth purification tax (*zakāt*) and the one fifth tax (*khums* – observed by Shiites), or they deal with both the self and wealth, like the pilgrimage (*hajj*) and striving or struggling in the way of Allah (*jihād*).

Allah is Ever-Perfect and Wise, while the Prophets and Messengers are the physicians of the self and doctors of the heart. The rules and laws with which they were sent are like the remedies and medicines which physicians give to heal the sick. If there had been a medicine more useful and more effective they would have sought it from Allah. For this reason we know that the medicine, which the acts of worship represent, is sufficient for removing the illness of ignorance, denial of Reality (*kufr*), doubt, and hypocrisy. The patient must take the medicine in the amounts prescribed, otherwise it may harm him or it may be insufficient. It is not permissible for the spiritually ill person to add to or subtract from these prescriptions; for example, if one prays five cycles (*rak`āt*) for the midday (*zuhr*) prayer as opposed to the prescribed four, it will be counter-productive and may produce undesirable side-effects, in spite of its being an act of devotion because it goes beyond the prescription of the doctor.

There are reasons for placing each of these actions in a particular order with one going before the other and one predominating over another, like prayer over fasting and fasting over the obligatory tax etc. Prayer is a combination of all the other four acts of devotion. The person offering

4. TRADITIONAL & TRANSFORMATIVE ACTS OF WORSHIP

prayer is in a state of fasting, *zakāt*, *hajj* and *jihād*. As for his prayer, it continues as long as he is in the state of the standing (*qiyām*), bowing (*ruku`*), prostrating and sitting during the prayer (*sajdah* and *jalsah*). During prayers one abstains from eating, drinking and all the other things that would invalidate the prayer. The tax which one pays during prayer consists of the payment from whatever he has jurisdiction over, and the body is included among his property – according to the Prophet's words:

~ Everything has a tax and the tax of the body is obedience.

The tax of the body is paid while performing the prayer, as long as one remains in the direction of the Ka`bah, facing the *Qiblah*, wearing the sacred garment of abstinence from any action which would invalidate his prayer, with the intention of seeking the contentment of Allah and obedience to Him, making the *tawāf*[21] around his heart to ensure that nothing enters it but Allah. As the Prophet said:

~ There is no prayer except when there is Presence of the Heart.

Hajj, or pilgrimage, is to journey to the Sacred House of Allah. Similarly prayer is also the journey to the Sacred House of Allah, which is the heart and the ultimate source of life within it. Outer *Jihād* has its rules and regulations, mostly based on self defense, or exerting oneself for the common good. Thus, while one performs prayer one is actually fighting against the lower self, which is indeed the enemy and the real rejecter of the *Dīn*, according to the

---

21   *Tawāf*, is walking around the Ka`bah during Hajj or `*Umra* (Lesser Pilgrimage).

Prophet who said:

~ Attack your enemy, yourself, which is within you.

Once, when he had returned from a military campaign, he said: "We have returned from the Lesser *Jihād* to the Greater *Jihād*." And when asked what the Greater *Jihād* was, he replied that it was the *jihād* of the self.

The fast takes precedence over the obligatory tax because it deals directly with the subject of the self, while the tax deals with the objects of wealth and possessions. It is for this reason that Allah stated in a *hadith qudsi*:

~ The fast is for Me and I shall reward it.

This is because it is an action into which ostentation or pride finds no inroad. Rather, it comes from sincerity, because whoever fasts is able to eat without revealing this to anyone. While it may be possible to deceive others, it is not possible to dupe Allah, the All-Seeing, All-Knowing. Thus, fasting is strictly for Allah.

The obligatory tax takes precedence over the pilgrimage, because it is specifically limited to wealth and possessions and is repeated annually. The pilgrimage, on the other hand, is only obligatory once in a lifetime if one has the ability to perform it. Whatever is obligatory annually takes precedence over that which is obligatory only once in a lifetime. The pilgrimage takes precedence over striving in the way of Allah (*jihād*) because it is obligatory upon everyone while the obligation of striving may be fulfilled if it is carried out by a part of the group of people to which one belongs.

From the viewpoint of *shari`ah*, however, prayer is given precedence over the fast because prayer is obligatory for all Muslims in various states or conditions, in contrast

4. TRADITIONAL & TRANSFORMATIVE ACTS OF WORSHIP

to the fast which is connected to a specific time period. Prayer is obligatory for every sane person who has reached the age of responsibility regardless of illness or health, whether at peace or at war, etc., while the obligation to fast is excused for those who are too weak, for young children and pregnant women. Prayer is repeated five times daily and the fast only once a year. Prayer thus takes precedence.

Fasting takes precedence over the obligatory tax because fasting is an obligation upon the self while tax is levied upon property. Not every Muslim possesses property or wealth on which he must pay tax but everyone has a self.

The obligatory tax takes precedence over the pilgrimage because the tax is obligatory a number of times throughout the year on property which does not have a once yearly payment as a condition.

The pilgrimage takes precedence over striving in the way of Allah because it is obligatory upon everyone, while *jihād* in the sense of military defense may be carried out by a portion of the people fulfilling the obligation for the others. On the level of inner meaning or *haqiqah*, however, *jihād* takes precedence over all other duties, because if one does not fight against the lower self one will not be able to rise to perform the ritual ablution or to pray. (For more detailed consideration of *jihād* go to the relevant section in chapter 4.6)

Prescribed Behavior

For centuries Muslims have used the terms obedience and disobedience when discussing the observation of God's laws and prescriptions. Cultures change and so do we. Until very recently cultures were based upon authority structures from within the household and the community.

This in turn was based upon limitation of resources and restrictions of mobility. It was easy, therefore, to enforce such authority. Much of the human drives in the past were based on fear and the need for survival. During the past few decades these drives have moved towards love and arrival at inner peace or enlightenment. Historically, most societies were composed of clans, tribes and extended families, but lately we are living a far more dispersed life, with more individuation and smaller family units. The mercy and grace of God, however, prevails at all times. We need to seek its map. Therefore we need to address the need of the individual to be liberated through personal awareness and experience, rather than through fear and heavy handed authority.

Quietening the limbs, humbling the body and controlling the senses are necessary for awareness to flourish. When there is least distraction, the heart and soul can ascend to the Divine Presence (*hadrah*) and Light (*nūr*). There is no doubt that the repetition of the actions and duties of worship and attaining the proper state of consciousness require good character and sustained, appropriate behavior. Appropriate conduct and refraining from inappropriate behavior are amongst the most important disciplines which enable the self to be prepared to take on what is suitable for it from knowledge and the states of knowledge of Allah, which is the desired goal.

The greatest of worldly activities is connected with teaching and guidance. After that come those related to the preservation of the physical body, and then those related to the preservation of one's livelihood and wealth. Thus the stages of obedience and disobedience, or rather, application and rejection, should primarily correspond directly to one's knowledge of Allah; then secondarily to

4. TRADITIONAL & TRANSFORMATIVE ACTS OF WORSHIP

the knowledge of whatever is related to the life of the soul; and finally to whatever is related to one's way of life by which the life of the soul is able to continue.

The first type of inappropriate behavior relates to whatever hinders one from attaining the knowledge of Allah and the knowledge of His Messenger. This is unbelief and rejection (*kufr*), and all Muslim scholars agree that there is no error worse than denial and rejection of Reality. The veil which lies between man and Allah is illusion and ignorance, while the means for drawing one close to Allah is knowledge. The deeper the knowledge and understanding one attains of the Attributes of Allah, His actions, His Books, His Messenger, and the Last Day, the closer one is to enlightenment.

Ignorance distorts the truths of faith, inducing a false sense of security and despair of His Mercy. Whoever has a deep and profound knowledge of Allah will never assume he is untouched by Allah's ways, nor will he ever despair of Allah's Mercy.

The second type of inappropriate conduct is rejection and it relates to destroying the self because its continued existence is what stands in the way of attaining this profound knowledge. This major deviation is referred to as 'the cutting off of the way'. Among other similar actions are adultery because these actions result in confusion concerning lineage and inheritance and natural generations are broken off. It is for these reasons that adultery and homosexual acts are not permitted and have to be dealt with according to the practices of *shari`ah*.

The third type of inappropriate conduct relates to livelihood and behavior. It is not permitted to rule over a people, subjecting them to oppression, tyranny, theft, or other abuses. Protection of the people is actually protection of their souls. Major abuses which fall into this category are theft, bearing false testimony, bribery, usury, and any act in which there is no mutual agreement.

The purpose of the path of Islam is to make the path to Allah smooth. The acts of devotion represent the journey of the seeker to Allah. The obligatory actions actually draw all who perform them towards Allah, to the expectation of His Generosity, to the all-inclusiveness of His Kindness and to the pervasiveness of His Mercy. If He had left the matter up to individuals, without them having an understanding of the law, they would have fought, argued, and disagreed, which would have distracted them from the Journey to the Creator. Such actions would only destroy them.

The divinely revealed code of conduct – or *shari`ah* – came with the necessary instructions concerning acts of devotion and mankind's transactions with his surroundings. Likewise, it established retribution to prevent the destruction of the soul and body. It provides for the proper punishment of crime to prevent harm to property and person and confusion over the matters of paternity or genealogy, which could affect successful reproduction of the species. The remainder of the *shari`ah* deals with the struggle (*jihād*) against those who reject the Truth, or the struggle against those who transgress, or other special situations. Its purpose is to protect the limits which Allah has set and revealed to the Messenger of the Lord of the Worlds.

4. TRADITIONAL & TRANSFORMATIVE ACTS OF WORSHIP

4.2 Formal Prayer (*salāt*)

Prayer constitutes the backbone of all the Abrahamic religions and teachings. The Judeo-Christian cultures are based upon personal and collective prayers, vocalized or silent. The words 'prayer' and 'supplication' are very general and encompass all human attempts to turn the mind towards the subtler and less tangible realm. Reflection and creative wonderings are the start of such an endeavor. A higher level of meditation begins when concerns and thoughts are reduced or cease for periods of time. As consciousness is experienced on different levels, so are meditations and prayers. In Islam supplication, prayers, and remembrance of God, are regarded as regular endeavors. *Salāt*, however, is a special package that has its own intricate rules and modalities.

The Arabic word for prayer itself may derive from '*tasliyah*' (*SLY*), which means to place a twig over a fire so as to straighten it. The following tradition is evidence of this:

> ~ Stand up before the fire which you have ignited upon your backs and extinguish it with your prayer.

That is, the fire which one has ignited by turning to other than Allah. Its derivation may also be from the word '*musalli*' (*SLW*), a term used in horse racing, to refer to the second horse that is following the first so closely as to overlap. *SLW* as a verb can mean to pray or supplicate, bless, follow closely, be in contact with.

While in the court of the Abbasid Caliph, alMansur, when Imam al-Sadiq was asked by him about prayer and its frontiers, Imam al-Sadiq replied:

~ *Salāt* has four thousand frontiers and you do not adhere to even one of them.

He was then asked: 'Tell me what is not permitted to leave out of prayer and by what action is prayer perfected?' He replied:

~ It is not perfected except by one who possesses the utmost sagacity and passion, who is not distracted and does not allow his attention to stray. He knows, therefore he is humble and steadfast while standing in resignation, longing, patience and anticipation; he envisages his goal and his heart is completely humbled before Allah.

Since *salāt* is the most noble form of worship which draws one close to Truth (from the root *SLW*, to pray or supplicate), it may also be semantically related to the Arabic word for 'bond' (*silah – WSL*), which joins one thing to another. If *salāt* bonds the seeker to his Lord then it also relates as a means of 'arrival' or 'attainment' (*wusūl*). If the seeker arrives at this destination, then he is performing the Prayer of Gatheredness (unification), in which there is no interruption or break, of which the Prophet spoke when he said:

~ The delight of my eye is in prayer.

☼ Those who remain steadfast in their prayer [70:23]

Prayer, then, represents nearness and connection between the worshipper and the worshipped. Its outer form is worship and its inner condition is that of witnessing. Because of its great value and high station it has been divided into obligatory and voluntary prayer according to the tradition of the Prophet.

4. TRADITIONAL & TRANSFORMATIVE ACTS OF WORSHIP

The ultimate purpose of the *salāt* in Islam is to be able to access the highest possible level of consciousness during the spiritual journey. However, *salāt* is beneficial at all times, even during the time of inability to concentrate or lose oneself in it. Attention is essential to begin with, but ultimately one would like to disappear in prostration for that is what the Prophet described as '*Mi`raj* of the *Mu'min*' ('night journey' or 'ascension' of the believer), which is transcendence to another zone of consciousness.

The great philosopher Ibn Sina divides *salāt* according to outer and inner. The outer is according to prophetic traditions and is based upon the Prophet's teaching that, 'He does not have *imān* who does not practice *salāt*,' and is performed according to specific procedures and at designated times, and is considered the most noble of all adherences to the requirements of formal worship. The outer procedure relates to the physical and involves specific readings and movements, such as standing, bowing and prostrating. As for the inner aspect, it is to do with the heart witnessing truth due to the self being purified, and is not subject to the restrictions and procedures of the outer.

The truth of *salāt* is to do with witnessing the Lord. And true worship is nothing other than divine love and spiritual realization. Outwardly the limbs express their humbleness and inwardly the heart expresses its utter reliance and connection to its essence. Thus the Qur'anic verse declares that *salāt* is a protection from wrongdoing but remembrance of Allah is of greater benefit [29:45]. Ibn Sina concludes that each aspect of *salāt* is essential in order for us to experience the transformation we are seeking.[22]

---

22 *Tafsīr Qur'āni fi Falsafah Ibn Sīna*, compiled by Dr. Hasan `Asi. University Foundation for Research and Publication, Beyrouth 1983.

Timings

Historical reports tell us that when the Prophet was taken up during the Night Journey various things occurred until just after high noon. At that time he was commanded to perform prayer with other prophets and angels, which consisted of two rak`āt for the noon prayer. This, then, was the first formal prayer ordained. The Night Journey, even though it occurred more than once, happened during the night, so the meaning of 'noon' is when the sun has reached its zenith and begins its descent. Everything external has its inward aspect, and inward aspects also have their own inner meanings on multiple levels. So just as outwardly the patterns of the sun conform with the outward cycles of day and night, so too do the inner suns comply with inner rules.

A tradition relates that the hour of the afternoon (`asr) prayer is the time when Adam was expelled from the Garden and his offspring were commanded to perform this salāt until the Day of Resurrection. The prayer of sunset (maghrib) occurs at the hour when Allah accepted the repentance of Adam who prayed three rak`āt: one rak`ah for his failings, one for Hawa' (Eve) and one for the acceptance of his repentance.

The evening (`ishā) prayer is symbolic of the darkness of the Grave, the darkness of the Day of Resurrection and the darkness of the Sirāt, which is the pathway leading to the Garden over which one must pass after death and which is finer than a hair's width. To fall from it is to fall into the Fire; and while some will pass over it instantaneously, others will find it laborious and difficult, and still others will fall.

The prayer of sunrise (fajr) symbolizes the rising to the heavens of the angels of the night and the descent of the

4. TRADITIONAL & TRANSFORMATIVE ACTS OF WORSHIP

angels of the day to the earth. Sunrise is thus the time when the angels exchange positions and obligations.

Preparations for Acts of Devotion and the Presence of the Heart

An act of devotion in the truest sense is praise of Allah, His Essence, His Names, and His Attributes. The measure of one's inner perfection or shortcomings is related to the level of the heart's purity, self-transformation and higher consciousness. It is the same with respect to acts of devotion, particularly prayer. Its perfection or deficiency correlates with the spirit in which it is performed. Sincerity and presence of heart are the two foundational pillars of transformative worship. Purity of the heart is essential if praise and adulation of Allah are to be tasted and deeply felt. If one knows the meanings and importance of the various acts and rituals of devotion, one's heart will be removed from laxity and distraction and one will awaken from ignorance to knowledge, as Allah has said:

> ✧ Those who have faith are successful, who are humble in their prayer. [23:1-2]

> ✧ So misery upon those who pray, but are neglectful in their prayer. [107:4-5]

The Prophet described the proper state in performing *salāt*:

> ~ Worship Allah as if you see Him, for if you do not see Him, indeed He sees you.

> ~ Worship as though it is the last act in your life.

Imam Ja'far alSadiq said the following concerning the meaning of the verse '...except those who come to Allah with a sound heart.' [26:89]:

~ The one who is sound is he who meets his Lord and has nothing within him other than Allah's pure light.

The importance of 'heart' is given in the verse:

☼ ...it is not the eyes which are blind but rather it is the heart within the breast which is blind. [22:46]

Imam Baqir has given the following example:

~ The 'heart' has within it a white patch which becomes slightly darkened with every wrong action. With repentance the darkness disappears. With persistent wrong action darkness prevails until it covers the heart after which point there is little hope for inner wellbeing.

All our outer actions and experiences have an immediate impact upon our inner state. In truth, the inner and outer, are in constant connection. You cannot express anger without its effect upon our heart.

☼ Allah has not placed two hearts within a man. [33:4]

The Prophet said:

~ Indeed, Allah has said in a *hadith qudsi*: "I watch over the heart of a slave and I recognize within it love for sincere obedience to Me and the desire for My contentment [with him]; I observe his demeanor and conduct. Whoever occupies himself with other than Me is one who mocks himself and it will be recorded in his Book that he is one of the losers."

4. TRADITIONAL & TRANSFORMATIVE ACTS OF WORSHIP

The following are extracts from 'The Secrets of Prayer'[23]:

The Prophet said:

~ Surely Allah will not answer a prayer from a heart which is distracted.

Imam Ja`far alSadiq said:

~ If the two qualities of longing and fear are combined within a heart it must be granted the Garden.

Imam `Ali said:

~ Blessed is the one who performs acts of devotion and supplicates sincerely to Allah while his heart is not occupied with what his eyes have seen, who does not forget the remembrance of Allah because of what his ears have heard, and whose breast is not saddened over what has been granted to others.

The Prophet said:

~ Surely, Allah does not look at your outward forms but rather He looks at your hearts.

What causes the lack of presence of heart are desires and attachment to worldly matters and whatever is related to them through thought and the outer senses. The most effective way to free oneself of this oppressive situation is to uproot this attachment and flee to Allah.

☼ ...so flee to Allah...[51:50]

---

23   In *Asrār al-Salāh* by Shaykh Zayn al-Din al-Shahid al-Thani. (d.1558CE/965AH).

The Prophet said the following about this:

~ The love of the world is at the head of every evil.

Whoever seeks the world is like the fly that has fallen into a pot of honey: however much it tries to escape, it only sinks deeper into it. When Imam Hasan was asked: 'Why do people honor those with wealth?' He replied: 'Because the wealthy person is in the company of their lover (i.e. wealth).' The cure is to remember at all times the ultimate purpose and meaning of this life which is the knowledge of eternal life and the presence of Allah's light and knowledge.

Preface to Prayer and the Meaning of Various Acts

The formal purification is performed with water which is the source of life – we have already looked at this in detail in chapter 3.5. Purification at the basic level is to remove outer impurities. At the next level it is to disassociate from spiritual impurity and to cleanse oneself from all despicable conduct. Then comes the purification of thoughts, inner desires and attachments.

Ultimate purification is to be freed from viewing the various states, stations, objectives and goals, and from all mental agitations and fantasies. All these are preludes to being pure at heart, free of hatred, fear, or sorrow. This purification leads to the realization that, in truth, there is no reality except that of Allah.

✿ None will touch it but the pure. [56:79]

That is, no one will touch the outward form of the Qur'an but the people of outward purity and no one will touch its inner meaning but the people of inner purity. Allah has given importance to the outward form of purity in His Book by including the body and clothing. Greater

4. TRADITIONAL & TRANSFORMATIVE ACTS OF WORSHIP

importance is given to the purity of the heart and the cleansing of the inner from impurities, which can be a greater hindrance than the physical impurities of the body.

The greatest of all impurities in the heart is the love for the world and its pleasures. By cutting off the inner and outer worldly distractions the heart will attain a presence which will enable it to become worthy of performing real acts of devotion. The self (ego) is like a bird which continuously flits from one branch to another. As long as the tree of hope and attachment to this world remain standing, the bird will remain in its branches. If this tree is chopped down by the *jihād* against the self and contemplation of Allah's signs, the heart will become tranquil, calm, and focused. The self becomes subservient to the soul within the heart.

This world itself represents samples of various aspects of the beauty of Allah. It is the cradle of training for the Friends of Allah and the Masters and the sowing field for the Hereafter. Many people have a little portion of the outward world, yet they are worldly people because of their love for and attachment to it. On the other hand, there are wealthy men and great kings, like the Prophet Sulayman, who are endowed with worldly wealth but their attachment is to Allah's light. Many a lover of the world is a pauper, while someone who has absolutely no attachment to it may possess wealth and honor, thereby winning both this world and the Hereafter. Imam Zayn al`Abidin said:

~ The world is actually of two types: one which is attainable and one which is cursed.

It is thus incumbent upon the person engaged in prayer not to be preoccupied in thought and heart. At the time of his worship, his mind should be clear and his heart tranquil. He must also ensure against outward disturbances so that he does not transgress the courtesies of the *shari`ah* with regards to his prayer, like turning his head or being distracted. One remedy for whoever is unable to concentrate or focus at the time of prayer is to pray in a dark place so that nothing will distract his senses. It may also help to pray next to a wall or in a corner or niche. Those who attend the mosques should lower their gaze, not glancing beyond the place of prostration, and consider perfect prayer to be one in which they are unaware of whoever is on their left or their right. In fact, it is not concentration per se that is required: one simply needs to go beyond the mind. Therefore, whatever helps to initially focus your mind is helpful. Become 'mindless', yet present at heart.

The meaning behind raising the two hands

One of the meanings of facing the *Qiblah* with open palms is that whatever is assumed to be owned by the seeker and all past desires and attachments have been cast behind him and his hands are now empty. In the magnification or *takbīr* (saying '*Allahu Akbar*'), which is performed throughout the prayer, his thoughts and mind are now submerged in the truth that Reality – Allah – Who is far greater than all our conceptions.

The raising of the hands may also indicate that one's hands are empty of any power or authority except what has been loaned to one. It is also said that raising the hands to the level of the breast is an indication that Allah is the focus and raising the hands to the ears indicates that Allah is above all.

In some Islamic traditions it had been explained that three *takbīrs* at the end of prayer are meritorious, as they symbolize the descent from the subtlest realms of *Jabarūt*

4. TRADITIONAL & TRANSFORMATIVE ACTS OF WORSHIP

(Kingdom of Light and Power) to that of *Malakūt* (Angelic Forces and Archetypes) down to the third level where we are, the earthly *Mulk*.

Allah's mercy encompasses the whole universe. As humans we can experience mercy at two levels. The first is the all-encompassing mercy which is not limited or conditional, of which Allah has spoken when He said:

> ✪ ...And My mercy encompasses everything. [7:156]

This mercy encompasses the whole of creation, good and bad, every animal, every plant, and all created entities or matter. This is the mercy which grants everything its rightful due and is referred to as the *Rahmān*, to which Allah refers in the following verse:

> ✪ ...the Merciful (*Rahmān*) is firmly established upon the throne. [20:5]

The second level of mercy is that which is experienced personally. Traditional scholars consider this mercy as special to the people of faith based on knowledge (*imān*):

> ✪ ...and He is Merciful (*Rahīm*) to the people of faith. [33:43]

and also:

> ✪ ...thus I will inscribe it for those who are in *taqwa* [cautious awareness of Allah] and those who give the obligatory tax. [7:156]

Obligatory Actions and Conditions

The difference between the conditions for prayer and obligatory actions is that the conditions are not actually a part of the prayer while the obligatory actions are a necessary part of the prayer. Prayer is composed of obligatory (*fard*) actions and actions recommended and performed by the Prophet (*sunnah*). Muslim scholars have listed five necessary conditions or stipulations for '*salāt*':

- *Faith based on knowledge (imān)*: that is, selfsurrender. The person of this station possesses the qualities of soundness in his words, purity of heart, and surrender to the All-Merciful, and follows destiny with inner contentment.
- *Maturity (bulūgh)*: Which is that one has reached the station where his words express the full and correct meaning, where he is surefooted, possesses deep understanding of the knowledge (of the men of Allah) and knows the sources from which they imbibe it. Whoever has not reached this state and knowledge would be ignorant in relation to those who possess this merit. The beginners on the Path are veiled from Allah's pervading Essence and whoever is veiled as such is not considered to be mature.
- *Reasoning (`aql)*: Any intellect which perceives other-than-Allah is not a fully evolved intellect and can be described as shallow, dull, or frivolous in relation to that possessed by the men of reasoning.
- *Cleanliness*: means that one must be clean and free of menstrual period, *janābah*, or any other outer impurity. The deeper meaning is to be clean and free of the dictates of the lower self and its whims so that one may be close to the Essence of purity – Allah.
- *Proper timing*: The time of prayer and witnessing refers to spiritual illumination. *Salāt* is based on illumined truth.

4. TRADITIONAL & TRANSFORMATIVE ACTS OF WORSHIP

The obligatory actions include specific actions, the performance of which is obligatory to the exclusion of other actions. Obligatory actions are those which are considered to be foundational (*arkān*), actions within the prayer which, if omitted, nullify the entire prayer, as well as those obligatory actions which, however, are not *arkān*. The *arkān* are five in number and are as follows: intention, the initial *Takbirat ulIhrām*, standing steadily (*qiyām*), bowing at the waist (*ruku`*), prostration with the forehead placed firmly on the ground (*sajdah*).

The obligatory actions which are not *arkān* include the recitation of *Fatihah* accompanied by another surah, or the fourfold glorification[24] in the third and fourth *rak`at*, the assumption of the sitting position between the two prostrations, and before standing, the declaration of the two *shahādat* (i.e. the *tashahhud*), the calling of blessings upon the Prophet and his family, and the *salām* at the end of the prayer.

Intention (niyyah)

The Prophet said:

~ The intention of the person of faith is better than his action.

He also said:

~ Actions are (judged) according to the intentions and everyone will have what he intends.

---

24   *Subhān Allāh wa'l-hamdu li'Llāh wa lā ilāha illa'Llāh wa'llāhu akbar* ('Glory be to Allah, praise be to Him, there is no god but Allah, and Allah is Most Great').

Intention has been described in the following manner:

> ~ Intention is considered by the general masses to be a firm intent to be obedient out of fear or strong desire, as Allah has stated: "They call their Lord out of fear or out of strong desire." [32:16] Intention with the illumined people is the determination to be obedient out of reverence and esteem. It is also the determination to be obedient out of longing and love. In the eyes of the Masters it is the determination to be obedient which follows as a consequence of their having witnessed the beauty of their Beloved (Who is entirely selfreliant in His Essence) and having become annihilated in Essence, Attributes and Actions, in the Divine Presence. ~ Imam Khomeini

Few people are constant in sincerity of intention and purity of actions. In the worship of people at the basic level this is considered to be the elimination of both outward and hidden *shirk*, like ostentation, conceit, and pride. In the worship of the intermediate stage it is the elimination of whatever adulterates the intention, such as desires, fears and expectations. For the more advanced, or what might be termed 'People of Heart', sincerity is the elimination of the impurities of 'Iness', because in the eyes of the men of awakened hearts, any image of the self is a great *shirk* which veils the Truth. Concerning the interpretation (*tafsīr*) of this verse '...except those who come to Allah with a sound heart' (26:89), Imam al-Sadiq said the following:

> ~ Whoever meets his Lord with nothing in his heart but Allah, that is, whoever has freed himself of the illusions of any other and there remains nothing in his heart but Truth; whoever has cleared the House of Allah (the heart) of any idols and emptied it of

Shaytan; whoever's *Dīn* and actions, both outwardly and inwardly are purely for Allah; Allah has chosen His own Attributes for us. Thus every heart in which there is any doubt or *shirk* has fallen.

He also said:

~ Whoever possesses a truthful intention likewise possesses a sound heart.

The Standing Position (qiyām)

The meaning of the standing position (*qiyām*) is to stand up to fulfill obligations for this world and the Hereafter. The seeker should mix with others so that he is one of them, looking after and fulfilling his responsibilities. When one has assumed the standing position his head must be bowed with his gaze fixed on the place of prostration, which is the dust of his humility and the basis of physical creation. He should remember his humble station, his faults and his shortcomings. He should see himself in the divine court of the physical and spiritual realms.

The Initial Takbīr (takbīr al-ihrām)

Imam Ja`far alSadiq said:

~ Allah is greater than whatever He could be described (or conceived) by. This is the meaning of *Allahu Akbar*.

The significance of the initial invocation (*takbīr*) is to invoke the magnitude of Allah with the heart of the worshipper, and to make himself utter it with his tongue, so that he becomes awestruck by the majesty of Allah and transfixed by His splendor. It is in this state that he should enter into the sacredness of prayer. It is not permissible for the worshipper to invoke any other qualities but those which express Allah's Magnitude and Majesty.

With reference to the invocations (the first being the *takbīr alihrām*, followed by six others which are considered to be *sunnah*), their significance is the lifting of the veils, which refers to the spiritual realms. With these invocations the two hands are raised for each *takbīr* in order to penetrate and raise one of the veils. The *takbīr alihrām* is referred to as the '*Takbīr* of Prevention', because it prevents the worshipper from concerning himself with anything else while in the Sanctuary of Majesty and Glory.

> ~ When you say the invocation, have a sense of the insignificance of everything between the heavens and the earth except His Majesty, for surely Allah observes the heart of his slave whose heart is not centered upon the true meaning behind his words when he says the invocation and Allah says: "O liar... by My Might and My Glory I will prevent you from My nearness and I will keep from you the sweetness of My remembrance and benefit in your whispered prayers to Me." ~ Imam Ja`far al-Sadiq[25]

Bowing from the waist (ruku`)

While the standing position represents the Unity of Actions, bowing from the waist (*ruku`*) represents the Unity of Names and Attributes, and the prostration represents the Unity of Essence. Since the bowing is symbolic of the

---

25   In *Asrār al-Salāh*, 'The Secrets of Prayer' by Zayn al-Din al-Shahid al-Thani.

4. TRADITIONAL & TRANSFORMATIVE ACTS OF WORSHIP

obliteration of actions, whoever witnesses the true nature of creation is without action and has thereby succeeded. Whoever sees creation as pure nonexistence has arrived. Since the bowing position is the first place of witnessing of the Near Ones, the seeker must praise Allah when he rises from the position, as Allah has said:

> ☼ Surely if you are thankful I will give you more...
> [14:7]

When the seeker attains the station of true gratitude and praise (both in word and in deed) then his faith will speak, saying, '*Sami`a 'Llāhu liman hamidah*' (Allah hears those who praise Him), that is, that Allah will accept this gratitude from you and He will reward you for it and He will transport you from the witnessing of His Acts to the witnessing of His Attributes. It is related in a tradition that when the following words of Allah were revealed: 'So glorify the Majestic Name of your Lord' (56:74), the Prophet said:

> ~ Use it in your *ruku`*.

Concerning the courtesy of the *ruku`*, Imam Ja'far al-Sadiq said:

> ~ Allah will illuminate any slave who has performed a true *ruku`* with the light of His Splendor and shade him with the shade of His Majesty.[26]

The true *ruku`* represents obliteration into the Attributes and the perception that no one is associated with Allah in them, because *ruku`* represents humility before Allah and the affirmation that what was fulfilled in the *qiyām* of service to Him is confirmed. It is recommended

---
26   *Misbāh al-Sharī`ah.*

to straighten the back in this position to demonstrate one's unbending lowliness and humble station. The bending from the waist represents one's fall from the station which he had assumed and the place he had considered his self to be in. The bending is also symbolic of the heart's fleeing from the whispering of Shaytan in as much as his attention in the *qiyām* was distracted. The *ruku`* of *haqiqah* is perfected by the bowing of every part of the body.

In the eyes of the gnostics it is the departure from 'the station of standing before Allah at the Resurrection' to 'the station of standing by Allah'; from the witnessing of the *qiyāmah* (Resurrection) to the Lights of Majesty; from the station of the Unity of Acts to the station of the Unity of Names; and from the station of 'Drawing Near' – 'then he approached and thus drew near' [53:8] – to the station of 'so he was the measure of two bows length or closer' [53:9].

Imam al-Sadiq has said:

> ~ No man performs the true *ruku`* unless Allah illumines him with the light of His Splendor. He will shade him with His Majesty and clothe him in the garments of His chosen few. *Ruku`* is first and prostration (*sujūd*) is second. Thus, whoever carries out the true sense and meaning of the first will do well in the second. Thus, there is courtesy in the bowing and there is nearness in the prostration, so whoever does not adhere to the courtesy will not attain to the nearness.

The Prostration (sajdah)

It is said that the one who performs prayer is seeking in prostration the origin of his own creation, which is dust. It is for this reason it is recommended to perform the

4. TRADITIONAL & TRANSFORMATIVE ACTS OF WORSHIP

prostration upon dust. Prostration represents the potential of the worshipper and also his nonexistence in that he falls down with the seven parts of his body (head, two hands, two knees and two feet) in dust with nothing remaining upright to claim his existence.

AlShahid AlThani mentions[27] that the reason for the repetition of the prostration in prayer is to affirm Allah's words:

> ☼ ...and from it (i.e. dust) We created you, to it We will return you and from it We will resurrect you. [20:55]

Imam alSadiq speaks of prostration as follows:

> ~ No one, by Allah, has gone astray who has carried out a real prostration, even if it was performed only once in his life, and no one has ever become remote and distant from Allah who has gained access and nearness in prostration...[28]

The following has been described as the prayer of the Mi`raj (the Prophet's Night Journey):

> ~ When the Messenger of Allah raised his head from the *ruku`* he said that the light which he saw astonished him so that he went into *sajdah*. When he lifted his head again he did not see that light. The light which he saw was that by which the heavens and earth are illumined and which is spread over the various forms of existence, both far and wide. The first prostration was mixed with the perception of phenomena and represented their negation. Thus, the second prostration was free of this adulteration.

---

27   In his book *Asrār al-Salāh* ('The Secrets of Prayer').
28   In *Misbāh al-Sharī`ah* or 'The Lantern of the Path.'

He did not see that light after the second prostration because there is no other station after that annihilation except pure beingness.

When the Messenger of Allah was asked the reason for performing the *ruku*` only once while the prostration is performed twice he replied:

> ~ Because bowing twice (towards prostration) from the sitting position is equivalent to a single *ruku*` performed from a standing position.

Prostration is the means to attaining nearness to Him with heart and soul. Whoever comes near to Him moves far away from others. Prostration does not become firmly rooted until everything tangible seems to disappear, and what remains is the essence of life.

Other Obligatory Actions

The most important of other obligatory actions is the recitation for which certain courtesies must be adhered to as well as certain stipulations. This also applies to the *tashahhud* and the *salām* uttered at the end of each prayer.

> ~ Whoever recites the Qur'an and is not humbled before Allah, and whose heart is not softened, and who does not experience remorse and joy in his Innermost, has degraded the majesty of the station of Allah and has clearly gone astray. Thus, the one who recites the Qur'an needs to have all three things: a humble heart, a body which is unoccupied, and a clear state. If his heart is humble before Allah, Shaytan will flee from him. ~ Imam Ja`far alSadiq

4. TRADITIONAL & TRANSFORMATIVE ACTS OF WORSHIP

The recitation of the Opening Chapter (*alFātihah*) represents a supplication which is demanded of the worshipper in the Presence of Allah, especially when he stands before his Lord and is showered by divine openings.

~ The recitation of the general masses represents a renewal for them of its form, its truth, and its perfection, and allows them the opportunity to contemplate its meanings and its traditional concepts. The recitation of the People of the Elect is an evocation of the subtleties of the divine words within the heart by the power of proof and the perfection of profound knowledge. The recitation of People of Knowledge is the expression of their own witnessing, after having attained the knowledge of the true essence of the divine words. The recitation of the Men of *Wilāyah* has three stations: one is understanding the stations of actions, the other is the station of names and the third is the manifestations of Essence. ~ Imam Khomeini

Surat alFātihah is divided between the worshipper and Allah. Thus, the beginning of the *surah* to the phrase 'You do we worship' (*Iyyāka na`budū*), is specifically for Allah alone, while the phrase 'From You do we seek help' (*wa iyyāka nasta`īn*) pertains to both Allah and His servant. Then from this point to the end of the *surah* the text specifically applies to the servant alone. Prayer itself is divided in the same manner. Prostrations specifically relate to Allah because the servant annihilated within them while the *qiyām* pertains to the servant because he is standing in the service of his Master. Bowing from the waist applies to both, where the divinely inspired lights manifest within the servant.

TRANSFORMATIVE WORSHIP IN ISLAM

Shaykh Ahmad ibn ʿAjibah (d.1809 CE) said the following in his explanation of the phrase 'Guide us to the Straight Path' (*ihdinaʾlsirāt almustaqīm*):

> ~ This is the combination of both *shariʿah* and *haqiqah* – that balance is obligatory. Thus one who is in this station must be balanced between the two aspects, the outer and the inner, and he must not allow one aspect to outweigh the other and become imbalanced, and, therefore, unjust. Justice is balance and Allah has commanded justice and goodness. Thus, one's inner should be witnessing while the outer is constantly striving and serving.

Further Obligatory Actions of Prayer

- ❖ Tranquility: In body, mind and heart, all agitations or concerns are left behind.
- ❖ Following a leader (*imām*): The leader represents guidance to what is right and awakening to truth. Thus, the traveler of this Path must follow his leader in the sacred sanctuary, which signifies the entrance into the hallowed and Sacred Presence.
- ❖ The intention to emulate: This means that the traveler is in unison with the leader at heart and by tongue.
- ❖ The proper sequence and order of the prayer: This means that none of the actions should be moved forward or delayed, and that no innovations should be made in the Path unless permitted. 'Enter the Houses through their doors' [2:189].
- ❖ The glorification (*tasbīh*): It is the declaration that Allah is apart from everything and yet the Creator

4. TRADITIONAL & TRANSFORMATIVE ACTS OF WORSHIP

and Controller of everything. The attainment of this most honorable of states occurs when one witnesses that the entirety of creation, with its limits of time and space, is apart from Allah. Annihilated into the Essence in prostration is the key to this realization.

When the seeker realizes that there is no other source of power and action in existence but Allah, then it is not fitting that he should be ignorant of Him in all actions. At the beginning of the act of prayers the seeker declares that nothing is greater than Allah (i.e. *takbīr*), and then takes hold of the strength and power (that is 'the firmest handle' [2:256]), which represents the outward adherence to *islām*, *imān* and *ihsān* combined with inward submission, certainty, and witnessing.

◈ Reciting aloud and *sotto voce* (under one's breath): The oral recitation or the whispering at various specific times throughout the prayer signifies that the seeker distinguishes between what is hidden and what is evident. The loyal worshipper does not reveal inner truths in the presence of strangers (ignorant beings), for that would be like throwing priceless pearls under the feet of sheep. Equally, a man of wisdom may not use a secret whisper when he should speak openly. Caution is advised here that what Allah has sent down is not used wrongly by people in high positions, or that one fears the reproach of someone who criticizes you on account of Allah. Rather, one must give to each his due, as has been said:

> Do not disperse wisdom to those who are not worthy of it and do not hold it back from those who are worthy, thereby depriving them.

- ◈ Calling blessings upon Muhammad: This is required of the leader (who has arrived at the station of witnessing) after he has finished his prayer and it has brought about the desired results for the seeker. The tranquility and unity which was attained after the unveiling of truth enables one to call Allah's blessing upon the Prophet. This call is the response to the yearning and love for the Prophet.

- ◈ The *Tashahhud* and the *Jalsah*: The meaning of the *tashahhud* is to go to the greatest lengths in witnessing, to the point where one is continuously testifying to the Oneness of Allah and affirming the prophethood of Muhammad. The *jalsah* represents humility, which one must assume prior to the *salām*, and by it the honor of the invocation is magnified before creation.

~ The *tashahhud* is a praising of Allah, so be a slave to Him in secret and be humble before Him in your actions, in the way that you are a slave to Him according to your words and claims. Join the truthfulness of your tongue with the purity of your Innermost Secret for, indeed, He created you as a slave and commanded you to worship Him with your heart, your tongue and your body. The realization of your state of slavery with regards to Him occurs through His Lordship over you. ~ Imam al-Sadiq

It has been said that whoever has witnessed the various lofty spiritual stations will not be content to witness anything else. Amongst the obstacles to the journey and to 'arrival' is having inner desires while not having concern for the actual state of the Innermost, so that one

4. TRADITIONAL & TRANSFORMATIVE ACTS OF WORSHIP

becomes worthless in the eyes of Allah – as the Prophet has explained:

> ~ Whoever is concerned with his inner will find that his worship is in proportion to what he extracts from it.

- ◈ *The raising of the two hands*: This action is symbolic of demonstrating that one's attention is directed toward Allah alone. One should recite the initial invocation aloud, and then raise one's hands to openly proclaim the action so that by doing so one combines both word and deed. With the increase in nearness, the worshipper becomes more absorbed and so his whole being undergoes a change and his illusion of his own existence begins to wane, all of which occurs because of his nearness to Truth, until the point when he reaches the furthermost extent of nearness, which is achieved in the prostration; as the Prophet has said:

> ~ The nearest that a slave comes to his Lord is when he is in prostration.

In prostration the enlightened seeker vanishes. Earlier he was standing, aware of existence, but after that he is annihilated with regard to his self and remains with his Lord. Sitting after prostration represents a return to the world of multiplicity without being veiled from the Oneness. Likewise, the *tashahhud* and the *salām* represent a return to the realm of multiplicity in both words and remembrance. This is why the *tashahhud* begins first with the testimony to the Oneness and Uniqueness of Allah and the negation of any partner with Him, and after that the attention is turned to the humble state of the slave, which is the state of the perfect Master, Muhammad.

- ❖ *The salām or taslīm:* these are given at the end of the prayer and represent a return to creation after one has died, as it were, in Truth. The Master of this station must turn his attention outwardly to creation. He must converse with it by his tongue whilst his heart is owned and possessed by his Beloved. Imam Ja`far alSadiq said:

~ At the end of every prayer there is to be found a security and a safety.

Whoever has carried out the commandments of Allah and the tradition (*sunnah*) of His Prophet with a humble heart will be secure and safe from the affliction of this world and free from the chastisement of the Hereafter. The word 'peace' (*salām*) is one of the Names of Allah which He has entrusted to His creation to make use of its meaning in their dealings, with whatever is entrusted to them as well as in their just treatment of each other.

- ❖ *The three invocations at the end of each prayer*: These are in consequence of the three unities which represent the reality of the prayer. They are a reminder of the invocations uttered at the opening of the prayer and are repeated as a reminder of the annihilation of everything. The first one signifies that Allah is the Greatest and that nothing occurs within His dominion without His Decrees. The second invocation signifies that He is greater than whatever is used to describe Him. The third invocation signifies that He is most exalted and that nothing exists within any realm or domain but Allah.

4. TRADITIONAL & TRANSFORMATIVE ACTS OF WORSHIP

✧ Thus wherever you turn, there is the Face of Allah. [2:115]

Additional Requirements

The following four requirements are essential for *'Salāt'*.

Facing the *Qiblah*:

The action represents turning the face away from all directions and directing one's total attention to the House of Allah. The meaning behind this is to turn the attention of the heart to the divine Presence of Allah. If one should deviate from it very slightly it is of no consequence because one who is veiled is not harmed by a slight deviation. If, however, one of the Near Ones deviates in his attention from the essence of the Ka`bah, his deviation would be considered great because it comes from one who possesses the certainty of truth, and this is called turning away from the Ka`bah altogether. The spiritual Ka`bah is symbolic of the Hallowed Presence, and the enlightened being cannot turn away from it even if he tries:

~ If I bothered to try to see other-than-Him I would be unable to do so.

Whoever is immersed within the truths of the Presence of Allah – who was unaware of the fact that he was outside and apart from it – would surely hear his heart cry, 'I am it!'

Imam Khomeini has said the Masters of Allah witness Allah everywhere. They see the Ka`bah of Hope in everything and the face of their Beloved everywhere. Thus he says: 'I have not seen anything in which Allah is not to be found within it and with it':

✧ And Allah's is the east and the west; thus wherever you turn, there is the Face of Allah. [2:115]

Imam alSadiq said:

~ When you face the *Qiblah* then renounce the world and whatever is within it, and renounce men and whatever they are up to, and empty your heart of every distraction.

Ritual Purity:

This stipulation is a requirement at the beginning and throughout the prayer. Thus it is incumbent upon the worshipper to be pure with regard to the place of prayer, his clothing and his body. Impurity here means any form of rebellion or opposition, wherever it may be. The cleanliness of the place of prayer is symbolic of one's outer; the cleanliness of the clothing is symbolic of one's inner heart; and the cleanliness of the body represents the purification of the inner, which is the Innermost. The outer is not purified unless it is cleansed and adorned by the *shari`ah*, by carrying out its injunctions, and by abstaining from its prohibitions. The inner is not cleansed except by the garment of *tariqah* or the original Path, and by abandoning envy, hatred, pride, conceit, and ostentation. The cleansing of the innermost will occur only after the heart is rendered empty of everything except Allah, as He has said:

✧ ...and your garments, cleanse them. [74:4]

Once the outer garment has been cleansed, then the inner garment (the heart) needs cleansing. At this station one must stand guard at the door of one's heart and reject every thought of anything other than Allah. One is then

4. TRADITIONAL & TRANSFORMATIVE ACTS OF WORSHIP

ready for the voice of True Unicity.

Imam Khomeini described impurity as being remoteness from the company of Truth and the Station of Purity. It nullifies prayer which is the spiritual ascent (*Mi`rāj*) of the people of faith based on knowledge (*imān*) and the method for achieving the station of nearness for the people of fear and awareness (*taqwā*).

> ~ By means of evacuating from the interior the harmful substances which represent the impurities of Shaytan and the abandonment of the 'accursed tree of uncleanliness' [17:60], by fleeing from the ego and 'Iness' and leaving anything other than Allah, the seeker then becomes worthy of the Glorious Presence and worthy of donning the garment of the *Khalīl Allah* (Intimate Friend of Allah). After this, the movement is directed towards Allah and annihilated in Allah, the ever-lasting.

The Qur'an tells us:

> ☼ Whoever leaves his house fleeing to Allah and His Prophet and is overtaken by death will have his reward guaranteed by Allah. [4:100]

It is said that this spiritual journey has two foundational pillars: One of them is contained within the act of purification, the basis of which is abandonment, and its secret is in renunciation. The veiled secret of renunciation, in turn, lies within the realization that Allah is above and apart from anything which may be attributed to Him (i.e. His incomparable transcendence – *tanzīh*).

The second pillar is contained within the prayer, whose roots lie in illumination. The secret of illumination may be found in the realization of Allah's singularity, and its veiled secret is found in Unity. Thus purification represents abandonment, the secret of which is renunciation and *tanzīh*, and that prayer is divine illumination, whose secret lies in the uniqueness of Allah and Unity – true abandonment leading to enlightenment.

Modesty and Covering:

Since prayer is a spiritual act which involves turning away from otherness, how one dresses for it should enhance that state of being sealed off from distractions of any kind. In prayer, what should be concealed is therefore covered, because whoever seeks to enter before Allah must conceal whatever manifests to him, the secret of which is hidden, because Allah's secret must be glorified by its concealment from those who are unworthy of it. Similarly, anyone who speaks of what should be concealed uncovers his `awrah (shame). Just as clothing is meant to cover the private parts and the shortcomings of men, it is impossible to conceal secrets from Allah. We must, therefore, remove these coverings and tear them off before Him.

Imam Khomeini explained the meaning of covering the `awrah in the following manner:

> ~ From the viewpoint of the general masses it means to cover the shameful (intimate) parts of the body before Allah during the time of Prayer. In the eyes of the people of *Tariqah* it represents veiling shameful actions with the garment of fearful awareness (*taqwā*) while in His Presence. For the People of *Haqiqah* it represents veiling the abominations of the self by restraint. For the People of Faith based on knowledge it signifies veiling the abhorrent qualities which may be found in the heart by the garment of

4. TRADITIONAL & TRANSFORMATIVE ACTS OF WORSHIP

Tranquility. In the eyes of the Men of Knowledge and illumination it signifies veiling the defilement of the Innermost Secret by the garment of Witnessing. And, finally, in the eyes of the *wali* it signifies veiling the contamination of the Secret of the Innermost by the garment of steadfastness so that it remains constantly within the Presence of Truth.

Imam al-Sadiq said:

~ The most beautiful garment of the people of faith based on knowledge is the garment of fearful awareness, and the most important is the garment of faith.

✪ ...and the garment of fearful awareness (*taqwā*), that is best. [7:26]

The best of garments are ones that will not distract the seeker from Allah, but rather will draw him near by way of his gratitude, obedience and remembrance, nor should it lead him to conceit, ostentation, pretence, arrogance and pride. These are obstacles to submission and lead to hardening of the heart.

When the seeker dresses he or she should remember how Allah has covered his or her wrong actions with His Mercy. He should adorn his inner with certainty in the same way that he adorns his outer with clothing. His inner should be clothed in awe and his outer veiled in obedience. He should contemplate the grace of Allah for creating the means to cover our outer selves and for opening the door of return and repentance so that we may cover our inner shamefulness. It is incumbent upon the seeker not to disclose the faults of others when Allah has already veiled greater shortcomings within himself. Let him busy himself with his own faults and save himself from what does not concern him.

Taharah from impurity (*hadath*):

Hadath is an event or occurrence implying temporariness. In *fiqh* it means 'impurity' or 'excrement'. Thus, the seeker needs to remove physical impurity first so that he can remove the greater impurity that is the veil between him and Allah. Anyone who stands to perform prayer whilst contaminated by this type of impurity will be hindered unless it is removed. He must renew his purification every time he comes into contact with such impurity. We need to start with outer purification until we reach the heart.

> ✪ Surely when those in cautious awareness come into contact with a pressing fancy from Shaytan they are reminded and so they see. [7:201]

Times of Prayer:

The concept of time involves specific periods when the prayer, the fast, and the pilgrimage, etc. must be performed. If these times are not observed, the act of worship is not valid; this is because certain specific times contain characteristics that distinguish them from other times. Prayer, for example, is invalid if it is carried out before or after its appointed time. If a person dies and wills his children a buried treasure which he has hidden in a specific location, he leaves directions which define a certain wall and a specific number of steps from it in such and such a direction in order to find the treasure. If his children take more steps than specified they will miss the treasure and the same applies if they take fewer steps.

4. TRADITIONAL & TRANSFORMATIVE ACTS OF WORSHIP

Consequently they must adhere to the specific numbers of steps and start from the exact point they were instructed to in order to discover their treasure.

Acts of devotion and the specific times and manner assigned are similar to this example. Time is composed of periods, stages, and portions of the night and day, all of this being dependent upon the position of the earth from the sun. Because man is a microcosm of existence which is itself a copy of the Gnostic (*wali* of Allah), the specific states of the Gnostic differ according to the differences in man's spiritual illumination, that is, the extent of his nearness or distance from Allah.

Closeness is likened to the bright sun of the morning. In the same way that noon does not occur until the sun has begun its descent from its zenith, likewise the noontime of *Haqiqah* will not be realized by the Gnostic until the decline and descent of the lower self has occurred. If the seeker is afflicted by his lower animal nature then it must be eliminated before he can move further on.

Nearness is the opposite of remoteness, being manifest is the opposite of being hidden. It is unavoidable that the seeker remains within these states for limited periods so that he might find within them what will join him to his Beloved. Afternoon and sunset represent the remoteness of the sun from the centre of the sky. It is the same with the sun of the seeker: if it begins to set in his heart (i.e. disappear from his heart) then he is required to leave that time period.

In truth, the Gnostic represents the manifestation of subtleties: as far as remoteness is concerned he is a dot of clay, and as for nearness he is the Vicegerent of the Lord of the Worlds and a responsible steward on earth (*khalifah*). To whatever extent an attribute manifests within him, his state will change according to the particular attribute, just as the color and state of the earth change in accordance with its proximity to or distance from the sun. If you were to question him while in a state of nearness and while in the Divine Presence, he would reply: 'I am the "House (Ka`bah) that is visited" [52:4]', and 'I am the "Overflowing Sea" [52:6]'. These words can only be uttered because of his nearness to Truth. Whenever something comes that is close it is as if it has become one with the Truth. If you were to ask him at the time of his return to his self he would look at his own weakness and insignificance before Allah and reply: 'I am cut off after having arrived, I have come out after having entered;' it could even be assumed that he had not tasted nearness.

Evening represents the middle stage between nearness and remoteness, as mentioned above, because it occurs between the rising and the setting of the sun. In this state the seeker is not required to hasten or to take his time because of the fact that he is in an inbetween state – he is at the point of the 'barrier (*barzakh*) between two seas' [55: 20]. The sun of *haqiqah* for him remains set in that 'eyes do not perceive Him yet He perceives them' [6:103], and it has not yet risen for him in that 'there are faces on that day which will be radiant, gazing upon their Lord' [75:22-23]. Those who have come to know their Lord's magnificence are speechless in wonderment.

The enlightened ones have certain times in which they are not occupied with anything but gazing upon their Lord in humility. When the eyes of the heart are gazing upon the sun of the appearance of their Beloved, they are not aware at that time of anything but their Lord; as the Prophet has said:

4. TRADITIONAL & TRANSFORMATIVE ACTS OF WORSHIP

~ I have a time in which I am encompassed by nothing but my Lord.

When existential veils and barriers are lifted then all that remains is the Divine Essence which encompasses one. In the same way that neither the heavens nor the earth can contain Allah, the hearts of such men contain Him (as Allah indicated in a *hadith qudsi*). These beings have pleaded to Allah and He has drawn them near; they have remembered Allah and He has remembered them, as the Prophet has said:

~ Keep Allah in your thoughts and you will find Him before you.

Disliked (makruh) Actions During Prayer

❖ *Reciting the phrase of 'Refuge from Shaytan'*: The uttering of the phrase 'I take refuge with Allah from the accursed Shaytan' (*a`udhu bi'llāhi min alshaytān alrajīm*) is disliked (*makruh*), for in the Presence of God there are only His manifestations. Thus, for the one from whom multiplicity has vanished and who has witnessed Truth, and absolute Oneness, there is no trace of Shaytan. He has already taken refuge with the *Rahman*. Shaytan cannot find a pathway into the sublime sanctum of the glorious Presence. The Prophet said:

~ I take refuge with You from You.

Thus, seeking refuge from Him is to seek refuge with Him, and this is the utmost level of affirmation; by it the awakened seeker has entered into the vastness of absolute Oneness. He will then be granted respite from the plotting of Shaytan and will join those of whom Allah has spoken when He said:

> ✡ Surely, with regards to my slaves, you have no authority over them... [15:42]

To paraphrase: 'You have no authority over them, for I am their Creator and Master, and I am their Protective companion. My Abode is within their hearts. You have no share of their inner or of their outer.' Thus whoever knows the *Rahmān* does not see any Shaytan with him.

◈ *Recitation of the Qur'an during ruku` and sajdah*: It is also disliked to recite verses from the Qur'an during the bowing and the prostration, that is, at the time of the death of the self, prior to annihilation in his Lord. While in this state it is not permissible or possible to recite Allah's words because the slave is overwhelmed by *fanā'*. After annihilation in the Essence of the Lord, and after one raises the head from the prostration, it is permissible to express whatever is worthy of the Essence of Allah, either of His Uniqueness or His other Attributes.

◈ *Thoughts about creation*: It is objectionable for the seeker to occupy his mind with thoughts of creation or to allow any part of them to enter their heart, because this type of contemplation nullifies one's state of humility before Allah and humility is not attained except after the manifestation of Truth. Whoever is occupied with thoughts of creation at this time will be veiled from Truth. Thought occurs with regard to creation and things within it, not with regard to the Essence of Allah, as the Prophet has stated:

> ~ Think about everything but do not think about the Essence of Allah.

Thus, when the existence of something vanishes into

4. TRADITIONAL & TRANSFORMATIVE ACTS OF WORSHIP

nothingness, one must beware of thinking of it. He must exchange his process of thought for a state of awe and wonder, because when he returns to the process of thinking he falls into something which is detestable to his former state. The Prophet used to make the supplication:

~ O Allah, increase me in wonder of You.

- ◈ *Frivolity*: The seeker should not be concerned with anything which does not concern him, even though this may be permissible for the general masses, in that the good actions of the righteous are the despicable actions of the Near Ones.

- ◈ *Turning Away*: Among the actions which are censurable for the Gnostic is 'turning away'. The Master must not turn to other than the Truth, especially after his arrival and confirmation of the absolute Oneness of Allah. An example of this type of turning away is the performance of various miracles or seeking to achieve the supernatural; so he prays to Allah to destroy whoever it is he wishes to perish and to grant safety to whomever he wishes, or he asks that someone be given provision, and so on. Whoever is in this station and acts in this manner has 'exchanged that which is good for that which is base' [2:61]. It is said in this context that whoever is not patient with the company of the Truth will be afflicted with the company of slaves.

Likewise Ibn `Ata'Allah said:

~ The best which can be sought for from Him is whatever He demands from you. What miracle is better than the knowledge of Allah?

The Prophet said:

~ Whoever is not content with the knowledge of Allah is indeed wretched.

Shaykh alShadhili[29] has said the following regarding miracles:

~ Miracles are not a condition of the confirmation of a Master so that he needs to request them from Allah, but, rather, miracles may seek him out. Because if one seeks to perform miracles, steadfastness (before Allah) will be demanded of him and where is the steadfastness of the one who has already turned away in his quest for miracles? What the Master seeks from his Lord is truthfulness in his acts of service and the carrying out of that which is the rightful due of his Lord, that is, if they request anything of Him at all. If not, they are too modest before Allah to turn to anything but Him or to request anything because they know of His Mercy and Kindness and of His concern for his slave, for Allah 'has inscribed for Himself Mercy' [6:12].

◈ *Supplication while bowing*: Making a supplication while in the bowing position is disliked. As has been discussed earlier, the *ruku`* symbolizes the removal of the attributes of the slave when the Attributes of the Lord become manifest. For the one who has had revealed to him the existence of the Attributes of Allah throughout His entire creation, and for whom matters have become gradually clearer, it is not proper for him to ask Allah for anything

---

29   The `Arif Abu'l-Hasan al-Shadhili, d.1258 CE/656 AH, founder of the Shadhili Tariqah.

4. TRADITIONAL & TRANSFORMATIVE ACTS OF WORSHIP

before its time. If this applies to those for whom the Attributes of Allah have been unveiled, what about those for whom His Essence has been unveiled? It is for this reason that Ibn `Ata'Allah has said:

~ Your requests of Him actually represent your suspicion of Him. Your requests of Him for less than Him are because of your lack of modesty and respect for Him, and your requests directed to other-than-Him are because of your remoteness from Him.

We are reminded here of when Prophet Ibrahim was cast into the fire. Jibril (Gabriel) asked him, 'Do you need anything from me?' Ibrahim replied, 'From you? No.' Gabriel then said, 'Then ask Allah.' Ibrahim answered saying, 'His knowledge of my condition frees me from asking.' This is the height of trust in Allah and exclusive reliance on Him.

One Master has said:

~ The Masters are silent throughout the course of destiny, while they possess nothing that would be either of benefit or harm to themselves.

✿ Say: I do not control anything for myself of benefit or harm for myself except what Allah has willed. [7:188]

◈ *Closing the eyes*: It is also disliked for the seeker to close his eyes after he has attained what the seeker sought, which is the arrival at Truth. Before that, i.e. during the remembrance, closing the eyes is demanded because the determination (*himmah*) of the seeker is not yet gathered and the senses will not yet be quietened except by closing the eyes. When his inner vision and insight are opened, purified and cleansed, then the senses will represent true meaning to him and vice versa; consequently it will then cease to be proper to close his eyes.

Meaning and States in Prayers

The obligatory actions in the first *rak`ah* of the prayer are: standing in the *qiyām* position if one is able to (or, if unable, to at least do what one is able to in its place), the intention, the initial *takbīr* (*takbīr alihrām*), the recitation of the Qur'an, the *ruku`*, the first *sajdah*, its invocation, the raising of the head from the *sajdah*, the second *sajdah*, its invocation, and the raising of the head.

The first obligatory stipulation is that the intention should accompany the initial *takbir*; this applies until the pronouncement of the words 'Allahu Akbar' is completed. This is followed by the recitation of *Surat alFātihah* and any other *surah* of one's choice. Those parts of the prayer which should be recited aloud must be recited as such and, likewise, those portions which are to be recited in a whisper must be recited in that manner. One must assume the bowing position completely when the body is firm and steady in that position. The same is true when one returns to the standing position. The prostration must be performed with seven parts of the body: the forehead, the two hands, the two knees, and the big toes of both feet. One must assume the first prostration fully, then rise up to the sitting, or *jalsah*, position, and sit firmly. The same is true of the second prostration. In all, this adds up to thirty-one actions and stipulations.

In the second *rak`ah* the actions and stipulations are repeated, with the exception of the renewal of the intention and the initial *takbīr* and its four stipulations. Thus, there

4. TRADITIONAL & TRANSFORMATIVE ACTS OF WORSHIP

remain twenty-seven and altogether they add up to fifty-eight actions and stipulations in both *rak`āt*.

Added to this there are six things: the *jalsah* of the *tashahhud*, sitting firmly and still in that position, the two *shahādat* (testimonies of the Oneness of Allah and the Prophethood of Muhammad), the calling of blessings upon the Prophet and his family. All these amount to sixty-four actions and stipulations. Added to this is the *taslīm* (*salām*) of the *fajr* prayer. The same actions and stipulations apply to the third and fourth *rak`ah* in the prayers of *zuhr*, `*asr*, and `*ishā'*, except for the renewal of the intention, the initial *takbīr*, and their stipulations (which are four), and the recitation of anything more than the *Fātihah*. Thus, this makes a total of sixty actions and stipulations. This is the order of the prayer according to the people of *shari`ah*, in the manner of the Ahl alBayt.

For the advanced Muslim *salāt* is a most desirable act of spiritual nourishment.

~ Prayer is the means of drawing near for every person of faith.

This is expressed by some of the men of Allah as 'the position without place'. It is reported that the Prophet said:

~ Prayer is service, nearness, and connectedness.

As mentioned before, the service refers to the *shari`ah*, the nearness to the *tariqah*, and connectedness to *haqiqah*. It is said that the *shari`ah* is to worship Him, the *tariqah* is to come to Him, and the *haqiqah* is to witness Him. Nearness to Allah is dependent upon the *sajdah* of *haqiqah*, which is also referred to as annihilation. It is this which Allah refers to when He says:

✧ ...and prostrate and draw near. [96:19]

The meaning is to annihilate your own essence and existence into the Essence of Truth and His existence, remaining with Him eternally. This is the station of the people of *haqiqah* or the enlightened.

The form of prayer was fashioned by the Lord of Lords. Its soul is the intention, sincerity, and presence of heart; its body is the actions; and its basic limbs are its pillars. Consequently, sincerity and intention are its soul; the *qiyām* and the *jalsah* are its body; and the *ruku`* and *sajdah* and their proper execution represent the head, hands, and feet. The calm and perfect performance of the *ruku`* and *sajdah* represents the body in its best condition. The remembrance and glorification of the prayer represent the sensory faculties that reside in the head.

The nearness of the worshipper in prayer is like the nearness of the servant to his king. Omitting the proper intention and sincerity in prayer is like the insincerity and infidelity of the lover. It is obligatory for everyone performing the prayer to pay attention to the soul and to carry out the prayer properly. Consequently, one should not bow or prostrate unless the heart is concentrated, centered, tranquil, humble, and in line with one's outward actions. The meaning here refers to the humility of the heart, not to the humility of the outward form. One should not utter the words *'Allāhu akbar'* unless the heart is completely concentrated upon Allah. One should not say *'alhamdu li'Llāh'* unless the heart is overflowing with praise, gratitude, and thankfulness for the grace which constantly showers upon one. One should not say *'iyyāka na`budu wa iyyāka nasta`īn'*, unless one is aware of their own weakness and helplessness, as was revealed to the Prophet:

> ✿ You have nothing to do with the matter whether he forgives or torments them. [3:128]

4. TRADITIONAL & TRANSFORMATIVE ACTS OF WORSHIP

Likewise, with regard to all of the remembrances and actions, Allah does as He wills and judges as He pleases.

✧ He cannot be questioned about what He does; it is they who are questioned. [21:23]

If this state is attained, then the intermediate level prayer, which comes about after their having successfully executed the prayer at the basic level, consists of focusing their heart upon the *Qiblah* of *haqiqah* and the Spiritual Ka`bah, which is the true heart, and which is referred to as the Sacred House of Allah, as Allah has said in a *hadith qudsi*:

~ My earth and My heavens cannot contain Me, but the heart of My servant who has faith contains me.

Likewise the Prophet said:

~ The heart of the one with faith is the House of Allah.

Also:

~ There is no prayer without presence of the heart.

✧ It is to Allah that pure faith belongs. [39:3]

✧ Say: my prayer, my sacrifice, my life and my death are for Allah, the Lord of the Universe. [6:162]

One should then execute the initial *takbīr* and deny oneself all that stand in opposition to Allah's commandments and all that is contrary to what pleases Him, in either word or deed. Then one should begin with the recitation which consists of: *alhamdu li'Llāhi rabbi'l`ālamīn* (praise is Allah's, the Lord of the worlds). This signifies fulfillment of gratitude for His grace, offering of gracious praise for Him, and carrying out of the responsibilities of worship due to Him in their various forms. It is the affirmation of His Oneness.

When one utters the words: *'iyyāka na`budu wa iyyāka nastaʿīn'* (You do we worship and from You do we seek aid), it is beseeching Him for His help and affirming one's own station of servitude or slavehood. Attributing the Acts and Attributes to Him at both stages is an indication of the Unity of Action and the Unity of Attributes, because 'You do we worship' is connected with Unity of Action, while 'from You do we seek aid' is connected to the Unity of Attributes.

The words, 'Establish us upon the Straight Path, the Path of those upon whom you have bestowed grace', follow directly after because of the granting of the request of the Prophets, Masters and the entire creation for guidance and grace, and for their being allowed to remain upon the Straight Path, and for security from being expelled from it. 'Not of those who are the object of Your anger nor the misguided': this applies to everyone who has deviated from the straight path which is the middle way between negligence and excess in true moral and ethical behavior, both inwardly and outwardly, which is wisdom, restraint, courage, and justice. If the word *'ihdina'* did not carry the meaning 'establish us' as opposed to 'guide us', it would be a foolish request because the Prophets and the Masters, all of them, were already on the Straight Path, as were (and are) those people of faith based on knowledge who followed them; as Allah has said:

> ✧ ...We have selected them and guided them to a Straight Path. [6:87]

As the faithful awakened ones are already guided, the word *'ihdina'* means 'establish us', or 'strengthen us'.

4. TRADITIONAL & TRANSFORMATIVE ACTS OF WORSHIP

Then one bows in *ruku`* before Allah and returns to your own self, broken and humble which are among the inherent qualities of the self, because bowing represents the return to original nonexistence, as Allah has said:

✧ I have already created you from nothing. [19:9]

It is for this reason that the next movement is an inverted one, that is, the prostration with the head facing downward. Because this position is peculiar to plants, which are continually in this inverted position, this act represents a return to the origin, the root, as it were. This is why the worshipper comes down from standing upright, which is a position peculiar to man, and assumes the bowing position, which is the horizontal position characteristic of animals. Then he assumes the prostration which is the position of plants. From the standpoint of form, humans have ascended from the level of plants, through the animal kingdom to the realm of humanity, which Allah indicates in His words:

✧ We created man in the most beautiful stature, then We reduced him to the lowest of the low. [95:45]

The upright stature relates to the nature of man and the lowest of the low refers to the animal and plant level, which is suggested in Allah's words:

✧ ...Turn back and seek light [57:13]

This is an indication of this return, because the 'light' – which is referred to as being behind one which results in perfection, is not attainable until one has returned to his origin in both form and meaning. Allah's words testify to this in the following verse:

✧ O tranquil soul, return to your Lord, contented

and the object of His contentment. [89:27-28]

Thus, both the return and experience of this state of need and humility are of great benefit on the pathway to annihilation, both outwardly and inwardly. They make it easy for one to abandon pleasures and desires. This continues to the point of witnessing the magnitude of the Creator and the insignificance of one's own self. Then one utters the words of glorification and veneration of Allah: 'subhāna rabbi'l`azīmi wa bihamdih' (Glory be to my Lord, the Magnificent, and praise be unto Him).

When one has witnessed the magnitude and glory of the Creator after having witnessed one's own insignificance and return to the original state of nonexistence, one then returns to witness one's condition in relation to Allah and Allah's relationship to oneself in changing one's own attributes for the Attributes of Allah and the refinement of one's behavior. Then one utters, `sami`a'Llāhu liman hamidah' (Allah hears those who praise Him), because this represents one's witnessing, the Truth and that everything is with truth, in that He hears the words of everyone without any difficulty, as if the words are coming from Himself; as it has been previously mentioned by Imam `Ali:

~ I used to repeat a verse until I heard from the One Who spoke it [originally].

And:

~ Whoever comes to know his own self has come to know his Lord.

Allah said:

✿ Is it not sufficient as to your Lord is a witness over all things? [41:53]

4. TRADITIONAL & TRANSFORMATIVE ACTS OF WORSHIP

✺ We are closer to him than the jugular vein. [50:16]

✺ ...and in your own selves [are signs], do you not see? [51:21]

These are all allusions to annihilation and the return to the original nonexistence, and then the remaining, referred to as 'The Divine Presence':

✺ Surely those who are cautiously aware are in gardens and rivers in the seat of honor with the Most Powerful King. [54:5455]

Then one prostrates, returning to one's origin in creation – the plant stage – because prostration means placing the highest and most noble part of the body into dust which is the lowest thing in creation, in order to break the self and humble it. The second breaking and humbling represents *fanā'* after *fanā'*. The first *fanā'* was the annihilation of Attributes and behavior, while the second *fanā'* is the annihilation of the very existence and essence. In this state of intoxication, the tongue utters the words, '*subhāna rabbi ala`lā wa bihamdih*' (Glory be to my Lord, the Most High and praise be unto Him).

As long as the seeker remains in the station of multiplicity, witnessing the manifestation of Allah's Attributes, he remains distant and remote from Him because he is worshipping his own limited illusion of his Lord and not the Absolute Lord. However, if he arrives at the station of Unity, he will be free of this and so he again says, '*subhāna rabbi ala`lā wa bihamdih*'. The Most High is the One Who is more lofty and exalted than one who is limited by Attributes. It is obvious that lords who are limited have no existence except from the Absolute Lord, and this is the meaning of Allah's words:

☼ ...and surely to your Lord is the final destination. [53:42]

He is the Absolute Lord and the final destination of every lord or master.

There one surrenders everything to Allah. One abandons the journey of one's self and remains with Him, which is the station of eternity. This is the result of contentment and surrender, which is the combination of the Unity of Actions and the Unity of Attributes, to which Allah alludes when He says:

☼ No indeed, by your Lord, they will not believe in Reality until they make you, a judge of that which has become a matter of disagreement among them, and then they do not find any resentment in their hearts as to what you have decided and completely submit. [4:65]

And furthermore:

☼ You have nothing to do with the matter... [3:128]

All patterns and relationships in the universe have been perfectly established from the time of creation. Our task is to witness perfection. Prayers of the Gnostics are true witnessing of what is eternally perfect.

Previously we said prayer could be divided into service, nearness and connectedness – that 'service' represents the *shari`ah*, 'nearness' represents the *tariqah*, and 'connectedness' represents *haqiqah*. Likewise, *shari`ah* means that you worship Him, *tariqah* means that you go to Him, and *haqiqah* means that you witness Him.

Worship can be divided into three categories: worship as the utmost degree of humility from the viewpoint of the people of *shari`ah*; a state of servanthood or slavehood

4. TRADITIONAL & TRANSFORMATIVE ACTS OF WORSHIP

(`ubudiyyah`) for the people of *tariqah* (representing the earnestness of their determination to reach Him by travelling His Path); and, finally, witnessing one's state of slavehood for the people of *haqiqah* who have witnessed their self standing before Him in a state of slavehood. The people of *haqiqah* are distinguished by their prayer which consists of witnessing their Beloved by means of the eye of their Beloved and no other, as the Prophet said:

> ~ I saw my Lord with the eye of my Lord and I came to know my Lord by way of my Lord.

It is also reported that he said:

> ~ There are three things of your world that are beloved to me: sweet scent, women, and my delight and joy in prayer.

The first is an allusion to the fulfillment of the *shari`ah*, both in knowledge and deed, that is, the sweet scent of one's proper behavior and its refinement in words and deed. The second symbolizes following the *tariqah* in one's inclination and feelings. As for the love of women, this indicates that one must extract the seeds of meaning and *haqiqah* from it (every man and woman has within themselves the essence of the perfect complementary opposite sex, for which they yearn); as Allah has said:

> ✧ People, be cautiously aware of your Lord who created you from one soul and He created from it its mate and dispersed from the two of them (both) men and women. [4:1]

The third represents witnessing the Beloved and the delight thereof. This is the prayer of *haqiqah*, as has been narrated from the Prophet in his description of goodness or the state of inner and outer excellence (*ihsān*):

~ Excellence (*ihsān*) means to worship Allah as if you see Him, for though you do not see Him, surely, He sees you.

With regard to the Prophet's words, '...and my delight and joy is in prayer': prayer is the witnessing and exchange of secret whispered words between Allah and His slave. It is an act of devotion which is divided between Allah and His slave; as Allah has said in *a hadith qudsi*:

~ I have divided the prayer into two halves between Me and My slave. One half is for Me and one half is for My slave and My slave will receive whatever he asks. The slave says, "*Bismi'Llāh arrahmān arrahīm*" (in the name of Allah, the Merciful, the Compassionate) and Allah says: "My slave has remembered Me."

~ Then the slave says, "*alhamdu li'Llāhi rabbi'l `ālamīn*" (praise belongs to Allah, Lord of all the worlds) and Allah replies: "My slave has praised Me." Then the slave says, "*māliki yawm aldīn*" (Master of the Day of Judgment), and Allah says: "My slave extols Me." Then the slave says, "*iyyāka na`budū wa iyyāka nasta`īn*" (to You do we turn in worship and from You do we seek aid), and Allah replies: "This is between Me and My slave and surely My slave will have whatever he asks."

It is clear from this why it is obligatory to recite the *Fātihah* in prayer, for whoever does not recite the *Fātihah* has not made the prayer.

Since prayer represents the secret whispered supplication of the worshipper it is in effect remembrance.

4. TRADITIONAL & TRANSFORMATIVE ACTS OF WORSHIP

He who remembers Allah is in the company of Allah, as He Himself has said in a *hadith qudsi*:

> ~ I am the Companion of whoever remembers Me and of whoever keeps company with one who remembers Me and possesses sharp vision and sees His Companion.

This is witnessing and seeing and from this the worshipper will recognize his own station: does he witness Allah accordingly in his prayer or not? In the words of the Prophet:

> ~ ...and my delight and joy is in prayer.

He does not attribute this joy and delight which he experiences in prayer to his own self, but rather, he attributes it to the fact that Truth has manifested for him from Allah and not from the one offering the prayer. The eye of the lover finds no delight except in the witnessing of the Beloved, thus his eye will find delight upon seeing the Beloved and will not gaze upon anything else. For this reason it is forbidden to turn away in prayer. The act of turning away represents something which Shaytan has stolen from the prayer of the slave, thus depriving him of witnessing his Beloved. If one were a true lover, he would never turn away from his Beloved in the prayer.

> ✿ ...but rather man has insight into his own self even though he may give excuses. [75:14-15]

The Prophet said:

> ~ You will see your Lord in the same way you see the moon on a night when it is full.

TRANSFORMATIVE WORSHIP IN ISLAM

Imam ʿAli said:

~ Would I worship what I do not see?

He also said:

~ If the veil was lifted I could not be any more certain.

These clear 'witnessings' or testimonies confirm the realized, divine state in their prayers. The state of continuous prayer is not achieved except by witnessing Allah in the manner described above. This is unique to the greatest of His slaves and the most sincere of Masters who are steadfast in witnessing *tawhīd*, which has been described in Allah's words:

✿ So be firm and steadfast as you have been commanded. [11:112]

The steadfastness (*istiqāmah*) is an allusion to the steadfastness of the perfect slave in the station of perfection, and to the journey in Allah after having completed the journey to Allah.

As for the initial *takbīr*, it symbolizes that one is unable to turn one's face and attention to other than the Door of Allah, and that one is unable to perform actions which are not pleasing to Allah; as it is declared in the Qur'an:

✿ Surely my prayer, my sacrifice, my life and my death are for Allah, the Lord of the Worlds, [6:162]

provided that he has acted in accordance with:

✿ I have turned my face to the One who created the heavens and the earth, as a true believer and I do not associate anything with Him [6:79]

The recitation of *Fātihah* in the manner mentioned

4. TRADITIONAL & TRANSFORMATIVE ACTS OF WORSHIP

above, that is, apportioned between Allah and His servant, including witnessing with the eye of the heart during this recitation, is alluded to in:

> ✧ And in this way We will show Abraham the Spiritual Dominion of the heavens and the earth so that he may have certain faith. [6:75]

Then one bows in *ruku`*, that is, one is humbled before Allah while the angels and all the spiritual regions are humbled before him on account of his being the vicegerent of Allah.

Then he falls into prostration. He annihilates the entire realm of existence and creation, including the annihilation of his own existence and the annihilation of this annihilation itself, because of his having been an eyewitness to the fact that:

> ✧ Everything upon it is perishing while the Face of your Lord remains, the Possessor of Glory and Generosity. [55:26-27]

Then he declares His Uniqueness and Purity by witnessing, in the executions of first the bowing then the prostration, by saying in the *ruku`*: '*subhāna rabbi al`azīmi wa bihamdih*' (Glory be to my Lord, the Sublime, and praise unto Him). Then in the prostration he says: '*subhāna rabbi ala`lā wa bihamdih*' (Glory be to my Lord the Most High, and praise unto Him). Then he testifies to the absolute Unity of His Essence and the pure uniqueness of His Oneness, in accordance with the verse:

> ✧ Allah, the angels and the possessors of knowledge supported by justice bearing witness that there is no god but Him. There is no god but Him, the Mighty, the Wise. [3:18]

TRANSFORMATIVE WORSHIP IN ISLAM

The *salam* means to submit to this Unity in one's heart and soul because of their (i.e. the heart and soul) having actually witnessed it. As the Qur'an tells us that all the souls have confessed when asked, "Am I not your Lord?" Submission to Allah is not completed except by surrendering to His Messenger, as Allah says:

> ✧ Surely Allah and His angels send blessings upon the Prophet. O you who believe do send blessings upon him and be in complete submission. [33:56]

Some ignorant Sufis have said that it is permissible to neglect the *shari`ah* concerning the carrying out of its obligations. They say that the responsibilities and obligations of outer worship are no longer applicable to enlightened Masters. This claim is clearly ridiculous, because whoever arrives at some level to Divine Presence will be even more passionate about worship, inwardly and outwardly. The highest example of this was the Messenger of Allah himself. He used to pray day and night to the point that his feet would become swollen. When asked why he did that when it was said that Allah had already forgiven him of everything he replied:

> ~ Should I not be a thankful slave?

When we truly love someone, that inward state will also clearly reflect outwardly. True love will always be expressed – what then of the worship and adoration of the Exalted Beloved?

Enlightened beings are those who have arrived at the knowledge that the only doer or actor is Allah. Allah has spoken about these people in a *hadith qudsi* saying:

> ~ My Masters are under My canopy; they are known to no one other than Myself.

4. TRADITIONAL & TRANSFORMATIVE ACTS OF WORSHIP

They are also alluded to in the revealed words:

☼ Thus, Allah will bring a people whom He loves and who love Him who are humble towards the believers and mighty against those who reject Him, who exert themselves in the way of Allah and do not fear the ridicule/blame from any quarter. [5:54]

In spite of this, the Prophets were not spared the tongues of the scornful and rejecters who, because of their ignorance of the real state of the Prophets, attributed their acts to magic, sorcery, and poetry. It has been said that anyone devoid of merit will not believe in its existence in others, in fact, they will even deny its existence. The Men of Allah are the perfect followers of the best example:

☼ Surely there has been a good example for you in the Messenger of Allah. [33:21]

4.3 Fasting (*sawm*)

Human interest in fasting is deeply rooted in our consciousness. Fasting has long been resorted to for maintaining physical and mental health as much as for cultural or political reasons. More specifically, fasting has been a devotional practice in most religious and spiritual movements throughout the ages.

Islam has prescribed the practice of abstinence and fasting as a means of self-purification and worship. The act of restraining the self from fulfilling its desires purifies and enhances awareness at physical, mental and spiritual levels and sensitizes human consciousness. The seeker realizes the weakness of the self and is gratified by the discipline, restriction and prohibitions, for these limitations are windows to Allah's limitlessness.

Fasting in History

In many cultures, such as the Indians of North America, tribes of Brazil, the people of the Pacific Islands and numerous Asian, African and European peoples, fasting has been used as a rite of initiation, marking puberty, prior to hunting and as part of the rites of marriage. In some cultures such as those in the Andaman Islands, Fiji, Samoa, China, Korea and others fasting is observed as a rite of mourning. In general, we find whenever human beings are in need, suppressed, or in fear, they seek God or higher powers through abstinence or penance. When our limited state of knowledge and consciousness is insufficient fasting guides us out of difficulties to find other means of inspiration and solutions.

Ancient Egyptians, Greek, Roman, and Chinese cultures practiced fasting to cure various illnesses. The

4. TRADITIONAL & TRANSFORMATIVE ACTS OF WORSHIP

Egyptians believed that fasting three days a month helped to preserve good mental and physical health. The Greeks learned the virtues of fasting from the Egyptians and fasted before battle and the Romans followed suit. Socrates and Plato are known to have regularly performed fasts of ten days duration. Today in the West, fasting is used by alternative and naturopathic systems of medicine and healing for curing a host of acute and chronic diseases and as a useful catalyst in helping the body mobilize its own natural immune system.

The Old Testament often refers to fasting: David chastened his soul with fasting, while Moses fasted for forty days when he ascended the mount to receive the tablets of the covenant. Daniel fasted for three weeks, supplicating and praying all the while. Jews observe six obligatory fasts during the year, one such being Yom Kippur.

The institution of fasting and abstinence from certain foods in Christianity has its origin in the New Testament as it relates to the fasting of Jesus' disciples for several days during Lent, the forty-day period before Easter. The duration of the fast during Lent varied throughout the ages, until forty days accompanied by strict rules became the norm. Additional fasts were introduced later in different parts of the Church, such as the fast of Rogation Days, the Ember Weeks, the Whitsun Week, and fasts were also ordained by the Roman Catholic Church. Considerable variations in the practice of fasting are noticed between the Orthodox Church, the Eastern Orthodox Church and the Reformed Churches of Europe.

Over time there has been a gradual mitigation in the frequency and rigor of the fasts and abstinences prescribed by Church laws due to extenuating circumstances such as age, health, poverty, hard or continued labor and changing social conditions. Today few are obliged to fast strictly, while some are excused even from abstinence. Roman Catholic legislation further provides for dispensations to be granted by the Church authorities. The overall result is that the practice of fasting has declined and is almost forgotten as a religious exercise.

During the twentieth century fasting has sometimes been used as a tool of political and social protest by individuals as well as groups. During the national struggles for independence from colonial rule, several leaders of the third world in Asia and Africa resorted to fasting to highlight their plight and struggle, often with some success.

The Islamic Fast

For Muslims fasting, or *'sawm'* in Arabic, was commanded in the Qur'an as a major obligatory spiritual discipline for the duration of the month of Ramadan. The Arabic word for fasting is derived from the root, *'sama'*, meaning to abstain from food, drink, smoking, sensual gratifications, wrong actions, harmful intentions, thoughts, words and deeds.

Islamic fasting is obligatory for one month in every lunar year, that is, Ramadan, the ninth month in the Islamic calendar. All healthy adults are expected to adhere to the proper rules of fasting. In addition to this obligatory fast, there are many optional fasts, some of which occur regularly every week or month, and some that are scattered throughout the year. These fasts are *Sunnah*, or the practice of the Prophet. Fasting is also used as a penance for breaking an oath and as a compensation for some other religious obligation.

The fast of Ramadan begins with the physical sighting

4. TRADITIONAL & TRANSFORMATIVE ACTS OF WORSHIP

of the new moon. Throughout the month a Muslim may not eat or drink from daybreak (when a fine strip of light may be seen on the horizon) until the sun has set. Before dawn a small meal (*suhur*) is usually recommended to be taken, although not obligatory, and the fast is broken just before the sunset (*maghrib*) prayer traditionally with dates and water, to be immediately followed by the prayer. Later on a larger meal is partaken by the entire family, often shared with relatives, friends and guests.

The daily fast is begun by formulating the intention to perform the fast as a rite by making a clear intention (*niyyah*) to observe the fast. No one should fast if their health cannot sustain it or if a fast should threaten one's health. Pregnant and nursing women whose health may be harmed are exempted, as are those who are travelling away from home. When health is restored or other conditions for not fasting are removed (such as menstruation) then the person is expected to make up the fast later during the course of the year.

Ramadan offers the believer an opportunity to mark an end to daily indulgences, or at least to impose clear limits on a daily basis for the duration of a month. This daily restraint breaks the habitual patterns of the self and constitutes a purification both of body and spirit, which brings about renewal of strength and greater spiritual awareness. Each and every ritualistic practice of Islam disciplines the individual and strengthens Muslim society if applied thoroughly.

Every year the month of Ramadan falls at different times because the lunar calendar is shorter than the solar by approximately ten days. This means that as the period of the fast is brought forward annually, Ramadan will fall during all seasons of the year in a gradual progression.

Despite the strict rules and restraint induced by the fast, Ramadan is usually a joyful time for Muslims everywhere. The last ten nights of the month, particularly the odd nights, are the spiritual highlights of Ramadan, for one of these nights is *Laylat al-Qadr*, the Night of Determination, in which the Qur'an was first revealed to the Prophet. During these nights Muslims spend their nights in supplication and prayer, hoping to favorably influence the course of events that will unfold subsequently.

Ramadan comes to a close with the celebrations and prayers of Eid al-Fitr. On this day a Muslim will give appropriate alms to the poor, and families gather for a light morning repast after the congregational prayer. The Eid prayer, usually performed outdoors is accompanied by a discourse delivered by the prayer leader after which people exchange good wishes and celebrate their success in performing a most important act of worship and attaining a heightened awareness and purposefulness in life.

The Prophet of Allah said:

> ~ The root of Islam is prayer, its branches are the obligatory tax, its height is the fast, and its expanse is striving in the way of Allah.

He also said:

> ~ The tax of the body is fasting.

A Jew who was one of the most learned of his people asked the Messenger of Allah: 'Why did Allah make it obligatory upon your people to fast throughout the day for thirty days?' The Prophet replied:

> ~ When Adam ate from the tree it remained within his stomach for thirty days, so Allah made it obligatory upon his offspring to experience thirty days of

4. TRADITIONAL & TRANSFORMATIVE ACTS OF WORSHIP

hunger and thirst. Whatever they eat at night is a grace from Allah. Thus it was with Adam, so Allah made the same obligatory for my people.

Then he recited the verse:

✧ The fast is prescribed for you as it was prescribed for those before you. [2:183]

Imam alRida wrote the following concerning the obligation to fast:

~ It is so that one may know the feeling of hunger and thirst, so that he will be humble and helpless, in order to be an indication of the difficulties of the Hereafter. Within it is contained the breaking of desires so that one will experience the deprivations caused by withholding from the poor and the needy.

Imam alSadiq relates that the Prophet said:

~ The fast is a shield, that is, a veil protecting one from the afflictions of the world and from the punishment of the Hereafter. Thus, when you fast, make the intention to restrain your self from its desires and cut off the thoughts inspired by Shaytan. Bring yourself to the place where you are content without the desire for food or drink.

The purpose of the fast is to deaden the desires of the self; it is a cleansing for the heart and the body and a revival of both the inner and the outer. It also includes given by those who stand in need before Allah gratitude for the grace and goodness bestowed. It increases humility, meekness, and tears, and causes one to seek refuge with Allah.

The reason food is permitted during the night is

because Allah does not make one responsible for more than one can endure. Allah has made it easy for us, which is the main characteristic of the *shari`ah*. Previously it has been said that Adam performed his fast in the daytime, that his repentance (*tawbah*) was accepted at the time of the afternoon prayer, and that he was freed of transgression at the time of the sunset prayer. This tradition is observed every day during one month so that during this time one may rid oneself of wrong actions and then be joyous in one's liberation from them by eating after sunset.

The degrees of fasting can be arranged in the following manner: The first and lowest of them is that the person fasting limits himself to refraining from those things which would render his fast null and void but not from doing those things which are considered reprehensible. This is the fast of the general masses. The second is to restrain the body from whatever is considered reprehensible. Consequently, one guards his tongue against slander, his eyes against desire, and so on with the rest of his body. This represents the fast of the people of *tariqah*. The third, in addition to the above, is to protect the heart from going astray and from the whisperings of Shaytan, limiting it to the Remembrance of Allah and the witnessing of Him in all His manifestations. This represents the fast of the Chosen Few and is perfection itself.

Meaning and Benefits of Fasting

The fast is to refrain from specific things during certain specified intervals of time. Among its stipulations is the soundness of the intention covering a specific time period, for example, the month of Ramadan, or for the purpose of fulfilling an oath (*nadhar*). The intention which specifies the type of fast must also be made at the time when it is begun.

4. TRADITIONAL & TRANSFORMATIVE ACTS OF WORSHIP

Making Up or Expiation

There are various categories of fasts and each has its particular regulations: obligatory fasts, recommended fasts, fasts for specific oaths, and fasts for nonspecific oaths. Those actions which require a fast to be made up (*qada'*) or expiated (*kaffārah*) are nine in number and are as follows (as per the teachings of Ahl ul-Bayt):

1. Eating.
2. Drinking.
3. Sexual intercourse.
4. Intentional ejaculation.
5. Intentionally telling a lie concerning Allah, His Messenger, or the Imams.
6. Complete submersion in water.
7. Intentionally taking in thick dust in the throat (e.g. flour or anything similar).
8. Intentionally remaining in a state of *janābah* (ritual impurity) until after *fajr*.
9. Going back to sleep after having already awakened before *fajr*.

The *kaffārah* or expiation consists of fasting for two consecutive months, or feeding sixty people in need, or freeing a slave (this ruling remains even though slavery is no longer practiced, while the more likely practice will be the two former). One may choose one of the above.

There are eight actions which will break the fast and will require the Muslim to make up a fast (*qadā'*) without expiation:

1. Eating, drinking, or engaging in sexual intercourse before confirming whether or not it is actually sunrise.
2. Not accepting it when someone (reliable) says that

it is sunrise.
3. Following someone else who says that it is not yet sunrise when one is able to observe it oneself that it is indeed already sunrise.
4. Following someone else who says it is night when one is able to ascertain it oneself.
5. Breaking the fast (*iftār*) before its time has arrived; e.g. when in the presence of some obstruction (such as clouds) in the sky which makes it appear to be dark, and then it becomes clear that it is not yet the time of *iftār*.
6. Returning to sleep after having already awakened once before taking a ritual bath from *janābah* and not awakening again until after the sun has risen.
7. Water entering the throat for those seeking to cool themselves (but this does not include the rinsing of the mouth in preparation for prayer).
8. Finally, taking an enema.

For the more mature Muslim, fasting means to abstain from anything which would be displeasing to their Lord and contrary to His commandment and prohibition, either in word or deed. The Messenger of Allah said:

~ Everything has a door and the door to acts of devotion is fasting.

The more advanced seeker abstains from whatever is forbidden and restrains the self. Fasting is a deep link between the seeker and his Lord which no one observes but Allah, in contrast to prayer, the obligatory tax, and the various other actions which are possible for others to notice (and therefore possibly motivated by the desire for acclaim or out of pride).

4. TRADITIONAL & TRANSFORMATIVE ACTS OF WORSHIP

☼ Whoever wants to meet his Lord, then let him perform good actions and not see anything other than Allah in the worship of his Lord. [18:110]

Seeing other than Allah (*shirk*) in this context refers to performing an act of worship for the eyes of someone other than Allah. The Prophet said:

~ The infiltration of *shirk* within my people is more hidden than the creeping of a black ant on a black stone on a dark night.

Islamic scholars say that this type of *shirk* refers to the performance of an act of worship for one's own reputation of piety or other worldly position. The men of inner knowledge say that it means 'to see anything other than the One', as Imam `Ali has said:

~ The lowest form of *riyā'* (worship performed to be seen by other than Allah) is *shirk*.

There is no question of *riyā'* if one sees no one but Allah. Open or hidden *shirk* will inevitably be weakened by cutting back desires and appetites, as Imam `Ali said:

~ Shaytan flows through man like blood so constrict his passageways by hunger.

The Messenger of Allah said:

~ The gates of the garden are opened when Ramadan begins and the gates of the Fire are closed.

Outward abstentions

◈ *Abstention of the Tongue*: This concerns useless, foolish, or discourteous speech, as well as anything which would be contrary to what pleases Allah. The Prophet said:

> ~ Whoever is silent is saved.

> ~ When the discussion reaches Allah, then be silent.

> ~ Whoever knows his Lord, his tongue becomes still.

That is to say, one is incapable of speaking about the absolute Source and Essence. Divine knowledge is to be tasted and witnessed personally and the tongue is incapable of expressing what is beyond the senses and the mind. The Messenger of Allah said:

> ~ Whoever speaks too much speaks frivolously. Whoever speaks frivolously has little modesty. Whoever has little modesty has little restraint, and whoever has little restraint enters the Fire.

> ❖ *Abstention of the Eyes*: This involves restraining them from seeing whatever is forbidden according to the *shari`ah* of Islam.

> ✡ Tell the people of faith to avert their eyes and to guard their private parts...[24:30]

Lowering the gaze is expected from the serious seeker. Desires that arise from seeing can cause distractions that can be subtle and subconscious as well as gross and action-oriented. A blind person may be spared these distractions (unless he or she regains his/her sight).

> ❖ *Abstention of the Ears*: The ears must be restrained from hearing whatever is forbidden in *shari`ah*, like slander and gossip, music and songs that entice lower tendencies, and listening to the talk of the

4. TRADITIONAL & TRANSFORMATIVE ACTS OF WORSHIP

misguided and the corrupt.

- *Abstention of the Sense of Smell*: This refers to abstaining from both foul odors as well as exciting scents. Foul odors cause aversion and disgust, whereas sweet scent may excite desires and pleasures.

- *Abstention of the Sense of Taste*: The meaning here relates to avoidance of whatever may veil the faculty of reason, such as imbibing intoxicating beverages, or by acquiring a taste for usury and unfair profit, abuse of orphans, the poor and the weak, and various other 'prohibitive' tastes and habits which will hinder one's spiritual progress.

✧ And do not approach the property of the orphan except in the best manner…[6:152]

✧ But those who take usury will rise up on the Day of Resurrection like someone tormented by Satan's touch. [2:275]

- *Abstention of the Sense of Touch*: This relates to abstaining from touching whatever may lead to forbidden actions, or to excesses in permitted actions, or to go beyond the limits of balance.

✧ They will say to their skins, "why have you testified against us?" They will reply: "Allah has caused us to speak, it is He who gives speech to everything and He created you in the first instance and to Him you will return." [41:21]

✧ Nor were you discreet lest your ears or your eyes or your skins testify against you. [41:22]

The senses have been created to function in harmony and balance regarding worldly interactions. Anyone who uses the body and its various parts in a manner for which it was not created is considered to be a wrongdoer and out of balance, which is the opposite of harmony, and, therefore, of justice.

One explanation of the following verse:

> ✧ And the places of prostration (*masājid*) are for Allah, so therefore do not call upon anyone with Allah, [72:18]

is that the human points of prostration include the seven points where the physical body touches the ground. These include the forehead, the two hands, the two knees, and the two feet. These places of prostration are for Allah: they belong to Him and are His slaves, so do not use them in anything which is not pleasing to Him or in anything for which they were not created.

Inner abstentions

Inner abstentions are five:

- ❖ *The First Abstention* refers to restraining the mind from being occupied with base or worldly concerns. The mind is where reasoning and intellect are developed for interaction with the world. When used properly they lead to rational and good understanding. The Prophet has taught that the contemplation of one hour is better than the actions of seventy years.
- ❖ *The Second Abstention* is to use the mind and intellect to learn about creation and appropriate boundaries and limitations.

4. TRADITIONAL & TRANSFORMATIVE ACTS OF WORSHIP

☼ ...those who preserve Allah's limits. [9:112]

◈ *The Third Abstention* involves restraining the imaginal power (*khayāl* – the faculty which enables us to construct entities or ideas which do not physically exist, such as a 'flying cat') so that its activity is limited to the purpose for which it was created, which is the perception of things in their true higher reality without being overcome by fantasy and foolish imagery. Allah did not create this power for any reason other than to deduce the meaning behind the world of matter. The power of imagination inspired the Pharaoh and his people to imagine that the transformation of the staff of Musa into a serpent was merely a result of magic.

◈ *The Fourth Abstention* is restraining the power of illusion (and values or meanings given to events or situations) which makes one hate someone one minute and love someone else the next. This *'wahm'* prevents one from steadfastness and perseverance on the path of spiritual evolvement. It will cause one to fall prey to the delusion of love and hate and other confusions.

Whoever possesses a 'Tranquil Soul' is free of all of this as he is in the station of witnessing his Beloved and His acts, and 'anything the Beloved does is loved'. Whoever is in this state of witnessing One Reality has no enmity for anyone nor concern. Allah addresses the one who has attained this station:

☼ O soul that art at rest! Return to your Lord pleased [with Him] and well-pleasing [Him]. [89:27-28]

Whoever truly fasts is the one who possesses a soul

that is at rest or tranquil and is not possessed or controlled by his lower self.

- ❖ *The Fifth Abstention* deals with restraining the combined senses as they manifest themselves, both in subjective thoughts (*wahm*) and in the imagination, and as they constantly appear to the self in both form and meaning. This is naturally an obstacle to progress on the Path, because anyone who is occupied with the senses is veiled from the real significance that lies behind them.

  Likewise, anyone who is preoccupied with their illusions and self-given values will be veiled from true meaning. The 'One who is veiled, is veiled, regardless of whether it is by one veil or a thousand.' Consequently, the one who fasts must abstain from the likes of these so that he may be free of all veils and witness his Beloved in the manner we have discussed.

The Men of Allah consider the self to be like a tree with ten branches. Each branch naturally takes its share of nutrients which the tree imbibes from the earth. If, however, we suppose that nine of these branches are cut off then the power of those branches and the nutrients which originally went to them would now go to the one remaining branch; it would grow larger and its fruit would be sweeter and bigger. So it is with the self of man. If man ceases to be attached to the world which surrounds him and his attachment is to the trunk then no doubt the fruits of his thought will be loftier, greater, more powerful, and more honorable.

The fast of the Gnostic consists of abstaining from witnessing anything other than Allah. Consequently,

4. TRADITIONAL & TRANSFORMATIVE ACTS OF WORSHIP

anyone fasting at this level abstains from anything other than their Beloved, for they assert that there is nothing in existence other than Allah (the Exalted), Allah's Names, Attributes and Actions; thus, everything relates to Allah, by Allah, and from Allah. This is because anybody who does not restrain his self from witnessing other than Allah is a *mushrik*, and the fast of the *mushrik* is not accepted, nor is his prayer, because praying and fasting cleanse the inner from the impurity of seeing another with Allah, and from the illusion of the grossness and the filth of 'otherness' with the water of Unity and the light of faith based on knowledge. It is obvious in prayer and other acts of worship that one cannot cleanse the inner unless the outer is cleansed by way of *wudu'* or *ghusl*. Likewise, the fast is not valid for the *mushrik*, whether his *shirk* be open or concealed, because every *mushrik* rejects Reality (i.e. a *kāfir*) and every *kāfir* is a *mushrik*, as Allah has stated:

> ✿ And whoever associates (others) with Allah has indeed gone far astray. [4:116]

The following verse elucidates the meaning of concealed *shirk*:

> ✿ Thus whoever seeks to meet his Lord then let him do good actions and not associate anyone in the worship of his Lord. [18:110]

If this is an allusion to one who was openly associating others with Allah, Allah would have said: '...and not associate anyone with his Lord.' But when He says 'in the worship of his Lord' we know that this is an allusion to one who secretly or inadvertently associates others with Allah, who are referred to as being 'believers' and 'Muslims', as Allah has said:

☼ And most of them do not believe in Allah without associating (others with Him). [12:106]

And recall what the Prophet said:

~ The infiltration of *shirk* into my people is more hidden than the creeping of a black ant upon a black stone on a dark night.

The awakened seeker must give up the illusion of seeing actions as coming from other than Allah so that by this realization he may arrive at the station of the Unity of Action. Then he must go past the illusion of seeing Attributes other than those of Allah. That is the station of the Unity of Attributes. Finally, he must go past the veil of 'independent' entities or events – in Truth, there is no Reality except the One Reality, Allah. That is the station of the Unity of Essence, which is the goal of the Path, and indeed, the goal of existence itself.

Shaykh Ahmad al`Alawi said that whoever has arrived at this station cannot see anything other than Allah even if he intends to do so. He also said that when it is established within one's self that it is an obligation to abstain from anything other than Allah, the self will begin to long for the knowledge of Allah, and this is like what occurs with the rising of the crescent moon of Ramadan:

☼ Whoever among you witnesses the month, let him fast... [2:185]

This station is that of witnessing or seeing, first outwardly and then in the subtle spiritual realms, and whoever does not raise his head will not witness the spiritual realms of the heavens and the earth. The determination and concern of the seeker should not be concentrated in the senses as this will cause the heart to

4. TRADITIONAL & TRANSFORMATIVE ACTS OF WORSHIP

turn away from witnessing the Lord. It is for this reason that he abandons everything which reaches him by way of the senses. The seeker will not be able to concentrate his will and direction until he is detached from his senses. The senses may dominate the outward, as one of the Masters has said that the senses will obliterate meaning unless the senses become the essence of meaning themselves.

Shaykh al`Alawi says that the self of the seeker is afflicted by separation which is often expressed as being in a state of *janābah*; absorption in Allah, then, is forbidden to him and the veil will descend upon him because of the existence of this obstacle. When the barrier is removed, then the seeker is obliged to make up whatever he missed. Allah has warned those who are not patient with 'one food' [2:61], that is, with the Unity of Essence, and who long for anything other than that from among the realms of creation, when He said:

> ✧ Would you exchange that which is good for that which is low and base? Then go down to a city and your wish will be granted… [2:61]

The significance of 'city' here is that it represents the consuming self with all that it contains of desires and expectations both open and hidden. This is alluded to in:

> ✧ …from whatever the earth causes to grow of greens, cucumbers, garlic, lentils and onions. [2:61]

Here Allah alludes to the desires of the self which lead to degradation:

> ✧ …and they were afflicted with degradation and helplessness and were forced to endure anger from Allah. [2:61]

This is the state when the lower self is in command and the way out is to take strength by way of the friendship of Allah. For this reason it is said that if you want strength which will not vanish, then do not take pride in strength which will vanish.

Whoever fasts the fast of *haqiqah*, and consequently abstains from anything other than Allah, is fasting according to the following *hadith qudsi*:

> ~ For every good action there is the recompense of ten to seven hundred times its worth except fasting, for, indeed, it is solely for Me and I shall surely be the reward.

At the earlier phases of spiritual evolvement, the fast is rewarded by the Garden, joy, houris and palaces, or by nearness, attainment, unveiling, and witnessing. At the advanced level the fast has its reward in Allah Himself, the Granter of rewards.

The difference between the fast of the people of *tariqah* and that of the people of *haqiqah* is that the former is a means for refining the behavior and taking on the Attributes of Allah, as the Prophet said:

> ~ Mould your character with Allah's Attributes.

The fast of the people of *haqiqah*, on the other hand, is a means of attaining annihilation and of cleansing oneself by Allah in the station of Pure Unity, which is referred to as annihilation in Unity; as Allah has said in a *hadith qudsi*:

> ~ Whoever has sought Me has found Me. Whoever has found Me has come to know Me. Whoever has known Me has loved Me. Whoever has loved Me I have slain. Whomever I have slain the payment of the blood money is on Me, and I will Myself be the

4. TRADITIONAL & TRANSFORMATIVE ACTS OF WORSHIP

payment for the blood money that I owe.

One relevant example often given is that of a lump of charcoal and fire. Suppose that there is a strong fire which is described in terms of light, burning, and heat, and that next to it lays charcoal which may be described as dark and cold. As this charcoal is gradually moved closer to the fire, we see that it begins to take on the same characteristics as the fire as fire begins to glow from the charcoal itself. Thus, the charcoal becomes fire and no longer remains charcoal.

> ☼ These parables We make for the people and they are not understood except by the wise. [29:43]

The Feast of Fast-Breaking (`Id al-fitr)

This feast that marks the end of the month of fasting alludes to the breaking of the fast which cannot be realized as long as the seeker's senses are suppressed, for during the correct fast the senses are made redundant. If the senses return to him from his Lord that is indeed what is sought after; it is this which is referred to as the `Id, 'that which returns' (from the word `ada, which means to return). The seeker abandons his senses because he abstains from sensual contact and worldly pleasures. But if the senses actually become conveyors of meaning rather than mere physical experiences, then he no longer needs to abandon them. When this occurs, the senses, the meaning, the uniqueness of Allah and His allegorical similarities become as one:

> ☼ ...Thus wherever you turn, there is the Face of Allah. [2:115]

It is with this same meaning that one Master has said:

I penetrated the outward and discovered the inward. I examined the inward and found it to be the outward. Thus, there is no inside to the inward and no outside to the outward and I found it to be in accordance with the meaning which is taken from Allah's words: 'He is the First, the Last, the Apparent and the Hidden.' [57:3]

We find that most of the great Masters in their later stages appreciate human companionship from which they were alienated earlier on. After spiritual solitude and meditation (*khalwah*), the entire existence for them becomes as if it were solitude in which they see only One Reality, and that is exactly what is sought after from the beginning.

If the seeker returns to creation and humankind before being immersed and absorbed in the witnessing of Allah, then he has broken his covenant and his fast is invalid.

4. TRADITIONAL & TRANSFORMATIVE ACTS OF WORSHIP

4.4 The Pilgrimage (*hajj*)

The word *hajj* literally means 'endeavor, aspiration, intention, destination, object, goal, aim'. In Islam it means: 'to intend to go to the House of Allah to carry out specific rituals which are to be executed within a certain time frame.'

In a spiritual sense *hajj* is endeavoring to reach a station whose meaning, magnitude and true essence cannot be expressed or explained because of the lack of words to describe it. For this reason there are few who speak of it. In 'The Lantern of the Path,' Imam Ja`far alSadiq said:

> ~ If you want to make the Pilgrimage then empty your heart before your departure of every distraction and concealing veil and turn all your affairs over to your Creator and trust in Him...

And also:

> ~ ...then wash your sins away with the water of sincere repentance and don the garments of truth, purity and humility.

Imam `Ali was asked about the reason for stopping within the sanctuary (*haram*).[30] He replied:

> ~ Because the Ka`bah is His House and the *Haram* [of Makkah] is His door. When they travel to it [i.e. the Ka`bah] they are stopped at the door and they implore Him.

Then he was asked why Muzdalifah[31] was part of the holy precincts. He replied:

---

30   *Haram*, meaning sacred precinct or sanctuary, should not be confused with '*harām*' which refers to whatever is forbidden by God.
31   Muzdalifah lies outside Makkah.

~ Because when they were granted permission to visit and enter, He stopped them at the second veil, and when their imploring had lasted a long time there He permitted them to offer their sacrifice. Then when they carried out their rites, they cleansed themselves by it of their sins which acted as a veil between Him [Allah] and them; then He gave them permission to reach in this state of purity.

Then he was asked why was fasting forbidden on the days of *Tashrīq*[32] and he replied:

~ Because people are the guests of Allah and His hospitality and it is not correct for the host to make his guests fast.

He was then asked what is the meaning of grasping onto the curtain of the Ka`bah. He replied:

~ It is like the man who has committed a crime and sin against another, so he holds onto his garment and beseeches him and is humbled before him so that he will overlook his wrong action.

The 'mountain' signifies the mountain of `Arafat which is outside of the Haram. As for *almash`ar ulharām*, or Muzdalifah, it represents the station of nearness, and this must be located within the sanctified area.

The Pillars of the Pilgrimage

The spiritual Pillars of the Pilgrimage are generally considered to be four in number: *alihrām* or consecrating oneself for the duration; the walking around the Ka`bah

---

32   The three days following the sacrifice which is performed at the Pilgrimage.

4. TRADITIONAL & TRANSFORMATIVE ACTS OF WORSHIP

(*ṭawāf*); hastening between the stations of pilgrimage (*sa`y*); and the pause on `Arafat (*wuqūf*).

1. Al-Ihrām

This is the act of entering the process of the Pilgrimage. It is thus called because the person making the pilgrimage abstains from shaving, cutting fingernails, hunting, and having sexual relations. It also refers to the donning of a garment, usually of white cotton, wool or linen, worn during the performance of the Pilgrimage. Its significance is that all things which are permitted (*halāl*) are forbidden (*harām*), in addition to what is already forbidden, to the person of this station while he is wearing the white garment, out of reverence for the sanctity of Allah. The people of gnosis consider it to mean the exodus from every circumstance, whether it be exalted or lowly or whether it be related to time or space. This is often referred to as 'Freedom from Surroundings'. If the person of this station does not exit from the limitations of time and space and from the external world of phenomena he will not arrive at his destination. All human experiences occur within the realm of phenomena. Outside of it there is no time or space, because Allah existed when there was no time and no space, and He remains unchanged. This entire realm of existence, with respect to His Magnitude and Glory, is no more than a mustard seed or smaller.

Makkah itself is the symbol of Oneness and thus worthy of the Divine. Here the seeker should assume new courtesies because every state and every station has its particular courtesy. Thus, the courtesy of Divinity (*ulūhiyah*) is not the same as the courtesy of Lordship (*rubūbiyah*). Among its strange wonders that indicate the difficulty of this station is that it demands of man to be both with existence and nonexistence at the same time. People have been excused from having to understand this because of its inherent contradiction. Ibn 'Ata'Allah has said the following concerning this condition:

> ~ The universe is established by His Essence, thus the universe is in reality non-existent with the form of existence – nonexistent from the standpoint of the Ever-Sentient Eternal Essence and existent from the standpoint of Attributes. Thus the person in this station [the pilgrim] can do nothing but submit and from there he concentrates upon entering the "Door of Peace."

It has been said with regards to this that the one who witnesses Allah does not remember Him, and that He will not be witnessed unless He is remembered.

The courtesy of this Presence is to be occupied with witnessing it and surrendering to its Right Hand (that is, surrendering to the Black Stone because of it having been referred to as the 'Right Hand of Allah'). Whatever comes from the acts of Allah are the traces. The Prophet said concerning this:

> ~ The Black Stone is the Right Hand of Allah.

When the Gnostic reaches this station he witnesses the heavens as being 'rolled up in His Right Hand' [39:67]. Thus, the Right Hand of Allah veils the Gnostic from seeing the world of objects, because they are not outside of the Right Hand of Allah.

2. The Walking Around the Ka'bah (*tawāf*)

This refers to the *tawāf* after stopping at 'Arafat and it signifies the return to the Manifestation of the Essence

4. TRADITIONAL & TRANSFORMATIVE ACTS OF WORSHIP

which is worthy of Divinity (*ulūhiyah*), and which is described in terms related to meaning and spirituality, travelling through the realm of meaning, and the various qualities of the manifestations of the Creator and the creation.

The *tawāf* is also a journey of reflection into the inter-relatedness of the seven key Attributes (the Living, Knowing, Willing, Able, Communicating, Seeing, Hearing), the characteristics of their composition, and the dependence of one upon the other. Because this station is the Station of Favor, general knowledge is unacceptable here as it has already been attained by the seeker. He should not neglect to perform the *tawāf* if he is able to do so, nor should he neglect to make a supplication here for what he wishes, because when the pilgrim enters the Sanctuary he finds the six directions (i.e. north, south, east, west, above and below) all facing towards the Ka`bah. If it is like this for the seeker, how is it for the Master who has vanished within the Essence of his Creator and who represents Allah in his words? Everything which issues forth from the tongues of the Masters comes from the beams issuing forth from the Presence of the Unique Oneness.

3. Hastening between the Stations of Pilgrimage (sa`y)

Hastening between the stations of the Pilgrimage, which are called *Safā* and *Marwa*, refers to the fluctuation of the Master between Allah's Beauty (*jamāl*) and His Glory and Majesty (*jalāl*) to the point where Glory becomes the essence of Beauty because of his having abandoned his self, not to mention his own will and freedom of choice. This fluctuation between Beauty and Majesty represents the Masters' rank of perfection. Their movement represents the Hand of Allah's concern and His protection in both states. In spite of the lofty position of the Masters, they are not seduced by what they have already attained from the *tawāf* and their immersion in the Presence of Oneness. Majesty and Beauty do not affect them because they are part of them, in contrast to others for whom this state would represent a tribulation.

> ✪ ... and We will test you with evil and with good as a tribulation. [21:35]

The Master is with Allah in all his conditions; thus, he enjoys Beauty and Glory to the same degree. Every time Shaykh Muhammad alBuzidi[33] experienced pain he would say:

> ~ My Glory coming from my Beauty.

He who is with Allah loves Allah's constriction as well as His expansion, and sees both of them as being natural occurrences like night and day, as they are both necessary conditions of experiencing being-ness. Constriction is an attribute of the physical while expansion is an attribute of the spiritual. The Master lets the station seek him out and does not try to seek it out. The station was created for him he was not created for the station. He is concerned exclusively with the glorification of Allah and allows everything else to serve him in his dedication.

Safā is symbolic of Beauty and *Marwa* is symbolic of Majesty or Glory, and the perfect Master is content with both states, as we have already said. Thus, whoever knows Allah by way of His Beauty but is ignorant of Him in His Glory has not attained perfection but has been distracted

---

33   One of the well-known North African Shadhili shaykhs of the 19th century, d. 1909.

4. TRADITIONAL & TRANSFORMATIVE ACTS OF WORSHIP

by the illusion of hastening between Beauty (*Safā*) and Glory (*Marwa*).

The person of intellect is the one who does not retreat or limit himself to only one of the two manifestations, causing himself to go astray or out of balance. He must advance regardless of the hesitation of his self or its anxiety about a station or a familiar condition. He is in the Divine Hand of Allah Who turns him from Beauty to Majesty, as Allah has said concerning the Companions of the Cave:

☼ ... and We turn them from the right to the left...
[18:18]

In effect, he is like the yielding corpse while being washed. He then may beseech Allah and call out to Him for whatever he wishes at the station of *Sa`y* and *Tawāf*, that is, when he has completed them, since it is not permitted to say 'I' before that. The limitation to one of these two manifestations brings balance, for which reason it has been taught that one will not have attained perfection unless the heart is the same in whichever of four circumstances: at the times of deprivation or bestowal or when one is either honored or humiliated.

It is incumbent upon the seeker to remain in a state of purity and to maintain concealment of the One Truth behind the two stations. This is the condition of discrimination between Glory and Beauty, which are referred to as the Hastening Between Stations, and the *Tawāf*, which are referred to as the two excursions within the interconnectedness of the Attributes. These stipulations accompany this station because one witnesses both the effect and its Cause – seeing the Attributes and what they are connected to.

The *muhrim* (one who is in a state of *ihrām*) continues

in a state of complete obedience, calling out the words of the *talbiyah*, *'Labayka'* (Here I am, at Your service!), until he arrives at the House of Allah, which is a state of Oneness. Then he discontinues the call because of his having completely vanished within the House: his presence melts into the unique oneness of the House, which is the focus of all creation. The black stone is a metaphor of universal relationships. It is a representation of star dust which is the structure of our earth and our bodies.

4. The Pause on `Arafah (**wuqūf**)

This is the stopping place or Pause of the Pilgrimage; as the Prophet said:

~ The Pilgrimage is `Arafah.

After completing the *Tawāf* and the Hastening, the Master is overcome by a state above which there is no higher condition or increase, which is the abandonment of anything known to him beyond the ability to describe. In this station of absolute abandonment, he is ordered to give up his physical form, his soul, his self, his reasoning, the names as well as the Attributes, and anything which has the scent of manifestation; he is commanded to gatheredness and to enfold the outward within the inward and the inward in the outward. When he has realized this state then he has completed the climb up the mountain, which is referred to as the Pause. It is also referred to as 'The Blindness' because it is absolute nonexistence, witnessing neither creation nor Creator.

The Pause is a station beyond reasoning, and therefore impossible to express, that it has been called the 'obscure', the 'amazement', the 'bewilderment', the 'obliteration', and the 'Realm of *Lāhūt*' (Pure Unity). Men of Allah are in

4. TRADITIONAL & TRANSFORMATIVE ACTS OF WORSHIP

wonderment at the mention of it, unable to describe it as if they were deaf and dumb and powerless to reason.

`Arafah, then, is the station of the Pause and the final goal of total annihilation (or complete vanishing from existence). The Pause occurs after *zuhr* (midday prayer time) and after the vanishing of existence (*zawwāl*):

> ☼ When the sun is rolled up and the stars are cast adrift. [81:12]

This is the station of obliteration and blindness, of which the Prophet said:

> ~ Indeed, it is the station of blindness (with) no atmosphere above it or below it.

As this station is incomprehensible and full of awe one must exit from it as soon as possible, remaining merely for a pause. The seeker must then hasten to the place of nearness: Muzdalifah.

> ~ Flee from it (`Arafah) to the Place of Nearness (Muzdalifah) lest you vanish within it.

Thus, it is cried out in bewilderment:

> ~ O my Lord, from the standpoint of the Truth of Existence, You are the Worshipper and You are the Worshipped, You are the Witness and the Witnessed.

After this, the seeker must hasten to Makkah, which is referred to as the Presence of Oneness, in order to cease his wandering, attain a sense of security, bathe, and pray his sunrise prayer.

Other Obligatory Actions

1. The Stoning of Shaytan

The casting of seven stones is symbolic of repudiating the deceptions of Shaytan. The act of casting a stone implies courage and determination to be spared of Shaytan's evils. Thus, if you stone him he will fear you rather than you fear him. You should fear Allah, as He has said:

> ✧ ...so do not fear them [friends of Shaytan] but fear Me if you are people of faith. [3:175]

Otherwise, beware because:

> ✧ ...and no one feels secure from the plot of Allah except the people who shall perish. [7:99]

In summary, the state of the Master is not steady until he reaches the House which is referred to as 'Oneness', and that is the station of Abraham:

> ✧ ...and whoever enters it is secure. [3:97]

For this reason it is said: Go to the House, make the *tawāf* and *salāt* in this manner. Outside this fortress there is no security. 'Fortress' is the Presence of *Lā ilāha illa'Llāh*, of which Allah has spoken in a *hadith qudsi*, saying:

> ~ *Lā ilāha illa'Llāh* is My Fortress and whoever enters My Fortress is secure from My chastisement.

This is a Presence which connects the worshipper with the Worshiped, and the witnesser with the Witnessed, in contrast to the preceding Presence which nullified both.

The one whose hand Allah has taken will never turn to Shaytan because his methods and tricks will become transparent. Every time Shaytan attempts to enter his heart,

4. TRADITIONAL & TRANSFORMATIVE ACTS OF WORSHIP

he is unable to do so because the station which the Master attained has unveiled the light of truth. For this reason it is obligatory for the Master of this station to stone Shaytan at the station of Jumarat three times, because Shaytan has three methods of diverting one on this Path that is full of danger. When the Master stones the pillar *'alJamrah'* for the first time, his ability to distinguish and separate truth from falsehood will then be established and thus it will be easy for him to block the remaining attacks of Shaytan.

2. The Prohibition against Hunting

Hunting relates to the senses, choice and survival. As long as the seeker remains in the unific sea of Truth he will not engage in such acts. When he comes back to the dry land of separation the capacity to discriminate between what is permitted and forbidden enables him to act accordingly. Within the sea of meaning there exists neither pattern nor time, yet when the seeker comes out of it he discovers inscribed upon all inanimate substances and all beasts: 'this is permitted and this is forbidden'. It is not possible, therefore, for him to harm anything of the game of the land when everything is submerged within the Sea of Absolute Oneness.

It is, likewise, obligatory upon the *muhrim* to harm nothing, not even a gnat, for how could one cause harm when one is in the Presence of Allah? In this Noble Presence nothing but the best courtesy toward all creation is possible.

3. The Prohibition on Sexual Intercourse while on Pilgrimage

Abandoning the company of women and abstaining from

intercourse is naturally practiced by men of Allah because of their intoxication with the Divine Presence, and thus they leave off worldly conjugal communion with their wives. The same applies to women in regard to their husbands. When they depart from this Noble Presence they return to their human state, and what was forbidden to them becomes permitted.

The Lesser Pilgrimage or `Umrah & the Ka`bah

This is the voluntary visit to the Ka`bah at other times of the year. The word `umrah is from the Arabic three letter root `AMR, which means to construct, build and inhabit, implying 'flourishing, inhabiting, giving life to, populating, and building'. Thus, `umrah means to cause to flourish and to be enlivened by one's presence at the Ka`bah.

The Ka`bah is a metaphor for divine impenetrability and for this reason there is no fear for the one who is present there. It is the Fortress of Eternal Truth – everlasting and perfect. Whoever performs the `Umrah is not obliged to perform the Pause at `Arafah, but only the *Tawāf* and the Hastening Between Stations, and does not leave Makkah before visiting the House many times. This represents the passion for Allah's Names and Attributes which encompass the universe and the Ka`bah is its centre.

Going to Madinah and to the Presence of Muhammad is not considered complementary to the House of Allah, because the prophetic presence is a manifestation of the Presence of Oneness. The enlightened seeker sees through the Muhammadi Presence, and his spiritual insight witnesses the Presence of Oneness – the Unique Absolute One. As his outer is within the *shari`ah*, his soul is within the *tariqah* and his Innermost is within the *haqiqah*. Reflecting upon 'Muhammad the Messenger of Allah' will reveal that

4. TRADITIONAL & TRANSFORMATIVE ACTS OF WORSHIP

'Muhammad' represents the Physical Universe and the 'Messenger' (*rasūl*) represents the Spiritual Realms, and that 'Allah' represents the Realm of Power. Thus, whoever knows the *haqiqah* of Muhammad knows the entire truth.

> ☼ ... and whoever obeys the Messenger has obeyed Allah... [4:80]

The Ka`bah

It is said that the word Bakkah (an alternative spelling for Makkah used in the Qur'an spelled with the Arabic letter *ba'*) refers to the exact location of the House (*alBayt*) and its meaning relates to the Arabic word for 'to weep'. As for Makkah (with the Arabic letter *mīm*) it refers to the rest of the city and its meaning relates to being sought after.

The cuboid shape of Ka`bah signifies the shape of the Throne, which consists of four directions or corners. This bears a relationship to the four realities of divine origins. Two of them are to the East of *haqiqah*, which are the `*aql* (intellect) and the *nafs* (in the sense of higher self, i.e. soul), as they originate from the rising lights and suns of knowledges. The other two realities of *haqiqah* originate in the West and are nature and matter. Thus the effulgent divine light begins from the first two realities in the spiritual day and end with nature and matter during the night of that day.

> ☼ ... the Lord of the two Easts and the Lord of the two Wests... [55:17]

By now we can understand the deeper meaning of the phrases which constitute the foundations of Islam: '*Subhān Allah, wa'lhamdu li'Llāh, wa lā ilaha illa'Llāh, wa'Llāhu akbar*' (Glory be to Allah, and the praise is Allah's, and there is no god but Allah, and Allah is Most Great). The reason for the House of Allah being shaped like a cube is because it runs parallel to the greatest Throne of Allah which, from one aspect, consists of the universal nature of all matters.

The number four is the basis of numerical elements, which are the basis in the combination of all numbers. The numerical elements are one to ten, which are then repeated. There does not exist within these numerical elements a number which, when combined, contains and includes the number ten, other than four. Thus, four with its true form '4', and within it 3 (four contains 3), thus become seven (4+3=7); and from it 2 (four includes 2), which thus make 9 (7+2=9); and from it 1 (four includes one), which thus becomes a completed 10 (9+1=10). It is for this reason that it is said that the wisdom of the secret of organizing things is based upon fourbased numbers.

The Levels of the Pilgrimage

The Pilgrimage of Revealed Law

The pilgrimage at this level is to go to the Sacred House of Allah to carry out the prescribed rituals which are to be performed at specific times. Pilgrimage consists of both obligatory actions and voluntary actions.

The Obligatory Actions are of two types: absolute and restricted (to certain circumstances). The absolute is that the pilgrimage should be the Pilgrimage of Islam, which is fulfilled when the following conditions are met: maturity, sound mind, freedom, health, easy availability of provisions and means of transport, sufficient funds and the existence of a means of obtaining one's livelihood, the emptying of the innermost distractions (great fears, attachments etc.) and the possibility of making the journey.

4. TRADITIONAL & TRANSFORMATIVE ACTS OF WORSHIP

Other basic conditions for Hajj are Islam, maturity of mind and the power of reasoning. If these requirements are met then one must perform the pilgrimage once within one's lifetime. With regards to obligations that are restricted in their scope, they are obligatory only if there is a cause which makes them binding (i.e. oaths or contracts).

There are three types of Pilgrimage: *tamattu`*, *qaran* and *ifrad*. The *tamattu`* pilgrimage is obligatory for whomever does not have his family living in the vicinity of the Ka`bah. The *qaran* and the *ifrad* are obligatory upon those who have come to the Ka`bah from a distance of 12 miles (or more) in any direction from the House of Allah.

The actions of pilgrimage are of two types: obligatory and nonobligatory (preferred voluntary actions). Furthermore the obligatory actions are also of two types: *rukn*, an action which if omitted nullifies the pilgrimage, and non*rukn*, obligatory actions which, if mistakenly omitted, will not nullify the entire pilgrimage.

Of the three types of pilgrimage mentioned above, the pillars of the *tamattu`* pilgrimage are eight in number; four of them are restricted to the `umrah and four to the pilgrimage. The pillars of the `umrah are:

1. Intention (*niyyah*).
2. Assuming the state of *ihrām*, including donning the garment at the 'Station for Commencing the Pilgrimage' (*miqāt*) at the proper time.
3. The *tawāf* of the `umrah.
4. The Hastening (*sa`y*) between Safa and Marwa.
5. Those which are relevant to Hajj are:
6. The Intention for the Pilgrimage.
7. The Pause at `Arafat.
8. The Pause at Muzdalifah.
9. The Hastening of the Pilgrimage.

There are eight actions which are obligatory but not considered to be Pillars: The uttering of the four phrases of *Labayk* (if one is able to; if not, whatever is said in its place); the two *rak'āt* of the *Tawāf* of the *'umrah*; the joined prayers after the Hastening; the uttering of the words *Labayk* at the time of assuming the state of *ihrām* for the pilgrimage (or whatever is done in its place); the sacrifice or that which takes its place in the way of fasting if one is unable to perform it; the two *rak'āt* of the *Tawāf* of the pilgrimage; and the *tawāf alnisā'* and its two *rak'āt*.

The Pillars of the *qaran* and the *ifrad* are six in number:
1. The Intention.
2. The *Ihrām*.
3. The Pause at 'Arafat.
4. The Pause at Muzdalifah.
5. The Circumambulation of the *Ziyārah*.
6. The Hastening.

The actions which are considered to be non-*rukn* are four in number:
1. The uttering of the words *'Labayka'* or what is done in its place.
2. The two *rak'āt* of the *Tawāf* of the *Ziyārah*.
3. The *tawāf alnisā'*.
4. The two *rak'āt* of the *tawāfalnisā'*.

The *qaran* is distinguished from the *ifrad* by the performance of the sacrifice. It is preferable (*mustahabb*) to utter the *talbiyah* (*Labayka*) at the beginning of each Circumambulation for both of them.

There are many actions that are considered to be voluntary, preferable actions. One should refer to the books which specifically deal with the pilgrimage for details concerning them. This, then, is the pilgrimage of

4. TRADITIONAL & TRANSFORMATIVE ACTS OF WORSHIP

the people of *shari`ah* according to the way of the House of the Prophet.

The Pilgrimage of the Adepts

At the next level the advanced pilgrim will visit the House of Allah – the Spiritual Ka`bah. This sacred House can be considered from two viewpoints: from that of the 'Horizons' (i.e. the macrocosm) and from that of the self (i.e. the microcosm). With regard to the 'Horizons', this refers to the original human (*insān*) heart, also called the 'Universal Self', 'the Visited House' [52:4] and the 'Preserved Tablet' [85:22]. The 'self' as used here refers to the heart of lesser man which is referred to as the 'heart, the breast, or the articulating self.'

The former of these two, that is, the 'Horizons', are the *Qiblah* of the people of *haqiqah* and the latter is the *Qiblah* of the people of *tariqah*. The way the people of *tariqah* go to and turn towards their *Qiblah* rests upon what has come to us in the tradition that the first House which extended over the water and appeared upon the face of the water was the Ka`bah. This was before the existence of the earth and whatever was made upon it, according to the Prophet's words:

> ~ The Ka`bah was the first House which appeared upon the face of the water at the time of the creation of the Heavens. He created it ... before the creation of the earth.

Allah said:

> ✧ Surely the first House which was established for the people was the one in Bakkah (Makkah), as a blessing and as a guidance for the worlds. In it are

clear signs, the station of Abraham, and whoever enters it is secure, and Allah has obliged the people to make the pilgrimage to the House for whoever can make his way to it, and as for him who defies the commandment, Allah is independent from all of the worlds. [3:9697]

The tradition and the verse demonstrate that there is both a physical Ka`bah and a spiritual Ka`bah and each of them has two aspects. One of its aspects is the physical *masjid* which is called *alMasjid ulHarām* (The Sacred Mosque). The other division is the physical heart, which is also called *alMasjid ulHarām*. Another aspect is the Greater Heart of Man, which is referred to as the 'Universal Soul', and the other division is the Lesser Heart of Man, which is referred to as the 'Differentiated Articulating Self'.

The first Reality which manifested within the spiritual realm from the Greater Soul was the Soul of Man, of which it is said that the first thing that Allah created was the soul or reasoning, and it was the *Qiblah* of *haqiqah* which was called the Universal Soul; as Allah has said:

✧ O people fear your Lord Who created you from one soul. [4:1]

Similarly, the first form which manifested within the physical realm, which is referred to as the 'earth', was the form of the physical Ka`bah; as Allah has said:

✧ Surely the first House established for the people was the one in Bakkah (Makkah), as a blessing and a guidance for the worlds...[3:96]

The first Reality which manifested within the spiritual realm from the Lesser Soul of Man, referred to in His words:

4. TRADITIONAL & TRANSFORMATIVE ACTS OF WORSHIP

☼ ...and when I formed it and blew into it by way of My Soul, [15:29]

was the *Qiblah* of *haqiqah*, which is referred to in the words of the *hadith qudsi*:

~ My earth and My heavens cannot contain Me, but the heart of My slave who has faith contains Me.

The first form which manifested within the physical realm, that is the 'body', was the form of the physical heart, referred to as the 'breast', of which Allah has said:

☼ Have We not expanded your breast? [94:1]

Thus, just as the spiritual Ka`bah may be understood from the physical Ka`bah, the existence of the spiritual heart, which is the lesser Heart of Man, may be understood from the existence of the physical heart, by virtue of:

☼ We shall show them Our signs on the horizons and in their souls so that the Truth will become clear to them. [41:53]

It may also be understood from the verse:

☼ It is He Who created the heavens and the earth in six days and His Throne was upon the water. [11:7]

The Throne (the structural blueprint) existed before the creation of the physical heavens and earth and is built upon the foundation of the spiritual essences consisting of reasoning and souls. 'Throne' here means the spiritual throne which is the Primal Reasoning. If the meaning of the word 'Throne' refers to the physical Throne, which is the greater cycle of the heavens, then the meaning of the term 'water' signifies physical water. It has also been said that the term 'water' here signifies divine knowledge which is the foundation of all phenomena. Distinguishing it by placing the Throne over it is to signify its vastness and greatness.

If we suppose the water upon which the Throne rests is a drop from the Greater Man (the Macrocosm), from the standpoint of form as it is determined to be among the Men of Allah, then the water represents physical water and its manifestation signifies its relationship to the drop from which all forms in the world spring. It is also thus with regard to the Lesser Soul of Man (i.e. the microcosm) which is derived from a drop of sperm. The microcosm is identical to the Macrocosm in all aspects of meaning.

The Pilgrimage of the Gnostic

This consists of spiritually turning in the direction of the greater Heart of Man, which is the Supreme House of Allah and which is referred to as the 'Visited House', the 'Sacred Presence' and the 'Universal Soul'. This is in contrast to the Pilgrimage of the people of *tariqah* which is directed to the Lesser Heart of Humankind.

The authority over the differential (individual) soul, which is the soul of the Lesser Man, cannot exist anywhere but within the mind. Likewise the authority over the Universal Soul which is the soul of the Greater Man, and which is referred to as the universe, cannot exist anywhere but within the Throne, similar, in this instance, to the mind. Furthermore, in the same way that it initially manifests within the Lesser Man as the physical heart, which is the fountainhead of life, so too it is that its initial manifestation within the Greater Man is the Fourth Celestial Sphere, which is the celestial sphere of the sun, the fountainhead of life in the world. Thus it is like the breast of the Greater Man with the sun being like the physical heart within it.

4. TRADITIONAL & TRANSFORMATIVE ACTS OF WORSHIP

The heart of *haqiqah* is the Universal Soul, which is also called the 'Preserved Tablet', the 'Clear Book' and 'Adam of the *Haqiqah*'. Allah alludes to it in the verse:

> ☼ O people, fear your Lord Who created you from One Soul and He created its mate from it. [4:1]

The Soul of the Fourth Celestial Sphere is like the animal soul which is in the heart. All parts of the body receive life from it. It is the well-known 'Visited House' of the *shari`ah*, the Fourth Heaven, and it is by it that Allah makes an oath in the verse:

> ☼ By the Mountain and inscribed Book on a fine outstretched parchment and the Visited House and elevated canopy and the overflowing sea. [52:16]

The 'mountain' represents the Throne, and the 'inscribed Book' represents the Universal Soul which is the heart of the universe. The 'fine outstretched parchment' represents the Eighth Celestial Sphere, which is its manifestation. The 'elevated canopy' may be the Throne or it may represent the earthly sky. The 'Visited House' may represent the Fourth Celestial Sphere and it may represent the Universal Soul. The 'overflowing sea' is filled with forms and may represent the Realm of the Barrier, or interspace or barrier (*barzakh*), which lies between the two worlds of the spiritual and physical, and is referred to as the shadow realm and is filled with the form of everything in creation.

The Ka`bah represents the Universal Soul which is called the Supreme House of Allah; its appearance on the water is an allusion to the spiritual realms which originate from it before the physical realms.

✧ It is He Who created the heavens and the earth in six days and His Throne was upon the water, [11:7]

This could mean that before the creation of the physical heavens and earth the Throne was upon their two spiritual counterparts, reasoning and the self, if by the term 'Throne' we mean the spiritual Throne which is the Primal Reasoning. It is possible that the water is an allusion to the basic matter from which the universe was created. Furthermore, it is possible that this was before 'the splitting asunder' during the time of unity when all primordial matter was in one state, when reasoning, the soul, and the Throne were one Reality.

The 'First House' which has been alluded to is the Universal Soul and the word 'Bakkah', is an allusion to the Eighth Celestial Sphere, which is termed the Dais (*kursiy*) and as 'Blessed' – an allusion to the blessing of knowledge and truth which surround it and which descend from it to the rest of creation below it. 'A guidance for the world' is an allusion to its overflowing grace and illumination for all of the worlds.

'The station of Abraham' is an allusion to the arrival of the spiritual traveler, by means of it, to the station of the allinclusive oneness of the *haqiqah* of Abraham. Allah says the following concerning this:

✧ And in this way We show Abraham the dominion of the heavens and the earth so that he may be among the certain. [6:75]

✧ ...and whoever has entered it is secure. [3:97]

These words indicate that whoever enters the House in the manner mentioned above will be secure from all suspicion and doubt regarding the cosmic Divine sanctity.

4. TRADITIONAL & TRANSFORMATIVE ACTS OF WORSHIP

He will be secure from the two forms of associating others with Allah, i.e. openly and secretly.

✧ ...and Allah has obliged the people to make the Pilgrimage to the House... [3:97]

That is to say, from the standpoint of spiritual knowledge, of witnessing, unveiling, and viewing an obligation rests upon the people who are ready for this station to go to that House in this manner. The verse

✧ ...whoever is able to make his way to it, [3:97]

is an indication of His having distinguished a particular group of people who are able to do it by virtue of their appropriate knowledge and good action.

Useful knowledge is attained in two ways. Either directly from Allah without any human intermediary, referred to as revelation, inspiration and unveiling, or through the medium of the men of knowledge, like His Prophets and Messengers. They are alluded to in:

✧ Read: And your Lord is the Most Generous, He who taught with the pen, [96:34]

and:

✧ ...and when Allah made a covenant with those who were given the Book: You shall certainly make it known to men and you shall not hide it. And they cast it behind their backs and took a small price for it; so wretched is that which they have purchased. [3:187]

Good actions also have two aspects: One relates to the people of *shari`ah* and *tariqah,* and refers to good and purifying actions, with no trace of doubt or suspicion and which is performed purely and sincerely for Allah. The other aspect is distinctly for the people of *haqiqah* and the people of attainment, and this is not known or witnessed by anyone in existence except by Allah:

> ✡ So whoever wants to meet his Lord, let him perform a good action and not associate anyone in the worship of his Lord. [18:110]

Thus, whoever desires to go on the Pilgrimage of the gnostics must assume the state of *ihrām* from witnessing the realms of the senses completely, by forbidding (i.e. making *harām*) his self from witnessing the physical universe and those worldly pleasures which are connected with it. Then he should direct his attention to the spiritual realm, which is the Sanctuary, Makkah or Bakkah, so that in fact he may attain it and become adorned with the Attributes of this spiritual realm and obtain its knowledge. Then he should direct his attention to the Ka'bah of *Haqiqah*, which is the Universal Soul and its knowledge and truths, and make seven *tawāfs* around it.

The seven stations of the self are:
1. The Commanding Self (*nafs alammārah*)
2. The Critical Self (*nafs allawwāmah*)
3. The Inspirational Self (*nafs almulhamah*)
4. The Tranquil Self (*nafs almutma'innah*)
5. The Contented Self (*nafs alradiyah*)
6. The Self which is the object of Allah's contentment (*nafs almardiyah*)
7. The Perfected Self (*nafs alkāmilah*)

The levels of knowledge of the physical realm correspond to what has been called the 'Seven Levels of Qur'anic Knowledge', of which there are numerous subdivisions, and have been indicated by the Prophet

4. TRADITIONAL & TRANSFORMATIVE ACTS OF WORSHIP

when he said:

~ Indeed the Qur'an possesses both an outward and an inward and its inward possesses an inward continuing to seven levels.

Then the attention is turned to the station of Abraham, which is the station of Unity, and the Presence of Oneness, known as the Primal Reasoning and the Supreme Soul. There he performs a prayer of two rak`āt in thanksgiving for having arrived at that Presence. The two rak`āt represent the annihilation from both the outer and the inner realms and whatever they contain of existence and creation, including himself.

Then he hastens between Safa and Marwa (outer and inner worlds), to observe them once again with his effort and struggle in order to discontinue looking upon multiplicity by carefully examining the One Existence which lies behind it, and to become firmly established in the station of unity or gatheredness, which is his desired destination. Then he directs his attention to the Ka`bah once again in order to witness the Universal Soul and to observe its truths. He takes the *ihrām* of the Pilgrimage from it, which is beyond rationality, in the prescribed manner.

Then he turns his attention to `Arafat (the station of the self). Turning one's attention to the `Arafat of the self is to turn the attention to the station of knowledge of *haqiqah* and there is no Presence after this Presence except the presence of the Essence, which no one can reach, for it has preceded and reached all before creation. In this station the arrival at the Unity of true gatheredness is attained, which is referred to as 'Muhammadi Unity'.

It is here that a man becomes a human (*insān*) where the perfected being is perfected, and where the Master becomes a Master. For this reason they are obliged to return to the task of bringing others to perfection by returning to the realm of multiplicity, as Allah has said:

> ☼ ...and to warn their people when they return to them. [9:122]

When Shaykh Junayd was asked about the end destination, he replied:

> ~ (It is) the return to the starting point.

This is the secret of the return of the pilgrim from `Arafat to Mina, because it symbolizes the return to the realm of multiplicity. Then he occupies himself with the performance of the rituals of Mina, that is, the business of the outward world viz. the stoning, the sacrifice and the shaving of the head. He casts the stone of `Aqabah, which represents the world and its provision, casting it away without the possibility of returning, now that he lives the life of *haqiqah* (the real life):

> ☼ Do not reckon that those who have been killed in the way of Allah are dead; on the contrary, they are alive sustained with their Lord. [3:169]

And:

> ☼ ...or is the one who has been dead and to whom We have restored life and made a light for him with which he walks among the people like the one who is within darkness from which he does not escape? [6:122]

He then shaves his head, that is, he cuts the head of his self from the love of the world and its provision, thereby symbolizing that he will never allow his self to return

4. TRADITIONAL & TRANSFORMATIVE ACTS OF WORSHIP

again. Then he returns to the station of eternity, which is the ongoingness after annihilation, and he goes around the Ka`bah again in order to examine it once more from seven aspects in accordance with the state of his own creation, which is in seven stages; as Allah has said:

> ☼ ...He created you in stages, [71:14]

so that he may glimpse or experience the light of truth by way of that free movement within the seven regions of the earth and the seven celestial regions, which are referred to as Spiritual Regions and the Realm of Power respectively.

Then he performs *salāt* at the station of Abraham, the Unity of Haqiqah, performing the two *rak`āt* prayer of the Feast (Feast of the Sacrifice and Feast of the Fast Breaking), because of having become annihilated from every feast and because of his remaining eternally in a constant state of feasting in divine light, in the station of the Unity of *Haqiqah*.

Finally he returns to Mina,to the world of multiplicity and the three stages which are mineral, plant and animal and stays there for three days of the Days of Allah, as Allah says:

> ☼ ...today I have completed for you your way of life (*Islam*) and I have perfected My Grace upon you and I am contented with *Islam* as a way of life for you. [5:3]

4.5 Obligatory Wealth Tax (*zakāt* and *khums*)

The word *zakāt* literally means 'growth, increase, nearness, goodness', as well as 'purification'. This obligatory charitable tax is given this name because it is the cause of increase in reward, in that one unit is valued as ten or more. It also brings about an increase and growth in wealth, as it is one of the actions which will increase nearness to Allah by obeying and carrying out His commandments. It is also given this name because it purifies wealth by giving Allah what is His due and by giving men theirs. It purifies the heart from the love of wealth and the inclination to amass it. It is also referred to as '*zakāt*' because of what it does to improve the lot of the poor and, likewise, the wealth of the rich, because He has given the responsibility of caring for the weak and ailing to those who are more endowed materially, as is related in the tradition:

> ~ If people would only pay the obligatory tax upon their wealth, there would not be any Muslims in poverty and need, and men are not stricken by poverty, need, and hunger for any other reason but the greed of the rich.

There are two forms of obligatory tax: the tax on wealth and objects of material value and the tax on individuals and family members, which includes the tax paid at the time of the Feast of Fast Breaking which may be paid in cash, food, or animals. Tax is payable upon crop yields because man contains within him a portion which is plant, as the Prophet has said:

> ~ Honor your aunt, the date palm.

And Allah said:

4. TRADITIONAL & TRANSFORMATIVE ACTS OF WORSHIP

☼ He has caused you to grow from the earth as a gradual growth [71:17]

As for the secret behind specifying that 'a quarter of ten' (the amount of obligatory *zakāt* is about 2.5%) should be given for anything other than crop yields, it is reported that Imam Sadiq said:

> ~ Allah has made the tax for every thousand dirhams (unit of currency) twentyfive dirhams, because he created men with the knowledge of the rich among them and the poor, and of the strong among them and the weak, and thus He made for every thousand twentyfive who were needy [and cannot earn for themselves]; if it were not so surely Allah would have given them increase, for He is their Creator and He knows of them.

This means for every forty humans there is one who is needy and is incapable of providing for himself. If the people of faith paid their tax they would improve the situation of their entire community. There are other interesting facts regarding the number forty, as the Prophet said:

> ~ Whoever sincerely dedicates his actions to Allah for forty days, the spring of wisdom will flow from his tongue.

The numbers seven, twelve, forty and seventy occur often in the culture of Muslims. Forty is the number of days in which the soul descends into the womb. The drop of sperm becomes a clot of blood (in the womb) after forty days. The number forty is also mentioned regarding wisdom and maturity in the following tradition:

~ Surely Allah bestows honor on the one who reaches forty.

And:

~ Whoever from my people memorizes forty traditions Allah will raise him up on the Day of Resurrection as a learned scholar.

Imam Baqir warns whoever reaches forty:

~ Beware for you [now] are not excused, so work for what lies before you and abandon foolish talk.

Imam al-Sadiq said:

~ There is an obligatory tax to Allah on every one of your component parts; in fact, it is due for each hair; in fact, it is due for your every glance. Thus, the tax of the eye is to be warned by what you see as well as to cast the eyes downward before objects of lust and desire. The tax of the ears is to listen to knowledge, wisdom, the Qur'an and things which are beneficial to your way of life. The tax of the tongue is to aid the Muslims ... [34]

Basic Legal Foundation and Purpose

At its root the legal taxation is levied on camels, cattle, sheep (and goats), gold, silver, wheat, barley, dates and raisins. The stipulations regarding the one responsible for payment of tax are that the person be free (i.e. not a slave or in custody), possessed of the power of reason, a Muslim and be able to pay the tax.

---

34   From 'The Lantern of the Path'.

4. TRADITIONAL & TRANSFORMATIVE ACTS OF WORSHIP

The items upon which tax is levied must meet the deadline (i.e. the completion of the year) and that the taxable item has reached maturity. The remaining stipulations are well known in the *shari`ah*. This represents the obligatory tax of the Muslims and people of *shari`ah*. Obviously the historical basis of *zakāt* was the Arab way of life in Madina and the surrounding areas. The economy was based on small scale agriculture and animal herding. The shift to urban life changed the basic calculation to one based on income rather than on a different basket of commodities.

The inner meaning of *zakāt* is cleansing the self from its love of accumulating wealth and the purification of the heart from attachments, especially avarice:

> ✿ ...and whoever is guarded from the avarice of his self, they are the successful. [59:9]

Those who spend their wealth in the way of Allah have been singled out in praise:

> ✿ The parable of those who spend their wealth in the way of Allah are like (a single) grain which has produced seven ears and on each ear there are a hundred seeds and Allah multiplies further for whomever He wills... [2:261]

When the seeker overcomes miserliness from his heart, the seeds of sacrifice and generosity begin to grow. Then other noble characteristics and desirable Attributes will bring success and liberation from base characteristics and despicable behavior.

The Gnostics have reasoned that because wealth is loved by us and the path to truth is to love Allah with passion and sincerity, everything will be sacrificed by the one whose love for his Beloved has overwhelmed his heart.

The giver must be careful not to reproach the one who receives. Real generosity is not to see oneself as the giver – only as a means of this action. Allah is the source of all generosity, i.e.:

> ✺ Do not negate your charitable gifts by reproach and insult. [2:264]

The Gnostic considers that the one who receives the tax has done a favor because of his acceptance of what is Allah's due, because the real purpose is to purify the heart from natural meanness and avarice. Pride, arrogance and insult of others (because of your giving) would add additional vices to the self which are subtler and therefore more difficult to be cleansed from. The Prophet said:

> ~ It (tax) is the filth of the people's wealth.

The Qur'an:

> ✺ You will never attain to righteousness until you spend of that which you love. [3:92]

There is no doubt that the most precious thing to man and the thing which he loves most, is his own soul or self. Spending of this soul in the way of Allah is higher purification and greater cleansing which is described in the tradition:

> ~ Everything has a tax and the tax of the body is obedience.

Man is described as being a microcosm which corresponds in every way to the macrocosm of the greater world. Human bones are equivalent to the mines found in the earth and the hair and fingernails to the plants. Seekers of truth will inevitably experience imprisonment in the

4. TRADITIONAL & TRANSFORMATIVE ACTS OF WORSHIP

human and the earthly limitations.

The Qur'an:

☼ And the soul and He Who made it perfect, then inspired it to understand what is right and wrong for it. [91:7-8]

Ultimately the heart's purification will reveal the Divine Power and its infinite lights which will overcome all earthly shadows. The Prophet offered the following supplications:

~ O Allah, make a light in my heart, a light in my hearing, a light in my vision, a light in my flesh, a light in my blood, a light in my bones, a light before me, a light behind me, a light on my right, a light on my left, a light above me, and a light below me, a light in my heart, O Allah, increase me in light and make me a light (I beseech You) by what is Your due, O most Merciful of the Merciful.

With the fulfilled requirements of the tax at the material and mental levels *zakāt* means liberation from earthly shackles and confinements, freeing oneself to the realm of all pervading oneness, which comes after the idea of 'otherness' has been transcended and the confusion of duality overcome.

It has been said that the way to release the *nafs* from its bonds of confinement is to extract it from the chains of complexity and take it to the realm of pure simplicity. Then one transports it to the simplicity of the exalted Celestial and Atomic Realms. Then it is transported to the Realm of the Universal Physical Nature by extracting it from the bonds of nature and taking it to the level of Simple Spirit, and then by extracting it from the spiritual bonds and taking it to the level of Sanctified Spirits, which is the level or stage of the Universal Soul and the Realm of Souls. From the stage of souls, which is referred to as the Highest Spiritual Region, it is taken to the stage of Pure Reasoning and from this point to the level of The One Unique Presence. This is the method of freeing these bonds and it represents true purification and complete cleansing.

The perfection (or evolution) of a mineral is attained when it reaches the station of the plant; the perfection of a plant is attained when it reaches the station of the animal; and the perfection of the animal occurs when it reaches the station of the human. The perfection of the human occurs first when he arrives at the station of angels, then at the station of spiritual vicegerency, then finally at the station of pure Unity, which has been referred to by Ibn ʿAtaʾAllah in the following words:

> ~ When *faqr* (the station of knowledge of one's complete dependence on Allah) is perfected, behold Allah.

Transformative *zakāt* is what renders man free and cleanses him from the shackles of material restrictions and limitations which are due to hidden *shirk*.

Types of Tax and their Significance

Shaykh Ahmad alʿAlawi describes tax as growth and increase, and that 'gratitude for the grace of Allah' is included in it. Within it lies a protection from the loss of this grace; as it has been said:

> ~ Preserve grace by gratitude.

> ☼ ...Surely if you are thankful I will grant you

4. TRADITIONAL & TRANSFORMATIVE ACTS OF WORSHIP

increase... [14:7]

Human expression of gratitude is according to one's level of illumination. There are those to whom Allah has become manifest through His Names; there are those to whom He has become manifest by way of His Attributes; and there are those to whom He has become manifest in His Essence.

Corresponding to these three levels, thankfulness is likewise divided into three types:

- *Thankfulness of the Tongue*: This represents praising and speaking about the grace of Allah; as He has said:

✧ And as for the grace of your Lord, speak (of it). [93:11]

- *Thankfulness of the Heart*: This consists of emptying the heart of everything but the Lord. This is alluded to by Allah when He speaks about Musa:

✧ I have made you for Myself. [20:41]

- *Thankfulness of the Body and Soul*: This is the thankfulness of the entire body and soul of man, which is referred to when Allah addresses the Prophet in the Qur'an, saying:

✧ ...So be steadfast as you have been commanded. [11:112]

The true meaning of this type of thankfulness is that the slave applies his body and his very essence to that for which he was created, as Allah says:

✧ ...and few of My slaves are thankful. [34:13]

The Tax of `ayn

The Arabic word `ayn (which has many meanings, among them 'eye') is used to describe a certain type of tax which is levied on the members of a household as opposed to the word 'head' which is used to count the number of livestock. The 'eye' is symbolic of insight into truth. The term 'eye' is also used to express different meanings.

The Divine Essence is very rarely perceived among men and it is above the general perception of insight or inner vision except for those 'whose sight, this day, is sharp' [50:22]. This occurs when the sight belongs to the One seen, which takes place within the Innermost and not within the realm of insight and visions. Insight gives meaning to outer vision, but when one's vision is turned inward by the power of insight, then the entire process becomes insight and only then can we understand the meaning of the verse:

- ✪ There is nothing like Him. [42:11]

- ◈ *Tax of the Eye*: has a stem which is `irfān and which possesses no branches. Among its qualities are that it is hidden from those who are unworthy of its significance. The tax of the eye is levied on its own kind and spent upon those who are worthy of it.

- ◈ *The Tax of Livestock*: this is an allusion to what Allah has bestowed of grace upon His slaves and consists of two basic forms of grace: the grace of the Ability to Procure and the Grace of Sustainment, each of which has various branches. The Grace of the Ability to Procure refers to the seven components or levels of the self. Whoever possesses mastery over them will be able to move about as he pleases without being obstructed by the assaults of Shaytan and the self. He will be obliged to pay

4. TRADITIONAL & TRANSFORMATIVE ACTS OF WORSHIP

the tax in order to firmly establish this dominion within him. The Tax of Livestock is an obligation upon the seeker at all times and in every instant if he possesses it and is sincere in his actions; if not, then it will not be due from him, because the Tax of Grace is not obligatory.

◈ *The Tax of Seeds and Fruits*: this is symbolic of the Grace of Sustainment which is continuously showered upon the Master after his having become firmly established in his station and after he has mastered the various forms of worship. This is dependent upon being firmly established within the Divine Presence.

Tax in kind becomes obligatory upon the seeker after he has become firmly established and is able to distinguish between the various stations and recognize the various types of illuminations; at that time he is asked to pay the tax, provided he has the minimal amount taxable:

✧ He who purifies himself and remembers the Name of his Lord and performs *salāt* has succeeded. [87:14-15]

This speaks of the purification of the self, that is, through knowledge of it. The one who conceals it has remained ignorant of it. There is much good and benefit in the knowledge of the self, as has been related in a tradition:

~ Whoever has come to know his (own) self, surely knows his Lord.

The knowledge of Allah is close to the knowledge of the self. One leads directly to the other. Consequently, the Masters occupy different levels: the Master who knows himself and the Master who knows his Lord. Thus, whoever knows himself is stronger in knowledge than he who knows only his Lord, as it says in the tradition:

> ~ The strongest among you in the knowledge of his Lord is the one who is strongest in the knowledge of his (own) self.

Whoever knows his self, as it is, will inevitably direct it to what it was created for and this, then, is the purification of the self which is referred to as grace.

◆ *Tax upon Grain and Fruit*: This is not obligatory except after they have become ripe:

> ~ Tax is not due except on those items whose time has come.

✧ And do not hasten with the Qur'an before it is revealed to you and say: My Lord, increase me in knowledge. [20:114]

Some Qur'anic scholars say that this verse refers to things which are subject to specific times or seasons, so beware that wisdom does not appear before its time. If your fruits have become ripe and are ready, that is, if your knowledge is sufficient and appropriate, then it is not permissible to conceal it, as the Prophet said:

> ~ Whoever conceals the knowledge he possesses Allah will bridle him with a bridle made of fire.

Someone asked him concerning this: Shall I speak about everything which I have heard from you, O Messenger of Allah? He replied:

> ~ (Everything) except a tradition which will not be comprehended by the intellects of the people.

4. TRADITIONAL & TRANSFORMATIVE ACTS OF WORSHIP

There may exist in this both a cause for difficulty and corruption. This is why we find that the tax is not obligatory except upon what has been stored up for the Day of Return and that it is not demanded of the Master to disseminate knowledge which he has not yet attained. His knowledge is what has been given to his heart, and it is not beneficial to the general masses at all times. Times and season differ – and for every illness there is a special cure – as do people's needs and intellects.

Whoever wishes to disseminate the knowledge of the twentieth century before the knowledge of the nineteenth century has been made available is mistaken in his action. This is similarly applicable to one who wishes to pay the *zakāt* upon grain which has not yet reached maturity, whose time has not yet come. Allah has stated:

> ✡ ...and there is nothing but that We possess its treasures and We do not send it down unless it is in a known measure. [15:21]

Furthermore:

> ✡ Let the wealthy spend from his wealth but he whose provisions are restricted should spend of whatever Allah has given him. [65:7]

The divinely revealed code of conduct is a treasure and everyone should spend of it in accordance to whatever he has attained of it. The enlightened one develops and changes by circumstances which are required by the season or the time. The color of the water is the same color as its vessel. This tax is not obligatory for anyone save those who possess taxable items of knowledge and on items in kind. This refers to those who are obliged to take this (task of disseminating knowledge) on and whose use of language is appropriate. It is not obligatory for whoever is unable to undertake this, for whoever possesses the 'taxable items' speaks correctly. He possesses this skill as an inheritance from the Prophet; if this is not so then the tax is not obligatory for him.

The Tax upon Livestock and its Categories

The word 'livestock' here symbolizes the various components of the self, which are divided into five categories:

1. The Lower Self (*ammārah*) which commands to evil actions
2. The Reproaching Self (*lawwāmah*)
3. The Tranquil Self (*mutma'innah*)
4. The Contented Self (*rādiyah*)
5. The Self or Soul which is the object of Allah's contentment (*mardiyah*)

Actions which originate with the last three are praised by Allah and are completely accepted. Actions which originate from the first one (i.e. *ammārah*) are rejected. The Reproaching Self (*lawwāmah*) is on the level of beasts (which are *harām* to eat) and thus there is no tax due upon it. If it is good then its actions will draw it near to the company of Allah because it indicates an 'actor who is absent from his actions'. It represents action which originates with the self, which has been described in the Qur'an as follows:

> ✡ And upon them they ride and from them they eat. [36:72]

> ◈ *Camels*: Camels are the first of the taxable livestock and represent the Tranquil Soul (*mutma'innah*), because the self has become tranquil, so it will

4. TRADITIONAL & TRANSFORMATIVE ACTS OF WORSHIP

accept work. It should then be loaded with various types of action which will draw it near to Allah and with various burdens of worship and obedience. The self is stronger in its ability to bear a load than a camel if it is given the sweet reward of obedience which it looks for when its actions are accepted in the beginning stages.

- ❖ *Cattle*: These are symbolic of the Contented Soul (*rādiyah*) because cattle and oxen, even though able to bear burdens, cannot carry the load of a camel. In addition, this level of the self does not, as a rule, transport its burdens to the heart; for this reason its burden is light upon the body.

- ❖ *Sheep*: Sheep represent the self that is the object of Allah's contentment (*mardiyah*) because of their docility and basic usefulness. When the self has attained this rank, all actions which originate from it will be useful for its owner in the same way that sheep are useful to their master – everything from the head to the feet. It is significant that the inability of sheep to carry a burden does not detract from their usefulness. Allah mentions this state of self as:

✧ O Tranquil Self, return to your Lord, contented and the object of His contentment and enter among My slaves and enter My Garden. [89:2730]

These are the righteous slaves and the men of Spiritual Knowledge.

The meaning of 'taxable limits' (*niṣāb*) in this context is that there are some 'People of Knowledge of Allah' who are obliged to pay *zakāt* by bringing out what they possess of hidden knowledge, and among them are those who are not obliged to because their 'taxable limits' have not yet been reached. He whose perception of absolute truth is not yet complete should not concern himself with other people's perception of truth.

Since tax is not obligatory for fruit which has not yet ripened or whose season has not yet come, it is similarly not obligatory for the incidental knowledge which is not connected with Divine Essence (referred to as 'fruits') and for this reason it has been said that one should not speak of what he has observed of that inscribed upon the 'Preserved Tablet' [85:22], because:

> ✡ Allah erases and establishes firmly whatever He wills and with Him is the archetype of the Book. [13:39]

All things are hidden in their opposites and the root is concealed within the branches; thus the 'taxable limits' are not complete and the gnostic is not perfected unless things are seen as joined to their opposites and that the root is indeed within the branches. The realization of the unity of opposites is not difficult if viewed from the standpoint of the inward meaning which is already one in essence, as Allah says:

> ✡ Neither your creation nor your raising is anything but as a single soul. [31:28]

So long as the seeker only sees the branches and not the roots, he is veiled by them from their Creator. How will the Creator become manifest to him when he is entangled within the nets of creation? In the realm of creation there are many opposing contrasts – long and short, big and small, good and bad, profit and loss, sleep and wakefulness, and gratitude and ingratitude. How can the Truth manifest to

4. TRADITIONAL & TRANSFORMATIVE ACTS OF WORSHIP

him among these opposites? He is manifest in the opposites only by way of illumination in various forms and by way of His Attributes. These are inherent within everything. This has been likened to water, which is the source of life for all.

~ Water is one and the same while flowers vary in color.

And:

~ The ocean is one and fish are multi-colored [one Source of creation yet multitudes of worlds].

Allah has said:

✧ ...They are watered with one water and We make some of them excel others in fruit... [13:4]

Some of us foolishly imagine that when we look at created things we are actually seeing their existence by their own essence. This is not possible because by their very nature 'things' are in essence nonexistent and the eyes cannot see that which is nonexistent; rather, we look upon the existence of their Creator Who has lent to creation transient reality. Consequently we imagine that we are actually witnessing the true existence of created things.

✧ Allah is the Light of the heavens and earth. [24:35]

Versatility in this type of divinely inspired knowledge is limited to a very small number of people. It is only granted to those who fulfill its requirements:

✧ Indeed charity is only for the poor and the needy and for those workers who have been [appointed] over it and for those whose hearts are made to incline [to Truth] and in the [ransoming] of slaves [or captives] and the indebted and in the Way of Allah and for the wayfarer... [9:60]

In short, whoever does not fall into any of the eight categories listed in this verse (explained further on) will not be worthy of the Divine Secret. It is obligatory for one who has been charged with the collection of tax not to distribute it to those who are unworthy of it, as the Prophet said:

> ~ Select those to whom you give your charitable donations in the same way you select [husbands] for your daughters.

It has also been said:

> ~ Do not give wisdom to the undeserving for they will do wrong by it and do not withhold it from the deserving for you will do wrong by them.

Khums

The practice of giving *khums* exemplifies the process of ratification that has taken place in the development of Islamic law. According to the verse in the Qur'an [8:41], one fifth of booty was supposed to be set aside for God and his Messenger, near relatives, orphans, the needy and the wayfarers. This practice was retained only by the Ja`fari school of law and the requirement to donate 1/5 of net income or profit to the Imam for the purpose of fulfilling the needs of those mentioned in the verse became a part of Shiite doctrine, while the other schools limited the obligation merely to *zakāt*, generally 2 ½ percent of profit.

Those Deserving of Spiritual Donations

The sincere seekers who deserve tax are as follows:

4. TRADITIONAL & TRANSFORMATIVE ACTS OF WORSHIP

◈ *The Poor or Needy (faqīr)*: This refers to those who are described as having the need for this higher knowledge, those whose hearts are empty of any pretence, and who see themselves as being devoid of knowledge or station; for this reason they are worthy to be given this knowledge:

✧ ...if they be needy then Allah will enrich them from His abundance... [24:32]

✧ Or who is it that answers the distressed when he calls upon Him... [27:62]

As for those who imagine that they are Masters of a certain state or station on the level of Men of Allah, it is not permissible to give them (i.e. those that *imagine*) this spiritual donation because their hearts are already inhabited, and truth cannot be established in a heart unless it is empty.

– *The Destitute (miskīn)*: The meaning here of the term '*miskīn*' (pl. *masākīn*) is not the one whose hand is empty of the world but, rather, one who is humble before Men of Allah. He sees himself as being destitute, helpless, powerless, and wretched. This person will be led by his humility to Allah, to the discovery of the illusion of his own independent existence. This opening will not come unless there is humility, an inner state of powerlessness, and genuine 'poverty'.

✧ Allah aided you at Badr while you were weak and small in number...[3:123]

Anyone who brags and boasts and sees himself as being free from Allah has no share in this spiritual tax:

☼ Certainly Allah helped you in many battlefields, recall the day of Hunayn when your great numbers made you vain, but they availed you not... [9:25]

If the seeker is indeed a *miskīn* Allah will inevitably take his hand by way of a Man of Allah and save him as he saved the boat of the needy one, according to His words:

☼ ...As for the boat, it belonged to certain poor people... [18:79]

Note how they have been described as being destitute and yet they possessed a boat – and perhaps they possessed even more than this. They are simply poor and miserable in a worldly sense only. On the other hand, you may discover someone who possesses absolutely nothing at all and yet possesses no traits of the *miskīn*. Such people are unworthy of this tax and do not desire the secret of the Elect.

◈ *The Raider (ghāzi)*: These are the people of determination and courage. They are described as possessing unequivocal resolve and outstanding truthfulness, and by virtue of their courage no obstacle will impede them nor will anyone enter their hearts but their Beloved. They are deserving of advancement by virtue of this characteristic in that they have drawn the sword of truth and cut through every anxiety and darkness. It has been said that the secret of Allah lies in the truthfulness of the search, as Allah says in a *hadith qudsi*:

~ If My slave draws near to Me an inch, I will draw near to him a yard. If he comes to Me walking, I will come to him running.

4. TRADITIONAL & TRANSFORMATIVE ACTS OF WORSHIP

The Prophet said:

~ Remember Allah and you will find Him before you.

Whoever is courageous before he has entered the Path will be so while on it, because his self has a natural propensity for seeking advancement in anything; as the Prophet has said:

~ The best of you in the *Jahiliyah* (time of ignorance preceding Islam) will be the best in Islam.

- ❖ *Those Whose Faces are Turned Toward Allah*: These are the seekers of freedom and emancipation, because all men are slaves in the grip of self's desires and anxieties and of worldly affairs, not cognizant of what is theirs in the way of eternal truth and spiritual illumination. If the seeker longs to escape the prison of servitude for the open field of freedom, then it is the duty of one who possesses the secret of his liberation to allow the spring of Unity to inundate him and save him from 'slavery to outer traces and effects', and to free him to witness the root cause of every effect. Only then will he become truly free. There is no greater reward than taking someone out of the prison of the self to the knowledge of his Lord.
- ❖ *The People of Action*: This refers to those who have no other intent but the Path of Allah and have consequently buried themselves in its service, their passion for its teachings, and their humility before its people. It is surprising to note that these are the most difficult people to move along the Path because of their being content with where they

are, that is, outwardly appearing like the People of the Path and having love for them. Among them are those who say: 'Our love for them and our connection to them is enough.' This acts as a veil between them and Allah. They are satisfied with merely the outward style of the People of the Path, like carrying a walking stick, a *tasbih*, or having a pious appearance, memorizing some poetry or relating some miracles, yet they have forgotten that the purpose of the Path is to reach the end, the ultimate destination of the ONE.

☼ And indeed to your Lord is the final destination. [53:42]

◈ *The Indebted*: Those who are indebted to Allah are those who are sick at heart because of having neglected to carry out the commandments of Allah and having failed to stay within the boundaries set by Him. The indebted one in this state is closer to Allah than others who appear good but are proud of their actions and arrogant in their acts of apparent goodness, as Ibn `Ata' Allah has said:[35]

~ Disobedience which causes humility and self abasement is better than obedience which causes conceit and arrogance.

Abu Madyan[36] said:

~ The humility of the disobedient is better than the

---

35   *al-Hikām li ibn `Atā'Allah* (The Wisdom of `Ata'Allah), by Ibn `Ata'Allah al-Iskandari, d. 1309 CE/709 AH.
36   One of the most influential Shaykhs of the Shadhiliyyah and Qadiriyyah, Abu Madyan Shu`ayb ibn al-Husayn al-Ansari was born in Andalusia in 1126 CE /509 AH just outside Seville and died 1198 CE /594 AH in Algeria.

4. TRADITIONAL & TRANSFORMATIVE ACTS OF WORSHIP

tyranny of the obedient.

No doubt whoever owes a debt which he admits to be just will be humble and broken in his heart, in contrast to the one who sees himself as being owed to by Allah because of his obedience and righteousness and who thinks that he is doing Allah a favor because of his worship and his faith. This is a deadly disease. Whoever possesses a broken and humbled heart is closer to Allah than the socalled stronghearted, as Allah has said:

> ✩ Allah loves those who constantly repent and He loves those who constantly purify themselves. [2:222]

> ◈ *Those who Hearts Have Been Reconciled*: This refers to those who have no basic desire or inclination for the Path like the others, and should they happen to come to it are like strangers because of their lack of longing. However, they are men of learning and the Path benefits from their knowledge. Usually they are not allowed access to this spiritual knowledge without the imposition of strict conditions so that they will not flee from it, in contrast to the others who oppose the imposition of conditions, as Shaykh alDarqawi[37] has stated:

> ~ It is not permissible to hinder men like these from spiritual enlightenment, because of its intrinsic goodness for mankind.

> ◈ *The Wayfarers*: This refers to those who need this discipline and are what is referred to as the 'Children of the Path' (*abna' alsabīl*). It is not necessary that one's ability to serve in this discipline be demonstrated; it is sufficient that

---

[37] One of the most famous Shadhili Shaykhs, Moulay Muhammad al-Arabi ad-Darqawi. d. 1823 CE /1239 AH Morocco.

one is a wayfarer in need of someone who will give him assistance in his journey to Allah. Therefore, if the Master of this secret (i.e. the Shaykh) encounters such a wayfarer, the Shaykh must take the wayfarer in and not deny him his right, which is merely a consequence of the Shaykh having encountered the wayfarer and having clearly seen his state – that is, that he is a wayfarer seeking Allah and that he is headed in the direction of Allah's Grace with his heart and soul. In these circumstances, nothing remains for the Shaykh but to give the wayfarer his elixir and to enfold him within his glance and from that instant the wayfarer will have found inner wealth.

It is stipulated in each of these eight categories mentioned above that one should be a free individual and a Muslim; that is, he or she must be firmly established in the station of submission (*taslīm*) which is considered to be the basic condition for the seeker. Likewise, the eight categories must be examined with regards to their state and the truthfulness of their claims before they are given the ultimate Secret. It has been said: Do not take into consideration the words of the *faqīr*, but look, rather, at his state.

4. TRADITIONAL & TRANSFORMATIVE ACTS OF WORSHIP

4.6 Striving in the Way of God (*jihād*)

The word *jihād* is derived from the Arabic root J H D, which relates to *juhd*, meaning 'strain' and 'exertion' and *jahd*, which means 'effort, attempt, exertion of energy'. In Islamic culture *jihād* means to strive in the cause of Islam and has come to mean calling to the path of truth, i.e. Islam. This act is obligatory upon Muslims.

There are clearly two forms of '*jihād*' in the way of Allah: the outer struggle and the inner striving. There are numerous prophetic references which allude to both kinds, and the Qur'an expresses this issue in different ways:

> ✧ And those who strive (i.e. undertake *jihād*) for Us, We will certainly guide them in Our ways. [29:69]

With regards to the outward struggle the Qur'an tells us to 'fight the polytheists (*mushrikīn*) all together, just as they fight against you' [9:36]. It is defense that is referred to, not offensive action.

> ~ In its most outward sense *jihād* came to mean the defense of *dār al-islām*, that is, the Islamic world, from invasion and intrusion by non-Islamic forces. The earliest wars of Islamic history which threatened the very existence of the young community came to be known as *jihād* par excellence in this outward sense of 'holy war'. ~ Sayyid Hossein Nasr[38]

Yet on returning from one of the battles the Prophet said:

> ~ We have returned from the lesser struggle and now what remains for us is the greater struggle.

---

[38] See 'The Spiritual Significance of *Jihad*' by Seyyed Hossein Nasr, at http://www.al-islam.org/al-serat/jihad-nasr.htm.

When someone then asked what the greater struggle was, he replied:

~ The struggle against the self.

Islam makes the outer struggle a legal obligation to strengthen His *Dīn*, to raise the 'word' high, and to embrace whomever He wills with His Mercy. The path is based upon confirming truth and denying falsehood in all situations. Establishing any aspect of living Islam in its fulsomeness implies exerting one's utmost effort. The invitation of Islam is to live a balanced life, with duties and obligations fulfilled as well as rights ensured.

While '*Jihād*' is an obligation in Islam, in the context of military defense it is nevertheless considered to be a conditional obligation, that is, if it is carried out by some of the Muslims of a community the obligation is lifted from the remainder. The following stipulations are to be considered: maturity, being male, sound of mind, good health, being free (in will) and that there exists a just Imam or one who has been appointed by the Imam to direct the struggle. If any one of these stipulations is not met then the struggle cannot be declared a true *jihād*. Lack of clarity about these stipulations has led to much confusion and misapplication of the idea of striving to one's utmost to establish Islam. Indeed, it has led to gross distortions both among Muslims and their largely hostile observers. Sayyid Hossein Nasr summarizes it thus:

~ By including the question of war in its sacred legislation, Islam did not condone but limited war and its consequences as the history of the traditional Islamic world bears out. In any case the idea of total war and the actual practice of the extermination of whole civilian populations did not grow out of a

4. TRADITIONAL & TRANSFORMATIVE ACTS OF WORSHIP

civilization whose dominant religion saw *jihād* in a positive light. On the more external level, the lesser *jihād* also includes the socio-economic domain. It means the reassertion of justice in the external environment of human existence starting with man himself. To defend one's rights and reputation, to defend the honor of oneself and one's family is itself a *jihād* and a religious duty. So is the strengthening of all those social bonds from the family to the whole of the Muslim people (*al-ummah*) which the *Shari'ah* emphasizes. To seek social justice in accordance with the tenets of the Quran and of course not in the modern secularist sense is a way of re-establishing equilibrium in human society, that is, of performing *jihād*, as are constructive economic enterprises provided the well-being of the whole person is kept in mind and material welfare does not become an end in itself; provided one does not lose sight of the Quranic verse, *'The other world is better for you than this one'*. To forget the proper relation between the two worlds would itself be instrumental in bringing about disequilibrium and would be a kind of *jihād* in reverse. ~ Sayyid Hossein Nasr

The Prophet said also said:

~ Your greatest enemy is your self which is within you.

The Qur'an tells us:

✧ And as for those who fear the station of their Lord and forbid the self from desire, the Garden is their refuge. [79:40-41]

The struggle of the self is to oppose it (the ego) in everything that it desires. The desires of the lower self are mostly in opposition to reason and *shari`ah*. Because the lower self commands to distraction and waywardness from pursuing the inner light, opposing it is therefore the essence of spiritual knowledge and justice, as it is reported in the tradition of the Prophet:

~ Consult with them and then do the contrary.

This tradition is generally given in reference to women in its outer meaning, but is an allusion to the self and its worldly desires. In that culture at that time it referred to attachment to and pursuit of worldly desire. The Fire is surrounded by the objects of desire and enticement while the Garden is surrounded by a wall of thorns. The fruit of opposing the self is the Garden:

☼ And those who struggle for Us We will surely guide along Our paths. Indeed Allah is with the doers of good. [29:69]

When the fight against the self is in the way of Allah, then it is on the path of truth. For this evolvement, the seeker needs someone who can give him guidance towards proper conduct and discipline. This guide is referred to as a Shaykh, Master or *Murshid*. This teacher reflects the seeker's real condition and motives to the seeker as he progresses. He reads the heart and reflects its state to the disciple.

For the Gnostics, '*jihād*' is to battle beyond rational reasoning in repudiating doubts and suspicions. Rationality always demands specifics and examples, while the sought after goal (gnosis or *ma`rifah*) will never be attained without stripping away every thought or rationale. As the Prophet

4. TRADITIONAL & TRANSFORMATIVE ACTS OF WORSHIP

has said:

~ Allah created reasoning so that the requirements of the slave may be fulfilled, not so that the essence of divinity may be understood.

The power of reasoning is restricted to a mental zone that relates to 'normal' consciousness and dualism. Higher consciousness belongs to a subtler realm. Reasoning, however, supports 'Higher Logic' or, to put it another way, 'Sacred Light'. Normal reasoning cannot perceive resurrection, but heavenly revelations give us the maps and pathways of the realms of the hereafter and the unseen worlds.

In the same way that physical war is waged against injustice, the Gnostic wages war against those who claim any reality other than Allah, with the spiritual 'sword'. Thus it is that the striving of the People of Allah is against the 'limitations of intellects' and against people of limited reason in order to eliminate their doubts and suspicions and to help them realize the limitations of rational reasoning. Higher consciousness and awakening to divinely inspired love – which are referred to as 'Revelation' and 'Inspiration' – is the '*jihād*' of prophets and enlightened beings. Everyone is in constant *jihād*, each according to their state and station.

4.7 Commanding Goodness & Forbidding Evil (*amr bi'l-ma`rūf wa'n-nahi `an al-munkar*)

Commanding or enjoining goodness and forbidding evil (*amr bi'l-ma`rūf wa'n-nahi `an il-munkar*) also fall under the heading of struggle or *jihād*. Concerning this Imam Ja`far alSadiq said:

> ~ He who has not been stripped of all his misconceptions and who has not been freed of the afflictions of his self and its desires, and who has not defeated Shaytan nor gone over to the side of Allah, to His *Tawhīd*, and taken refuge in His protection, should neither command others to goodness nor forbid them from evil. Because if one is not of this quality anything which he expounds will be used as evidence against him and people will not benefit from it.[39]

Allah says:

✧ How can you command the people to righteousness while you forget yourselves? [2:44]

In a *hadith qudsi* Allah says:

~ O Deceiver, do you command the people to the deception of your own self, while you have slackened its reins?

It is related that someone asked the Prophet about the interpretation of the verse, 'O you who believe! Take care of your souls; whoever goes astray cannot harm you when you are guided on the right way...,' [5:105] to which he replied:

---

39 'The Lantern of the Path'

4. TRADITIONAL & TRANSFORMATIVE ACTS OF WORSHIP

~ Command goodness and forbid evil, be patient with whatever afflicts you even if you witness avarice obeyed, desires followed and the pride of the opinionated with their views. Beware of your self and do not concern yourself with the affairs of the masses.

Whoever commands to goodness must know what is permitted and what is forbidden, and he must be free from his self when he commands and forbids. He must be one who can advise people, who is merciful with them in his sensitivity and in giving good counsel. Commanding to good and forbidding evil are obligatory in what is incumbent or forbidden, and they are preferable with regard to the Sunnah and whatever is detestable, provided that the following four stipulations are met:

1. That one has knowledge of the courtesies and obligations.
2. That (in the case of an evil action) the perpetrator is insistent on the wrong action.
3. That there is a possibility of its being effective.
4. That one is secure from injury.

When these stipulations are met it is then incumbent upon one to directly command people to goodness or forbid them from evil, whichever may be applicable. If not, then one ought to begin by reprimanding and forbidding them indirectly in a way that they will understand.

There are varying levels to forbidding evil: By way of the heart, conditional to which is that one knows the regulation involved and that the perpetrator persists in his evil act; by making openly known the displeasure of the heart, and if this is insufficient then turning away from him; by way of the hand, for example, the pouring out of wine or disposal of other intoxicants; by striking and the like, provided one has the power and ability to do so, as well as the prior knowledge that a person will not be restrained in any other way.

Just as divine laws have an outward form they also have an inward reality which is known by those who possess knowledge of Allah. As long as one has not examined the inward reality the outward form will not be effective.

In the same way that there are four stipulations for commanding to goodness and forbidding of evil in the outward, there are also four stipulations for the inward.

In the words of Imam Sadiq: 'He who has not been stripped of his misconceptions' parallels the first stipulation, that is, knowledge of the courtesies and obligations or the knowledge of what has been commanded and what has been forbidden.

His words: '...and who has not been freed of the affliction of his self and its desires ...' are parallel to the second stipulation, which is that the perpetrator is persistent in performing the act; while: '...and who has not defeated Shaytan ...', coincides with the third stipulation, which is that there should be a possibility of its being effective.

Finally: '...who has not gone over to the side of Allah, to His Unity and taken refuge in His protection...', is parallel to the fourth stipulation, which is that one should be secure from injury.

The Imam has defined the stipulations which must be met by the one who commands goodness and forbids evil in the following manner:

- That he knows what is permitted and forbidden. If he does not know this with regard to whatever he commands, then what will he be able to forbid?
- That he himself should be in compliance with

4. TRADITIONAL & TRANSFORMATIVE ACTS OF WORSHIP

commanding to good and forbidding evil.
- That he should advise people without any motives related to his self.
- That he should be merciful to those with whom he is dealing, be kind, sensitive and adopt the appropriate manner of speaking.
- That he recognizes the difference in people's behavior so that he commands one and forbids another according to their state and spiritual station.
- That he possesses insight into the intrigues of Shaytan to ensure that his commanding and forbidding will not give rise to pride whereby he supposes himself to be above people and of having reached the lofty station where he command goodness.
- That he should be patient with abuse that is leveled at him in the cause of his commanding goodness, that he should not attempt to take vengeance, and that he be careful not to be a fanatic or harbor feelings of malice.
- That he makes his intention strictly for Allah and for achieving nearness to Him.
- That he completely entrusts himself to Allah in this, and that he does not fear criticism.
- That he continually examines his own shortcomings and that every time he commands someone else he must first begin with himself.

CHAPTER 5

Appropriate Conduct

5.1 Islam & Reforming the Lower Self (self/soul dynamics)

The Qur'an has described the human make-up as composed of a spectrum, at one end of which is a slippery and ever demanding ego (or lower self) and at the other end a sacred soul or spirit. It is by self-discipline and grooming that human behavior and conduct become refined and are able to reflect the qualities transmitted from the soul within the heart rather than the whims of the lower self.

It should be clear by now that the overarching goal of following the path of Islam is to turn basic human nature into the gold of a noble and elevated state. The purpose of clear understanding and insight into the foundational truths of this revealed path is complemented and realized by the living practice of the designated acts of worship which, if performed with sincere intention, attention and deepening awareness, will bring about a transformation in human conduct. In the words of the Prophet:

~ I was sent to perfect noble character.

Both the form and the multiple meanings of the different acts of worship gradually tether the lower tendencies of the self and align them with the qualities of the Divine Names that are reflected in the human soul.

When conscious awareness is brought to worship it thus becomes transformational. This is the ultimate alchemy worth struggling for.

The Remedy for Grooming the Self

In traditional Islamic societies a key process in upbringing was grooming the young – *tarbiyah*. The foundation of that was to act appropriately under the guidance or authority of responsible family members or teachers. In order to change, we know that you need to either change your mind or actual behavior. In our modern age, we tend to lean towards understanding and the mind, rather than authoritatively changing the conduct. Since family or community authority has waned, voluntary acceptance of acts of worship can be of great therapeutic use in reducing natural egotistic tendencies.

In the same way that a doctor or physician treats the body, the Prophets, Masters, and Gnostic teachers are the physicians of the self. Thus, just as the medical doctor knows the method of removing an illness by way of treatment and medication, the physicians of the self know how to recognize and remove the causes of illnesses related to the self. In the same way that a person who is physically sick should not object to what has been given to him by his physician, it is not correct for the sick self to object to the guidance and instruction received from a spiritual teacher or Master. This objection will only delay or prevent the remedy from taking effect and the illness will only worsen. The doctor of the heart may sometimes act in a manner which appears to be harsh, but the purpose is to break the trap of egotism and enable the connection and synchronicity between self and soul. Many an effective medicine also burns healthy cells and many a remedy can

5. APPROPRIATE CONDUCT

be bitter but the effect will more than compensate for that initial unpleasantness. The Prophetic teaching is that if a wise person is given two choices, he or she should choose that which is heavier upon the lower self.

Health, wellbeing and light belong to the soul and are emitted through a purified heart towards the rest of the human being. All disturbances, sicknesses and unhappiness are due to lack of ongoing connection between the light of the soul (which is the source of life) and the mind and remaining faculties of cognition and perception. A healthy mind relates through the senses what is observable and connects that through memory and the brain with the source of life from the soul. A healthy being is he or she that is in constant remembrance of Allah and in constant awareness of Allah's trace and Presence as a light in the heart. A knowledgeable jeweler cannot place a precious necklace around the neck of a swine. This is the meaning of Allah's words:

> ✧ ...in their hearts there is an illness and Allah increases them in illness... [2:10]

> ✧ To God belongs all that is in the heavens and earth. Whether you reveal what is in your hearts or hide it, God will hold you to account for it. He will forgive whom He wills, and chastise whom He wills; God is powerful over everything. [2:284]

> ✧ O you who believe! Take care of your souls; he who strays cannot hurt you when you are on the right way; to Allah is your return, of all [of you], so He will inform you of what you did. [5:105]

✧ On the day when it shall be heated in the fire of hell, then their foreheads and their sides and their backs shall be branded with it; this is what you hoarded up for yourselves, therefore taste what you hoarded. [9:35]

✧ If you do good you will do good for your own souls, and if you do evil, it shall be for them. So when the second promise came [We raised another people] that they may bring you to grief and that they may enter the mosque as they entered it the first time, and that they might destroy whatever they gained ascendancy over with utter destruction. [17:7]

✧ And in your own souls [too]; will you not then see? [51:21]

✧ How is it that when a misfortune befell you, and you had certainly afflicted [the unbelievers] with twice as much, you say: Where does this come from? Say: It is from your-selves; surely Allah has power over all things. [3:165]

Self-Knowledge and Its Refinement

The self is imbued with its own light of consciousness:

✧ ...Then He inspired it (the self) to understand what is right and wrong for it. [91:8]

It is usual that the emerging self follows its own desires and whims and other disruptive influences. The lowest level of the self, the commanding self (*alnafs alammārah*), falls prey to countless forces of attractions and repulsions.

5. APPROPRIATE CONDUCT

When the self is disciplined and subdued it begins to see wisdom behind the natural forces and Attributes. When the self is purified and resonates with its soul wisdom and fulfillment are experienced:

> ☼ He will be successful who purifies it. [91:9]

The lower self is a mere shadow veiling the soul and thus is a serious hindrance for spiritual progress. Once we experience this truth the spiritual journey takes us across over the desert of darkness into light and the soul's tranquility. The self can be the means by which one fails and perishes, or by which one is elevated and liberated from the veils of this transient world.

It is related that the Messenger of Allah said:

> ~ The human form is the greatest gift of Allah in His creation. It is the Book which He has inscribed with His own hand, it is the totality of all of the forms of the universe, it is the sum total of the preserved tablets [cf. 85:22], it is the testimony to all that is unseen, it is the Straight Path to all spiritual knowledge, it is the bridge which is extended between the Garden and the Fire and the banner of Unity, it is the basis of all knowledge and the foundation of the knowledge of the Hereafter.[40]

As mentioned earlier, the purpose of all divine revelations is to follow the natural patterns of life to direct us towards the joy of contented submission, and to ascend from the degradation of the self to the summit of perfection in abandonment. This path is to save us from falling into gross materialism and to reveal to us the realms of exalted

---

40 Mulla Hadi Sabzivari in his book *Hidāyat alTālibīn* ('Guidance of the Seekers').

spiritual illumination. Living the path will lead to the knowledge of Allah through His Attributes, and the belief in His Angels, His Messengers, His Books and the Last Day. The outcome is to realize the natural state of perfect beingness. The Prophet taught that whoever knows himself will know the Truth (i.e. the Lord).

If one does not know the nature of the lower self and does not bring it to complete submission (to the soul) then one knows neither self nor Lord. By witnessing one's meanness, for example, one may recognize the immense Divine Generosity. By witnessing one's weakness one may realize the Divine Power. By recognizing one's impatience, one seeks refuge in Allah's infinite patience. To know 'how base is the self' is the key to realizing 'how glorious is Allah'.

The spiritual evolution of the self depends upon the realization that its nature is base and humble and that it is completely subjugated to worldly existence, from which it needs to transcend by discipline, will and dedicated work. As the Prophet cautioned us:

~ The worst of your enemies is your own self within you.[41]

He also said:

~ The self is the greatest of idols.

Likewise:

~ I take refuge in Allah from subtle association [shirk – seeing other than Allah].

---

41   From the book *Risalāt alSayr wa alSuluk*, (Treatise on the Journey and Behaviour) by Sayyid Bahr al`Ulum.

5. APPROPRIATE CONDUCT

The seeker on this path will come to recognize the deep meanings of these traditions with greater self-knowledge and transcendence of the lower nature.

The hidden ailments of the self cannot be treated except by continuous vigil over it and seeking the help of a Master who has had experience in these matters and has succeeded. Upon examining the ailments of the self, we find that there are those which are so subtle and hidden that they exert their influence upon the seeker without his knowledge. Among the most important of these are caprice and pride in their various forms. It is related that Imam Ja'far alSadiq said that whoever allows pride to enter within him shall perish. The Prophet said:

> ~ There are three things which will bring destruction: greed to which one submits, a desire which is followed, and a man's pride in himself.

Imam `Ali had said that whoever does not take his own self to account daily, is not one of us. Thus if he does good he praises Allah, and if he commits evil he seeks Allah's forgiveness.

The basis of hidden *shirk* is when a man sees his self and says 'I' and thus remains continuously lost in the illusion of his own independent existence. The words of the testimony of faith (*shahādah*), '*Lā ilāha illa'Llāh*' (there is no deity but Allah) in this instance will remain unrealized. The Prophet said:

> ~ There is nothing between them and their Lord which prevents them from seeing Him but the veil of pride.

Ultimately reforming the self implies transcending it. Ibn `Arabi explains that early-on the seeker needs to go against the lower self and reap the benefits of that. The mature person will then begin to use the self to help him to the realization of the prevalent soul and its perfection. It is like cracking the outer shell of a seed and then nurturing the plant.

5. APPROPRIATE CONDUCT

5.2 Transformation through Self Accountability & Reflection (vices & virtues)

Without self-awareness and reflection man is reduced to a mere primate. Self-awareness begins with the basic consciousness of a baby, moving its hand around and being fascinated by it, and entering the stage of developing its own personality and identity until the realization dawns that all of that was a mere shadow of the light of Reality, whose presence is in the heart as a soul. Self-awareness begins by seeing shadows (material or illusory) and ends up with soul-awareness which is directly connected to truth. Then comes the realization that there is none other than the One and to that Oneness all returns:

☼ ...And to your Lord is your return... [6:164]

The fabric of life is like layers of dualities which are intricately connected. Vices, such as anger, greed and fear, can be keys to their complimentary opposites of virtue through awareness and appropriate clear intention and actions. Through self-awareness and self-knowledge, we realize that our root and origin is a sacred light, which we call soul. That realization will relegate the self or ego into its banishment. The challenges of dualities, good and bad, vices and virtues, are resolved by experiencing soul which is beyond judgment – that is the Nūr of Allah, where absolute Oneness prevails without any shadow or association. The key issue is for the individual to be real and honest regarding their actual inner state, with the hope that eventually clarity will come about regarding this perfect sacred Presence.

Among common human vices are those related to desire and attraction, including indulgence and shamelessness, volatility, extravagance, immoderation and instability. The main vices which relate to the power of repulsion or anger are cowardice, pettiness, despair, being quick to anger, apathy, and lack of endurance. *Salāt* and *sawm* help us to transform indulgence to modesty, which is self-restraining conduct and self-discipline. It also brings about mildness, steadiness and magnanimity. All acts of worship will stop us from pursuing anger or greed. The preparations for acts of worship also enable us to go past apathy and refresh our orientation towards the true *Qiblah*.

As a result of becoming aware of the lower tendencies, the enhanced state of modesty, honesty and courage will produce the flowers of wisdom and justice. As a result of acting and thinking wisely, intelligence and retention improve, and thereby improve clarity of understanding and the capacity to learn more. Rationality, friendship and harmony will also ensue, bringing a greater sense of justice and fair play. This reformed character will, no doubt, increase the capacity to spontaneous awareness and higher consciousness.

In his 'Makkan Revelations', Ibn `Arabi, devotes a section on the importance of experiencing a virtue, such as that of patience, and then going past it. The attitude of piety is a key issue in Islam. Once a person considers him or herself as pious then a difficult blockage is formed which can lead even to material spiritualism. The danger is to fall into the personality of the 'do-gooder'. The real hero acts without realizing that action is heroism. It is only others who label it as such.

The basis of the power and strength of the self are the force of attraction (manifesting as desires) and repulsion (often manifesting as anger). These two forces are behind every agitation and attachment and the constant disturbance that results. However once these energy drives

5. APPROPRIATE CONDUCT

are brought under control these natural forces will assist one along the spiritual path to the final goal of awakening to the original source and purpose behind life's forces.

The following characteristics spring from the force of repulsion or anger: cowardliness, pride, fear, lack of determination, weakness of spirit, rage, and other similar traits. Likewise, the following traits originate from attraction or desire: love of the world, greed, avarice, miserliness, treachery, and the like. However, when these two forces of anger and desire are brought under control and the heart is brought in line with its true original nature, then the force of anger will lead to bravery, spiritual strength, determination, forbearance, steadfastness, and the like. When the force of desire is harnessed it produces kindness, modesty, patience, generosity, contentment, reverence, restraint, and so on.

The main objective, then, is to know the nature of the self, guarding over it with vigilance, holding it to account and treating it with the proper remedies. Progress in directing one's conduct and actions towards noble traits will result in greater awareness of the self and awakening to ever-increasing insights and knowledges.

The basis of *shari`ah* is to restrict the lower tendencies of the lower self in order for the higher (consciousness) to be the leader and guide for appropriate intentions and actions needed for wholesome living. The thrill of experiencing the inner light of the soul will then lead the seeker towards perfecting worship and maintaining a high level of self-awareness and clear boundaries for actions. Thus, higher consciousness will lift all the veils and shadows which were the cause of previous confusions and darkness. A paradigm shift in behavior will be the clear sign of enlightenment.

5.3 The Relationship between Mind, Brain & Conduct (emotions & rationality)

We relate and interact at all these levels: the first realm is that of the senses, the second realm is that of imagination, visions and insights, and the third realm is that of reason or intellect (`aql), which exists for the purpose of comprehending the realm of Lordship and Power.

The material world and our senses are like a metaphor representing the unseen world of the Hereafter (ākhirah), and other spiritual realities. The senses, therefore, are like a stairway by which the seeker advances to the point of subtle witnessing beyond the limitations of physical realities. By knowing the nature of the senses the seeker withdraws from their influence in order to discover the world of meaning which lies behind them. Whoever does not know the nature of the world and the baseness of its origins will be unable to reject it and go beyond. For this reason the men of knowledge and wisdom have concerned themselves with the study of the material realm and the conditions of the senses in order to proceed from there to what lies further ahead.

The knowledge of the material world and its shortcomings is the beginning of the knowledge of the spiritual realm and its wealth. It is said that as long as the self remains within this world it is like a passenger aboard a ship; that is, the self utilizes the body to make the journey from one world to the next, witnessing and experiencing various conditions over the seas until it reaches the shore of peace and awakening. The ship (the body) has fulfilled its duty when it brings the self to its goal and returns it to its original shore. The self by its nature increases in its egotistic tendencies through endless desires, attachments

5. APPROPRIATE CONDUCT

and whims.

☼ Know that the worldly life is only frivolity and a game and finery and boasting among yourselves... then it withers away and you see it turning yellow then it becomes dried up and broken... [57:20]

The material realm has been created so that one may come to know what lies beyond it in the spiritual realm. The former acts as an allegory for one who has not witnessed the latter. For this reason we find that men of knowledge encourage the seeker to hasten in his quest for annihilation of the self and to make use of this human body before the termination of its allotted time.

It is said that death represents the manifestation of Allah before the Moses of the heart. Thus the 'mountain' of the body disintegrates because it belongs to the material realm, and He becomes manifest before the self within the spiritual realm after the gross material has been stripped from it. This world and the next are opposites which, therefore, cannot manifest together or coexist. The self is disinclined to physical death due to its fear of annihilation and nonexistence because it has a goal and a purpose, which is to seek its state of eternity in the Hereafter and to reach the realm of nontime and non-space. By its very nature the self loves existence and abhors and fears nonexistence.

Concerning this Ibn Miskawayh Razi has said:

~ Death of the body in this physical existence is life to the soul in the existence of the Hereafter. The soul has a natural inclination toward the transition into the realm of the Hereafter. The self's disinclination is because the beginning of the growth of the soul occurs simultaneously with the physical growth of the body and the physical senses predominate over the soul as long as the connection between the body and the soul remains. Because of this connection the soul experiences pain and injury by whatever it is that causes pain and injury to the body. Everything which gives contentment and ease to the body is derived from health and favorable physical circumstances.[42]

There is also another reason for the self's disinclination towards death and its desire to preserve the body: the body may serve as a vehicle by which the soul comes to know the Hereafter, and thus realize its own potential perfection. Thus sensory perceptions such as pain and fear are experienced by the animal self to encourage the self to care of the body. The body, in essence, has no feelings and no potential of its own that could prevent or ward off harm. If it were not for the existence of pain and fear within the self, it would have neglected the body and left it to perish before it had fulfilled its mission, which is to nourish and awaken the self, to rise from the physical to the spiritual.

---

[42] *Tahdhīb al-Akhlāq, wa Ta`thīr al-A`rāq*, Abu Ali Ahmed Miskawayh al-Razi (d. 1030 CE).

5. APPROPRIATE CONDUCT

5.4 Relationships

In all religions mankind is encouraged to be gentle and courteous to others, especially to parents and elders. The Qur'an unequivocally commands us to uphold this. As a *'khalifah,'* or steward on earth, it is our duty and honor to act responsibly and with presence of mind and heart. Acknowledgement and respect for our biological roots is a step towards realizing our spiritual origin. We are all connected at source, all bound by our humanity, all in need of mercy, understanding, support and comfort. Not only are there ideals to be observed in relationships between individuals, but also in larger units such as the family, the extended family, neighborhood and community. At the core of all these relationships, however, is the relationship with oneself. If that is in order, then all other relationships will also fall into place.

Islam reveals the appropriate paths for correct relationships and duties towards people and God. We have duties towards parents, neighbors, humanity and all of creation. This implies boundaries and limits. We also cannot accuse someone of mistakes that someone else has committed. Gender also has a role to play in maintaining clear boundaries in personal relationships. Complementarity and collaboration are emphasized over sameness. Marriage between man and woman is an attempt to unify complimentary opposites; therefore there is an element of sacredness in the act. If, however, due to earthly reasons the relationship is not workable, then amicable separation is acceptable. A family must be respected and strengthened.

Ultimately, relationships between human beings will reach their best level when people realize that every heart contains a sacred soul that is the same as every other human soul. If the individual has not submitted to the inner ruler – the soul – then to exercise authority over others will only bring about greater disorder. Whoever is not under control is not fit to bring order to others. A good action multiplies ten-fold, whereas wrong action will only bring about its equivalent reaction.

To exercise courtesy towards others and to be kind and helpful is in fact a generosity towards one's own real self. Self-concern can only increase the egotistic tendencies, whilst through concern for the wellbeing of others, one is on the path towards understanding similarities that lead to unity in essence.

Amongst courtesies to one's own self is to be watchful with every thought, intention and action and not to waste time or energy in speculation of frivolous actions and risky gambles. The ultimate courtesy is to live fully in the moment and to have insights to the perfections therein. Contentment here and now reflects an aspect of the perfection of the Creator of all space and time. If one's relationship with God is right, then all other relationships will fit in appropriately.

All worldly relationships are relative. We progress from a very existential one, like that between a baby and a mother, to that of husband and wife, towards the ultimate harmony in the relationship between the lower self and the soul. When that inner relationship is in steady unison, then most other levels of relationship are likely to be in a better state. The progress from one relationship to another is a natural graduation, like a ladder one is climbing upon. Adam's descent to earth from the zone of perfect paradise is in order for us to experience all aspects of the relativity of relationships, aspiring towards that which is absolute. The mother weans the baby in order for it to establish a

5. APPROPRIATE CONDUCT

wider connection of dependency and interrelationship, and sometimes an enlightened teacher may also do that.

5.5 The Necessity of Living Teachers & Guides to Realize Oneness

The Prophet has said that the mother is the school, and that the whole of life is a process of grooming and learning and acting upon what is important. Therefore the process begins before birth because we constantly relate and associate with what is close to us. The sages teach us not to ask about the person, but who his friends and family are. In our modern times we give much emphasis to the environment and the effect of nurture, because as far as nature or the genes are concerned, many of their tendencies can be overruled.

As we develop from childhood to adulthood we realize the importance of the references offered by our immediate environments and teachers. There is a relentless drive in us for connectedness and harmony and therefore we adapt and adjust in order to fulfill that need. If a youngster keeps the company of thugs he would naturally like to outdo them in thuggery. Equally, if he is in the company of a group who serve the poor community, he would also want to outdo them. We all desire excellence in whichever endeavor we are in.

Ibn `Ajiba in al-Bahr al-Madid says that in the early decades of Islam, upbringing was achieved through companionship and by being in the circle of evolved beings, because in those days the desire for knowledge of Allah and experiencing it was as strong as the desire to purify the heart. As the period of dynastic rulership took over, upbringing took the course of increased litanies and acts of self responsibility. During this period the Sufis played an important role until the 9th century (14th CE) where most of the personal tutelage and upbringing through teachers

5. APPROPRIATE CONDUCT

and enlightened beings was replaced by reliance on a more literalist interpretation of the Qur'an and Prophetic teaching, without personal experience of illumination in the heart. As such, effective upbringing ceased. What has remained are hollow formulae and excessive attention to ritual rather than meaning.

The qualification of a true teacher or guide is that he should not desire any outer or inner reward for his teaching. At best he is a reflector of the truth that pervades all. The enlightened person is in constant reference with the 'inner' timeless authority – the soul within the purified heart. The seeker of truth is on the path of unison with this 'inner' authority. The child's 'ignorant' rebellion is an innate indication of refusing any 'outer' authority. Yet the first steps towards transformation are to groom the self by going against the egotistic tendencies in order to be able to receive the 'authentic' signals of the perfect soul or spirit within.

Every human being is composed of a perfect immortal soul which is the source of its temporary life on earth. We all have a beginning and end on this earth, but the soul carries on beyond its limited manifestation in time shaded and colored by its earthly experiences. The ultimate purpose of life is to realize that in truth there is only the soul and the so-called self, ego or *nafs*, is only a shadow which indicates the presence of that perfect Light. The early period of childhood allows this shadow or so-called personality to develop, influenced by its DNA, culture, religion and other environmental factors. Developing and maturing implies the beginning of an understanding that there are similarities between all human beings, in that everyone seeks wellbeing and happiness.

The usual human drives towards wealth, power,

dominance and social acceptance are all attempts of the self to take on the colors of the soul, which in itself beams out all the Divine Attributes. It is Allah who is all-Knowing, and the soul emits that field of energy, while the self desires it. The same thing applies to all the other Attributes. For a mature seeker it is immensely helpful to realize that whatever we are doing is an attempt to unify the self and the soul, and it is in this context that a living teacher and guide can be vital. There are no doubt exceptions to every rule, but you would hardly find a truly wholesome human being without the grooming and help of an enlightened teacher. Every aspect in life acts as a mirror, reflector and challenge. It is only the truly enlightened teacher who reflects an appropriate image at the time in one's own evolvement and awakening. It is that appropriateness, which is due to truth and love between the teacher and the disciple that brings about effective changes and ultimate transformation.

It is often asked how one might find an appropriate teacher. Every aspect in life has in it a teaching. You may even learn from a fool. According to your sincerity and diligence you will progress with a lot of trial and error and a time may come when you will come to know the appropriate teacher who has no ambition or expectation, because he or she is basking in the Presence of utter Perfection, for where is it that Allah's Light is not present?

Discovering the authority of the Divine Teacher is already within your own heart. Earlier on in one's journey one good teacher brings about balance and quick progress, and more than one can cause confusion, whereas later on, for a mature seeker, one can take from different teachers because by then you have the foundation established.

CHAPTER 6

Transformed Beings

6.1 Return to the Beginning

The word 'beginning' here means the original state of the universe and human beings before existence. The word 'return' here signifies completion of the cycle of birth and death.

> ☼ This is the primordial nature that Allah implanted in mankind; there is no altering of Allah's creation. [30:30]

> ☼ I have created you before when you were nothing. [19:9]

The original natural state (*fitrah*) was nonexistent before Reality brought it into existence. First there was Allah and there was nothing else with Him. That is to say, in the beginning Allah brought creation into existence from complete nonexistence and in the end He will take it from the realm of this apparent existence and return it to nonexistence (in terms of time and space). Thus, the end is a return to the beginning, and the goal we hope to reach was already present at our starting point:

✧ As We began the creation so will We cause it to return. [21:104]

The first state of existence for man was the garden in which Adam and Eve resided. The next stage was the fall from the paradise 'state' into this world of duality, of opposites, of time and space. The next state after this worldly existence is annihilation in the Oneness, which is the paradise of the people of Unity.

✧ O Tranquil Soul, return to your Lord, well-pleased and well-pleasing. So enter among my servants, and enter my paradise. [89:27-30]

To come from the state of paradise into this world is to experience imperfection and constant change. The departure from this world to paradise is to go from imperfection to perfection and to return to one's natural, originally desired state of unitive bliss. This represents the Return (ma`ād) of creation and its ascent to the Creator. The beginning is from Him and the end is with Him, and He is the First and He is the Last.

The physical world belongs to the material realm of the senses and the Hereafter belongs to the realm of meaning and Attributes which is not perceived by the senses, for it lies behind the physical world. The Hereafter is perceived through reasoning, insight, and reflection.

The true nature of man combines these three realms. If worldly attachments and sensual pleasures are predominant then he suffers disappointment and insecurity because worldly pleasures do not last. Sensual pleasures are symbolic and represent a minute example of a lasting attribute in another zone of existence. Thus, whoever is attached to or desires a state that by its very nature is transient and false, he will never be able to

6. TRANSFORMED BEINGS

maintain the elusive situation and thus will only fail and be disillusioned. When reasoning predominates, and one acts according to the spiritual path, one refrains from anything that would deflect one from it.

✪ For the likes of this let those who would act, act. [37:61]

✪ Let those who would compete, compete in this. [83:26]

The entanglement of the self with the external senses and powers of arousal prevent it from witnessing the inner realities. Those realities are much brighter and stronger and more durable than the outer ones, which are perceived by way of the sense organs in the material world. The men of spiritual knowledge are those who have arrived, through the strength of certainty, at the perception of truths by way of reasoning and insights. The lifting of the veil at the time of death will not increase them in certainty and knowledge except in clarity and freedom.

The fall of Adam, or his descent to earth from paradise, is a metaphor implying the human need to evolve through transient life back to the state of eternity or timelessness. Besides limited free will and self-awareness, Adam was given the knowledge of Divine Attributes and qualities; his yearning for them made him restrained and self-correcting. Adam's soul carries the imprint of paradise and his offspring will always yearn for the garden of comfort and ease.

The rise of Adamic consciousness may be related to the evolution and addition to the frontal cortex of the brain that enables the transcendental dimension of the human psyche. Before that, Adam was in paradise, the perfect garden where there were no needs, fears, or the cycles of life and death. Paradise is devoid of time and space; as such it is a state of eternal bliss.

6. TRANSFORMED BEINGS

6.2 Maps & Boundaries & Life's Topography

God has created everything according to a measure and with limitations. If we transgress the natural limits or boundaries then we risk injury, even irrevocable damage. The outer natural drive for freedom from limitations implies the existence of boundaries and outer limitations. Inner freedom and joy can only be contained within clearly defined borders. For that reason, both at the individual as well as societal levels, we need to adhere to a recognized system of law and order. Balance, equilibrium and peace are desirable at all levels.

A serious Muslim will realize the wisdom of boundaries of what is permissible and what is not, both ritualistically as well as according to customs and habits of the Prophet Muhammad and his faithful followers. Certain matters are clearly good and others are not; the areas of doubt and uncertainty in between are best avoided until clarification. Scholarship and relevant reference to the Islamic laws and jurisprudence are essential. What is permissible is *'halāl'* and what is not is *'harām'*. In between, there are some grey areas better avoided if there is choice.

Whatever is discerned in the universe exists within some limitations imposed by time and space. God's light and will, however, is free of all limitations. Boundlessness can only be realized within the purified heart, where the soul resides.

It is the intelligent person who accepts whatever governs society's wellbeing and stability; then he or she dives into the spiritual boundlessness and the unseen realms. Without acknowledging terrestrial realities and wisdom, celestial lights and insights cannot reliably take place. Adam's descent is only to bring about a well-earned ascent.

The topography of human life is defined by its limitations. While life on earth is limited and finite, Life is eternal, as is its Essence – Allah. Adam's soul is imprinted with that knowledge. Thus every person is driven to a better destiny and wholesome life on earth and in the hereafter.

All of our experiences here take place within time and space; thus, everything has a beginning and an end. Everything in our life is transient and subject to change and dualities, some of which are constructive and attractive, whilst others are undesirable and destructive. Life on earth is a constant struggle to bring about what is considered good and durable and to repulse that which is considered bad or difficult. We truly love stability, although deep down we know that it is unattainable on earth. Yet still, the futile outer search continues for better, secure situations.

With spiritual maturity, we can come to terms with outer transience as experienced in body and mind and discover constancy at heart. Permanent life is beyond earthly experience and death is its entry point. As for the quality of that life, it is dependent on the extent of our spiritual awakening in this life and realization of Allah's Lordship and perfections.

All life on earth is an intermediate stage between the eternal Source of life before creation, the material and physical realities, and identifications on earth. Every self leaves this world when the power of the soul departs to another realm carrying with it the residues of personality and the extent of its surrender and faith to its Creator. The urgency of this life is manifest in that the lower nature of the human being can never be content or satisfied, whilst the soul is ever secure. Our purpose is to unify self and soul and coast along towards the inevitable destiny.

6. TRANSFORMED BEINGS

6.3 Transition to Infinite Boundlessness

We are heavenly souls transiting through earth back to heaven. Human life on earth begins with the development of outer and inner senses, then to the development of faculties of imagination, reflection, thinking and higher intellect. Initially a child needs to be helped, protected and guided. The Lord of the universe has endowed parents with demi-lordship for their children. With maturity, greater self-awareness, acceptance of responsibility and inner guidance, the new person can take over.

The gift of life and the treasure of the soul are glorious and sacred and must be treated with caution, reverence and love. The mature seeker looks for meanings in events and is confident in God's guidance, mercy and forgiveness. A wholesome life implies living fully in the world of dualities and their challenges by constant reference to the soul that brings about constancy and stability along the journey.

A person's life is wholesome and healthy when everything in creation is seen as an example of the Creator's perfection. An awakened seeker of truth is in constant reference to the voice and signals of the heart whilst responding to outer stimuli and events. An enlightened person's heart is pure from all attachments and anxieties, for it is illumined by the sacred effulgence of the soul.

Inner freedom is the real indicator of wholesome living. A wholesome life is the unification of body, mind, heart and soul due to constant reference to the unifying light of God. This life is given by Allah, sustained by Him and returns to Him – there is no God but the one and only God.

6.4 The Complete Person – Mulla Sadra's Journey

The notion of the complete human being or the '*Insān al-kāmil*' was established by early Islamic scholars and Masters following the model of the Prophet and his exemplary conduct. Great beings like some of the companions, their followers, the Imams and Sufi Masters have elaborated upon a life fulfilled by enlightenment and God-realization.

A good life begins when the individual is always aware of intentions and accepts responsibility and accountability. A mature person submits to the fact that human needs and desires are endless. Submission, or Islam, is the first. Then comes living faith and trust in God's Perfect Mercy, and Justice, irrespective of circumstances. Then one basks in the security and knowledge of Divine guidance through one's own soul.

All Prophets and Messengers have perfected their own journey and attained the purpose of life, which is to witness the light of Allah and live according to it. With living faith and trust, the faithful seeker will realize the constant presence of Allah's mercy and grace, and with that realization, the enlightened person can only be in ecstatic gratitude. This is the complete person. Prophets and enlightened beings have reached that station and as such are appropriate guides and role models to be followed.

There are numerous enlightened Masters acknowledged by the scholarly teachers and theologians of Islam. Several of these beings are considered as founders of Sufi chains of transmission (*silsilahs*); till today there are thousands of seekers who follow along their footsteps. Several such Masters have been mentioned in the text. Mulla Sadra (d.1640 CE) described the stages of this journey of ascent

6. TRANSFORMED BEINGS

as four phases, saying:

> ~ Know that the seeker among the Masters and the *awliyā'* has four journeys. The first journey is from the creation to the Truth. The second is the journey by Truth in Truth. The third journey is directly opposite to the first because it is from the Truth to the Creation by way of Truth. The fourth journey is the opposite of the second in that it is by Truth within the Creation.[43]

The First Journey is completed by the lifting of the veils of tranquility which are connected with the self, as well as the veils of illumination which are connected with the heart and the soul. This is the ascension from the station of the self to the heart and to the soul; then one proceeds onward to the Highest Goal. The realms of the self, the heart and the soul have within them veils that lie between the seeker and Divine Truth, so one must pass through all of these obstacles. After passing through these realms, the seeker reaches the station of spiritual knowledge and begins the second journey of annihilation into the Names and Attributes of Allah, so that he embodies the words:

> ~ ...thus through Him (Allah) one hears and by Him one sees and by Him one walks and by His hand one grasps...

The First Journey, then, consists of traversing the material regions, the spiritual realms, and arriving at the realm of Essence. For this reason we find that the majority of the difficulties and pain which the seeker encounters occur within the First Journey.

---

43   In *AlHikam alMuta`aliyah fi Asfar al-`Aqliyah alArba`ah.*

There are three stations or milestones in the Second Journey. The first is the station of the Innermost Secret, which is the Station of Annihilation into the Essence. The second station is referred to as the 'hidden one' and it is the Station of Annihilation into the Attributes and Names of Allah. The third is the Station of Utmost Abundance, which is Annihilation into the Essence and the Attributes. Describing this further Mulla Sadra wrote:

> ~ If one wished, the secret of the annihilation of one's own essence could be described as being the end of the First Journey and the beginning of the Second Journey. The term 'Hidden' here refers to annihilation within Divine Power, while the term 'Utmost Abundance' refers to the annihilation of both of these annihilations and completes the cycle of Perfection. The Second Journey is likewise completed, its annihilation perfected, and one begins the Third Journey.

Al-Hakim Mirza Hasan Nuri further explained Mulla Sadra's meaning, saying that as long as man does not traverse the practical and theoretical Path of the Master, he will continue to see multiplicity and remain unaware of, and unable to see, Oneness. Multiplicity is the veil which conceals Unity. Multiplicity gradually begins to vanish when the seeker begins his search for the cause rather than the effect and to search for the Creator rather than what has been created. The seeker comes to the point where he does not see any duality or multiplicity and witnesses nothing but the One Ultimate Reality, the effulgent Truth. This condition is attained when Oneness cloaks all forms of multiplicity within its own light. At this stage the journey is from the creation to the Truth, from multiplicity to

6. TRANSFORMED BEINGS

Oneness.

After arrival at the realm of Oneness and the vanishing of multiplicity, and after discerning the True Essence within the Names, Attributes and works from one level to the next, one is said to have completed the Second Journey, 'in Truth, by Truth'. Concerning this Mulla Sadra has said:

~ The words 'in Truth' refer to the journey within the Attributes of Allah, His Names and His special traits.
'By Truth' refers to when the seeker has realized the true essence of Truth and has removed any sense of 'Iness' from himself and likewise the illusion of all multiplicity. It is then that he realizes the essence of Allah, His Names and His Attributes.

The Second Journey is the traversing of the Spiritual realms where one witnesses the Sublime Beauty of Oneness within its manifestations in the universe. Here the heart of the seeker is opened and made aware of Oneness within multiplicity and multiplicity within Oneness. He then stands between the two stations in that he has joined the two opposites. Thus, he is qualified to give guidance to sincere seekers.

The Third Journey is from Truth towards the creation 'by means of the truth'. This is called the Station of Refinement of Behavior (*sulūk*). It is the station of witnessing the Realms of Power (*jabarūt*), the Spiritual Realms (*malakūt*), and the Material Realm (*nāsūt* or *mulk*), and illumination by way of the knowledges from the Essence, from the Attributes and from actions.

The Fourth Journey is 'by Truth' within the Creation. This is the highest, most subtle, most complete, and most perfect of the stages discussed. The Master is himself veiled by the multiplicity of creation while he is simultaneously immersed within Oneness.

The four stages resemble the ritual of pilgrimage in Islam: the first, going towards the cave – `Arafah; the second, being in `Arafah with Truth, by Truth; the third, returning, testing one's *sulūk* by sacrifice; and the fourth, returning to creation.

The prayer of Shaykh `Abd alSalam Ibn alMashish (d.1227 CE), the well-known North African gnostic, is an example of a prayer made by a Master who has reached the highest stage:

> ~ O Allah! Let me be immersed within the Sea of Oneness, deliver me from the mires of *tawhīd*, and drown me in the sea of Unity until I see nothing, hear nothing, perceive nothing, feel nothing, except through it. Make the Greatest Veil of my soul and its spirit the secret of my reality and its reality the sum total of my existence, by way of the confirmation of the Primal Truth.

The Master alSabziwari has discussed the journey to Allah and added that the journey consists of focusing and directing the heart to Divine Reality.[44] The four journeys he mentions are: The first journey is 'to Allah' from the regions of the self, until one arrives at the clear horizons, which are the furthest extremity of the station of the Heart and the beginning of the heavenly manifestations. The second is the journey 'in Allah' by merging with His Attributes and realizing His Names, then travelling to the 'loftiest horizons'[45] and the furthermost extreme of Unified Oneness (*Wahdāniyah*). The third journey is the progression onward to pure gatheredness and Absolute Oneness

---

44   In the book *Sayr wa Sulūk*, compiled by Sayyid Mahdi Bahr al-`Ulum.

45   [53:7].

6. TRANSFORMED BEINGS

(*alHadrah alWahdāniyah*). This is the station of 'two bows' length',[46] as long as duality continues to exist. When it is lifted it then becomes the station of 'or closer',[47] which is the furthermost extreme of the station of nearness. The fourth is the Journey 'by God', the station of eternity (*baqā'*) which occurs after annihilation (*fanā'*) and is the differentiation after unification.

It is inevitable that at times the sincere seeker will experience states in which the meanings behind these journeys will be reflected to him and he will perceive them inwardly. However, a state (*ḥāl*) or a momentary spiritual illumination (*ishrāq*) is different from a station (*maqām*), the latter being when the seeker is firmly established within this condition and is thus able to remain steadfast on the Path of the Return to the Divine Essence from whence he originally came.

---

46   [53:9].
47   ibid.

6.5 No one but ONE

In countless ways the Universe and all of creation praises Allah – the incomparable One. The Divine qualities, Names or Attributes are like a web or fields of energy that permeate creation and give every entity a sense of direction, which fills in the gap between birth and death. Human beings love and adore (worship) God through all of His glorious qualities and countless Attributes, and relate to each other at the highest level. The seven key Attributes which contain all the others are: life, ability, will, knowledge, seeing, hearing and communicating. At the point of Oneness, it is love that fuses them all and that is how we experience the meeting of diverse entities or opposites in unity. He is the One, the Real, who is self-sustaining and envelops the whole universe, which is encompassed within the limitations of space and time.

Adam descended from the realm of perfect boundlessness in order to rise again and return to that state of eternal paradise. From that One cosmic source emerged multitudes of qualities and Attributes that are like fields of energy that envelop conscious creations. God's sacred, unifying light permeates all that is known and unknown and appears at numerous levels of diffusions and fusions. The human soul has had exposure to and knowledge of the original light and is, therefore, sacred. To kill one person unjustly is like murdering all people, while to bring life to one person is like giving life to all humanity.

All human souls are created with the same potential. Once the lower self is harnessed, then the person is far from the confusion of 'otherness' and is secure in 'Oneness'. God's supreme consciousness and light overflows into multitudes of channels that manifest as energies, matter and physical entities – all of which carry the memory of

6. TRANSFORMED BEINGS

the original state of unity, and yearn for it.

The ultimate spiritual experience is to resonate with Allah's supreme light through God consciousness – the station to which we all aspire. That is where bliss and joy are constant.

CONCLUSION

We have dwelt on some of the meanings and reasons behind various acts of worship and their significance with regard to the state of the seeker and his spiritual station. In this conclusion we shall present a brief description of the benefits of correct worship according to Islam. We will also relate some of the qualities and the state of the gnostic Master as an example to follow.

The most important foundation of Islam is Allah's Unity. Knowledge of this is not perfected except by the knowledge of Him, which in turn is not perfected without complete adherence to the Prophetic way of life and Islam. Allah says the following concerning this:

> ✧ ...and whoever wants other than Islam[48] as a way of life, it will never be accepted from him. [3:85]

> ✧ So set your face sincerely to the upright [Islamic] way of life, the nature of Allah by which He has made men. There is no altering of Allah's creation, that is the right way of life, but the majority of the people do not know. [30:30]

Contained within this verse is the path and prescription for human awakening. The Arabic word for 'nature', i.e. innate nature (*fitrah*), comes from the word '*fatara*' which means 'to bring forth or to crack (open)'. As a luminary once said, the meaning of *fitrah* relates to the action of

---

48   i.e., submission to the Reality.

bringing forth⁴⁹⁴³. Thus human *fitrah* is based on bringing about the discovery of *Haqq*, the Truth.

It is noteworthy that all human endeavors on earth are directed towards bridging space and time. We love immortality or whatever is eternal. We also are driven to discover whatever space there is in the universe. It is as though at the beginning of creation there was only absolute consciousness and oneness, and then the crack of creation occurred, and then the rise of humanity, which is constantly motivated to return to that original singularity. It can be viewed as a consequence of *fitrah*.

Man's knowledge of his self (i.e. his soul) is the means by which he completes his return to his true nature, which is from the realm of Allah's command, and will; as Allah says:

✪ ...say the soul is from the command of my Lord... [17:85]

As for the knowledge of man concerning his own direction, this refers to that which man faces outwardly, which is the Ka`bah:

✪ Set your face in the direction of the Sacred Precinct (*Masjid alHarām*). [2:144]

With his body man faces the body of the Ka`bah, while with his heart man faces the Creator of all bodies and the universe, with which He surrounds and envelops them.

As for the *Dīn* of Islam, Imam `Ali has said:

~ The first and foremost of the *Dīn* is the knowledge of Allah...

---

49   ⁴³Ayatullah Mirza Muhammad `Ali Shahabadi (d.1949 CE/ 1369 AH) in his book *Rashahāt al-Bihār* ('Droplets from the Oceans').

CONCLUSION

Allah is not accessible by human senses, mind or imagination. Those who seek to know Allah by the power of the senses are like those who seek to look at the sphere of the sun in the darkness of the night by starlight. As for the Gnostics, they see the 'suns of truth' by way of its own light, as the Prophet said:

~ I have known my Lord by way of my Lord.

Concerning this one of the Masters has said:

~ Not everyone who travels [the Path] arrives, not everyone who arrives attains, and not everyone who has attained is joined [with his Beloved].

Imam `Ali has said:

~ Allah has prepared for His *Awliyā'* a nectar which if they imbibe of it they become intoxicated, and if they become intoxicated they become transported with joy. If they become transported with joy they are exceedingly pleased. When they become pleased they dissolve. When they dissolve they are purified. When they become pure they ask. When they ask they find. When they find they arrive. When they arrive they are connected. When they are connected there is no distance between them and their Beloved.

This state is described by the Sufis as the Station of Annihilation in Allah (*fanā' fi'Llāh*). It is the annihilation of the knower into the Known, of the lover into the Beloved, of the witnesser into the Witnessed, of the transitory into the permanent. It is this which obliterates 'otherness' and duality, and removes the 'Iness' which is an obstacle and veil in experiencing eternal Beingness. This annihilation is transcendence in spiritual knowledge (*`irfān*), as the

Prophets and Masters have been annihilated in it and have remained eternally within it. Their bodies existed within the material world while their souls have acknowledged in the eternal Truth. The Prophet has said:

> ~ People are asleep and when they die they awaken.

If the seeker attains this annihilation and his ongoing existence by Allah, his essence within His Essence, his Attributes within His Attributes, and witnesses the truth by way of the Truth, then he will know the meaning of the verse:

> ☼ Everything perishes but His Face. [28:88]

At that time he will know the transformative meaning of the divine truth that it is only Allah who is before, after, and within all creational realities.

The basic purpose of religion and acts of worship is to refine the *nafs*, and transform it to be in harmony with Truth. In the tradition of the Night Ascent, it is reported that the Prophet asked Allah: O Lord, what is the first worship? Allah replied: Fasting. Then He said: Do you know, Ahmad, what the legacy of fasting is? The Prophet replied: No, O Lord. Then Allah said:

> ~ The legacy of fasting is eating little and speaking little. And the second worship is silence. Silence will bring about wisdom, wisdom will bring about knowledge, knowledge will cause certainty and if the slave finds certainty he will be unconcerned with whether or not he awakens in the morning in difficulty or ease. This is the station of contentment. Whoever acts to please Me I will bestow upon him three characteristics: I will make him know gratitude which is not mixed with ignorance, and remembrance

which is not mixed with forgetfulness, and a love which is higher than the love for all creation.

In another part of this same *hadith qudsi,* Allah says:

~ ...and if he loves Me I will cause him to be beloved to My creation, and I will open the eye of his heart to My Glory and Might, and the knowledge of the Elect of My creation will not be concealed from him, and I will be his close Companion in the darkness of the night and in the daylight so that he will discontinue his connection with the creation and keeping company with them. I will cause him to hear My word and the words of My angels and I will make him know My secret which I have concealed from My creation.

As for the state of Unity of the enlightened Masters and their *tawhīd,* we hear different descriptions of its outward manifestations and qualities. This diversity gives rise to some suspicion and doubt among the general public when they discuss the virtues of enlightened Masters. The reason for some of these differences may be traced to the general rule that there exists great expansiveness in Allah's Beauty and Majesty; if it were repeated it would be restricted and defined. Concerning this it has been said that:

~ Something does not bear a fruit which is exactly the same as itself. Fruits are not exactly the same in every way. If this were so, then existence itself would have manifested in one type and format over and over again. This is impossible because it would be useless and devoid of benefit and meaning. It would be foolish and Allah, the Real Doer and Actor, is far exalted above that.

In the same vein it has been said that Allah does not manifest Himself to two people in the same way twice. Concerning this the great sage Sabzivari has said:

~ There is no repetition in His manifestations because each manifestation is new.

As it says in the Qur'an:

✿ ...In every 'instant' He is engaged in regulating a different affair. [55:29]

The subject of spiritual knowledge, then, is closely connected to certainty. It is when the relative leads to the absolute. Some have described the 'Knowledge of Certainty' as similar to knowing that there is a fire somewhere in a forest, while the term 'the Source (eye) of Certainty' is like having actually seen that fire directly. The 'Truth of Certainty' is when you face that fire and experience it with the totality of all your senses and being. The state of the Truth of Certainty is not perfected until the inward eye of insight is opened and the two realms of the seen and the unseen approach each other within the heart. This is the true path of *tawhīd*.

It is related that Imam Zayn al-`Abidin said:

~ The slave [of Allah] has four eyes. Two eyes he uses to observe the affairs of his way of life (*Dīn*) and his world, and two eyes he uses to observe his Hereafter [the Unseen]. Thus, if Allah wants goodness for His servant He opens for him the two eyes in his heart and with them he observes the Unseen.

~ When the Master is cut off from his self and is connected with Truth, he sees every individual possibility as part of the 'original' possibility which

CONCLUSION

is connected with all things decreed, and every individual knowledge as being with His knowledge in which nothing in all of existence is missed or overlooked. He sees every individual volition as being within His will and there is nothing within the entire realm of existence and possibility which is outside of its scope. Everything flows forth from Him, the entirety of existence and its perfection is from Him. [Thus when one reaches this state] Allah becomes the eyes by which he sees, the ears by which he hears, the strength by which he acts, the knowledge by which he comes to know His existence by which he himself was brought into existence, and then the Master at that time, takes on the Divine qualities in truth. ~ Khwajah Nasir alDin atTusi

There are some people who don the garments of the Master and claim to possess spiritual knowledge, or claim to be Sufi Shaykhs and appear to be enlightened because they emulate the outward actions of the Sufi. Such people have not arrived at the desired goal nor have they taken on these rare characteristics and inner qualities. Many of them do not even know the laws of the *shari`ah* or follow them, while they take pride in their clothing, their lineage, and their false claims, even though there might exist among them those who have attained certain stations by way of disciplines. Thus 'spiritualized' egos can cause more damage than simply ignorant human beings.

It is said concerning the state of the Master that he has not arrived until he is unmoved whether he is deprived or receives, whether acknowledged or ignored – he remains the same in censure or praise.

~ The Master does not attain to the station until

> deprivation becomes more beloved to him than receiving, because deprivation represents the right of Allah due to Him by His slave, while receiving represents the right of the slave due to him by Allah. The true lover is the one who places his own wants behind the wants of his Beloved. ~ Shaykh Shibli

Lā ilāha illa'Llāh: there has never been and there is none other than the One. The worldly confusions and distractions are the gifts that drive human beings towards the final solution and unveiling. One cannot deny the veil for it was created by the Master of all Creation, until one is ready for the most blessed shock of infinite light and the knowledge that there is no existence other than the perfect knowledge of being created, designed and sustained by Him. There has never been other than the One, and the infinite varieties and multitudes of creation are permeated by the One for the purpose of acknowledging and worshipping the One, Allah subḥānahu wa ta`ālā.

May we experience and acknowledge His Mercy, Bounty and Perfection in every glance, in light and darkness. May Allah make our Dīn and life in Islam and all the prophetic practices natural and easy for us so that we constantly experience His Oneness. May Allah immerse us in the truth that our existence and all our experiences are only possible because of His Grace, everlasting Light and perfect decrees. May Allah show us His absolute perfection and our constant need and shortcomings so that we seek His glory and celebrate in that state of true submission, acceptance and service, light upon Light, endless joy and bliss – in the perfect present.

Glossary

`Abd:* Servant, slave, worshipper, bondsman, from *`abada, to serve, worship, venerate.

Abna' al-Sabīl: pl. of *ibn al-sabīl,* wayfarer, traveler, literally 'son of the way'.

Ākhirah: The Hereafter, literally, *'what comes last.'*

Akhlāq: Refined conduct.

al-`Ām: The Common People.

Allāhu Akbar: 'Allah is Most Great.' A phrase known as the *takbīr,* or magnification.

`Ālim: Learned, knowledgeable; a scholar.

Anbiyā': Prophets, pl. of *nabiy,* from *nabba'ā,* to give or bring tidings, inform, advise, reveal.

`Aql:* Faculty of intellectual perception, from *`aqala, to realize, understand.

`Ārif:* One who has mastery over his self and has been given knowledge of Allah; from *`arafa, to recognize, perceive, discover.

Arkān: pl. of *rukn.* Cornerstones or fundamental principles, as applied in the practice of acts of worship, without which the action is invalidated.

Awliyā': pl. of *wali.* The Friends of Allah; those who follow the Messengers with insight and clarity from their Lord.

`Awrah: Nakedness and therefore shame.

Āyāt: pl. of *ayah*, literally sign; commonly refer to the 'verses' of the Qur'an, but also refer to cosmic signs as they also point to the Reality.

Baqā': State of ongoingness after *fanā'*, the station of eternity, from *baqiya* to remain, continue (in a state). Divine Name: *al-Bāqi*.

Barzakh: Interspace; a zone between the seen and unseen; and between physical death and resurrection on the Day of Judgment.

Basirah: Insight, inner vision; from *basura*, to look, understand, perceive.

Bulūgh: Maturity, of age: a condition for when fulfillment of prescribed acts of worship become obligatory upon a person.

Dhawq: Taste or tasting, specifically of spiritual experience of inner transcendent realities.

Dhikr: Remembrance or invocation of Allah.

Dīn: The life-transaction of Islam; from *dana*, to owe or be indebted to. Thus translated the term reflects the all-encompassing path of Islam.

Du`ā': Supplicatory prayer, calling on Allah; as distinct from the prescribed prayer of worship (*salāt*).

Fadl: Favor, blessing, not in the sense of preference but of the sheer bestowal of grace.

Fard Obligatory.

Fanā': Annihilation or extinction of the self. *Fanā' fi'l dhāt*: annihilation in the Essence.

Faqr: Poverty; the state of knowing one is utterly 'poor', i.e. without means, and in need of Allah; hence *faqīr*, someone who has declared himself committed to the path of total

GLOSSARY

dependence upon Allah and therefore of enlightenment.

Faqih: One adept in *fiqh* (qv), the science of prophetically revealed principles and laws governing appropriate and desirable behavior in all spheres of life; a judicial specialist.

Fiqh: Jurisprudence, the science of deriving laws in keeping with the essence of Islam, from *faqiha*, to comprehend or have knowledge of something.

Fitrah: Original nature of man, deeply imprinted within him, from *fatara*, to split or cleave, break apart (hence *futūr*, fastbreaking), to bring into being.

Furu': Branches, specifically of applied Islamic practices.

Ghusl: Major ritual ablution, which involves bathing the whole body with the intention of making it pure.

Hadith: Tradition from the Prophet, from *haddatha*, to relate or report and *hadatha*, to happen or to occur.

Hadith qudsi: Sacred Tradition, i.e. from Allah via the tongue of the Prophet.

Hadrah: The Presence of Allah.

alHadrah alWahdāniyah: Absolute Oneness.

Hakīm: Wise. See *hukama'*.

Hāl: State, passing in nature.

Halāl: Permissible, allowed.

Harām: Forbidden. *Haram* is a sanctuary or precinct designated as inviolate and sacred.

Haqiqah: Truth, inner *reality*.

Hawa: Worldly desires.

Himmah: Determination and spiritual commitment.

al-Hukamā': The wise ones, endowed with knowledge,

insight and guided judgment (pl. of *hakīm*).

'Ibādah: Worship and of Allah and acts of devotion dedicated to Him, from *`abbada*, to worship, adore.

Ihrām: The state of ritual consecration taken on for the duration of the Greater Pilgrimage (*hajj*), symbolized by the wearing of two unstitched pieces of white cloth and other conditions. The *muhrim* is the person in the state of consecration.

Ihsān: Inner and outer excellence in thought and conduct in which one automatically acts in the knowledge that although we do not see Allah, one has absolute certainty that Allah sees us. From *ahsana*, to do right, act well, do good, be proficient, derived from *hasuna* to be beautiful, good, fine, fitting. Also translated as perfection.

Ijtihād: Arriving at legal decisions through reasoning based on Qur'anic injunctions and Prophetic precedents.

Ilhām: Inspiration as opposed to revelation.

Imāmah: Leadership, successorship; *Imām*: he who stands at the fore.

Imān: Faith based on knowledge. It is not blind belief.

Insān: Man, mankind.

'Irfān: Inner knowledge or gnosis – the same as *mā`rifah*.

'Ishā: Evening, hence evening prayer.

Ishrāq: Spiritual illumination that occurs in momentary flashes.

Islām: Submission; from *aslama*, to surrender one's will to that of Allah.

Jabarūt: The Realm of Absolute Power. (See *Mulk, Malakūt* and *Lāhūt*).

GLOSSARY

Jalāl: Majesty or glory; one of Allah's Divine Attributes *al-Jalāl*.

Jalsah: The seated position during prayer; a sitting.

Jamāl: Beauty; one of Allah's Divine Attributes *al-Jamāl*.

Janābah: Literally meaning 'remoteness', i.e., from a purified state. The state of ritual impurity following sexual intercourse, which is removed by *ghusl*.

Jihād: Struggling or striving for the sake of Allah; from *jahuda* to exert one's utmost.

Jizyah: A tribute or tax levied on non-Muslims who fell under Islamicate rule, in lieu of protection and military duty.

Kayfiyyah: Methodology; how to go about something as prescribed.

Khalifah: Steward or Vice-gerent of Allah.

Khalwah: Emptying out, or solitary vigil, usually practiced for the sake of opening the inner eye and awakening unto Reality.

al-Khās: The Elect.

al-Khās al-khawās: The Chosen of the Elect

Kufr: Rejection, denial, or covering up of the One and Only Reality. *Kāfir:* rejecter or denier of Reality.

Lāhut: The Realm of Pure Unity.

al-Lawh al-mahfūz: The Preserved Tablet, or the firmly protected knowledge in the unseen of everything in creation, past, present and future.

Ma`ād:* (or *mi`ād) The Return to our Source, from `*ada*, to return.

Madhhab: School of law (pl. *madhāhib*).

Maghrib: Sunset (literally the place where the sun sets).

Makrūhāt: Reprehensible actions, but not forbidden.

Malakūt: The Realm of the Angels or Angelic Forces and Archetypes.

Mandubāt: Non-obligatory actions, but authorized.

Maqām: Station, as opposed to state (*ḥāl*). A 'permanent' condition or level of attainment.

Ma`rifah: Gnosis, knowledge of Allah, spiritual knowledge, esoteric science.

Marwa: One of the stations between which the pilgrim hastens, symbolizing Majesty.

Mi`rāj: Night Ascension, or Night Journey, specifically of the Prophet, but symbolically and potentially of every worshipper who prays sincerely ('The prayer of the believer is his Night Ascension' – The Prophet).

Miskīn: pl. *masākīn* Destitute, not purely literally but metaphorically, so they are utterly humble before Allah.

Miswāk: Toothbrush made from a twig of the Arak tree (Salvadora Persica), the regular use of which was the practice of the Prophet for its hygienic properties.

Muharramāt: Forbidden actions.

Mulk: The Material Realm.

Mujtahid: One adept in *ijtihād*, the application of independent reasoning to arrive at new legal rulings, but derived from a grounding in the other sources of law, namely, the Qur'an, the Hadith, and *ijmā`* or consensus.

Murshid: A guide on the Path of Allah.

Mushrik: An idolater, someone who associates partners with God (see *shirk*).

GLOSSARY

Muttaqi: One who possesses the quality of *taqwā*, which is, cautious, even fearful awareness of Allah that inhibits one from wrong actions and hastens one to good deeds.

Nabiy: Prophet. One charged with delivering tidings or news (*naba'*).

alNafs alammārah: The lower self which commands to evil. It is the lowest aspect of the human ego, but above the vegetal, mineral and animal.

al-Nafs al-kāmilah: The perfected self.

al-Nafs al-lawwāmah: The critical or reproachful self.

al-Nafs al-mardiyah: The self that is pleasing to Allah. At this level self and soul are in alignment.

al-Nafs al-mulhamah: The inspired self.

al-Nafs al-mutma'innah: The reconciled or tranquil self.

al-Nafs al-rādiyah: The contented self.

Najis: Ritually impure.

Nāsūt: Another name for *Mulk* or the Material Realm.

Nawāfil: Supererogatory acts of devotion, namely prayer.

Niyyah: Intention; the essential and first part of any act of worship or, indeed, undertaking.

Nubuwwah: Prophethood.

Nūr: Light.

Qiblah: The direction of Ka`bah, symbolizing orientation to the Presence of God.

Qiyām: The standing position during prayer.

Rahmān: Merciful, a divine and key Attribute of Allah.

Rak`ah:* Cycle of prayer, which comprises standing, bowing, and prostrating twice; pl. *rak`āt.

Rasūl: Messenger; entrusted with delivering a message from the Divine.

Riyā': Self-admiration, especially in the performance of pious acts for the sake of being seen and admired.

Risālah: Messengerhood; message; epistle, treatise.

Rubūbiyyah: Lordship, the function of the *Rabb*, which is to raise each `abd to attain his true potential.

Rukū`: The bowing position during prayer.

Rusul: Messengers, pl. of *Rasūl*.

Safa: One of the two stations between which the pilgrim hastens, symbolizing Beauty.

Sajdah: The prostration of prayer in which one's self is obliterated in the glorification of Allah.

Salām: Greeting of peace.

Salāt: Prayer; the Islamically prescribed form of prayer.

Sawm: Fasting.

Sa`y: The hastening between the two stations of *Safa* and *Marwa* during *hajj*, commemorating Hagar's search for water for her infant son, and symbolizing running after worldly sustenance.

Shahādah: Testimony of faith; literally witnessing that there is no god but Allah and that Muhammad is His Messenger.

Shari`ah: Divinely revealed code of conduct, as bestowed upon the Prophet Muhammad (S).

Shirk: Seeing other than Allah or associating others with Allah. Hence often translated as idolatry. From *sharika*, to ascribe partners.

Silsilah: Chain of transmission with reference to Sufi brotherhoods.

GLOSSARY

Sirāt: The bridge leading from death on the final day of judgment to the Garden, said to be finer than a hair's width, from which, if one falls, one descends into the abyss of Hellfire.

Sulūk: The refined behavior expected from the committed wayfarer on the path of enlightenment.

Sunnah: Custom or life pattern, usually in reference to the Prophet Muhammad (S), but also in reference to Allah (cf. 33:62).

Tahārah: Ritual purity, from *tahura* to be pure, clean.

Tāhir: Ritually pure.

Tahūr: Purifying; having the capacity to purify.

Takbīr: Magnification of Allah by saying *Allāhu Akbar* 'God is Most Great'. At the beginning of the *salāt* it is known as the *Takbīr al-Ihrām*, or the *takbīr* of Prevention, for by its utterance one enters into the sacred communion of prayer.

Talbiyah: The formulaic call to Allah invoked while undertaking the rituals of Hajj. 'At your service O Allah, At your service!'

Tanzih: Affirming Allah's transcendence of humanity; declaring Him pure and free of otherness.

Taqlīd: Following a *mujtahid*'s guidance in matters of law. From *qallada*: to emulate, follow.

Taqwā: Fearful or cautious awareness; God consciousness.

Tarbiyah: Grooming, raising; the process by which a child is brought up to realize his inner potential as `abd Allāh.

Tariqah: Path, literally 'way', of the committed seeker of enlightenment. A term also used in Sufi brotherhoods.

Tasbih: Glorification of Allah, from *sabbaha*, to glorify, to extol. Hence, it is the name given to the Muslim 'rosary' (also known as a *sibhah*).

Tashahhud: Witnessing or testimonial of faith: i.e. There is no god but Allah and Muhammad is His Messenger.

Tawāf: Walking around, specifically of the Ka'bah during the rituals of lesser or greater pilgrimage. Also referred to symbolically.

Tawbah: Repentance, literally turning to Allah.

Tawhīd: Unity, the Oneness of Allah.

Tayammum: Dry ritual ablution with clean earth or stone, in the absence of water.

`Ubūdiyyah: state of conscious slave-hood to and worship of Allah.

Ulūhiyyah: Divinity; from *ilah*, God;

Usūl: Roots, foundations, or tenets of belief.

*Al-`Ulamā':* The learned, pl. of `*ālim*.

Wahdāniyah: Unified Oneness.

Wahy: Revelation; divine in origin.

Wājibāt: Obligatory actions.

Waswās: Whisperings of Shaytan.

Wilāyah: 'Friendship' with God, the state of being fully awakened to higher consciousness; hence, *wali*, an enlightened, awakened, saint.

Wudu': Ritual ablution involving washing the face, forearms and feet to consecrate the self before prayer. The Prophet advocated maintaining a constant state of *wudu'*.

Wuqūf: Literally the standing on the plain of `Arafat, the pivotal and seminal act of *Hajj*.

Yaqīn: Certainty.

GLOSSARY

Zakāt: Tax due as one of the essential acts of faith; from *zakiya* to purify.

Zuhd: Abstention, frugality, or doing without.

Bibliography

- al-`Alawi, Shaykh Ahmad, *Al-Manh al-Quddusiyyah* (The Sacred Bestowal).
- al-`Amili al-Shahid al-Thani, Shaykh Zayn al-Din ibn Ahmad ibn `Ali ibn al-Juba'i, *Asrār al-`Ibādah* (The Secrets of Worship).
- *Asrār al-Salāh* (The Secrets of Prayer).
- al-`Amuli, Shaykh Haydar, *Asrār alSharī`ah wa Atwar alTariqah wa Anwar alHaqiqah* (The Secrets of the Shari`ah, the Stages of Tariqah and the Illuminations of Haqiqah).
- Ansari, Khwajah `Abdullah, *Tafsir alQur'an alMajid* (Commentary of the Qur'an).
- *Manazil alSa'irin* (Stations of the Wayfarers).
- ibn `Arabi al-Hatimi, Shaykh Muhyi al-Din ibn `Abdallah, *Al-Fusus al-Hikam.* (The Bezels of Wisdom).
- al-Futuhat al-Makkiyah (The Makkan Revelations).
- `Asi, Dr. Hasan (compiler) *Tafsir Qur'ani fi Falsafah Ibn Sina,*. University Foundation for Research and Publication, Beyrouth 1983.
- Ibn `Ata'Allah al-Iskandari, Shaykh, *al-Hikam* (The Wisdom).
- Bahr al-`Ulum, Sayyid Muhammad, *Risalāt alSayr wa alSuluk*, (Treatise on the Journey and Behavior).

BIBLIOGRAPHY

- al-Farabi, Abu Nasr Muhammad ibn Muhammad, *al-Mabda' wa al-Mi`ad* (The Beginning and the Return).
- al-Harawi, Shaykh Abu Isma`il, *Manazil al-Sa`irin* (The Stations of the Wayfarers).
- al-Naraqi, Shaykh Muhammad Mahdi, *Jami` al-Sa`adat* (The Compendium of Joys).
- Nasr, Sayyid Hossein, *Al Serat*, Vol IX, No. 1, The Spiritual Significance of Jihad.
- al-Qummi, Sayyid Sa`id, *Asrar al-`Ibadat wa Haqiqat al-Salāt* (The Secrets of Worship and the Reality of Prayer).
- al-Razi, Abu `Ali Ahmad bin Muhammad bin Ya`qub Ibn Miskawayh, *Tahdhib al-Akhlaq wa Ta'thir al-A`raq*.
- Sabzivari, Mulla Hadi, *Hidayat alTalibin* (Guidance of the Seekers), published by the Dept. of Religious Endowment (*Awqaf*) of Khurasan.
- al-Sadiq,Imam Ja`far, *Misbah al-Shari`ah* (The Lantern of the Path).
- Shahabadi,Ayatullah Mirza Muhammad `Ali, *Rashahat al-Bihar* (Droplets from the Ocean).
- al-Shirazi, known as Mulla Sadra Sadr al-Din, *AlHikam alMuta`aliyah fi Asfar al-`Aqliyah alArba`ah* (The Four Journeys).
- Tabataba'i, Sayyid Muhammad Husayn, *Al-Mizan fi Tafsir al-Qur'an* (The Balance in the Exegesis of the Qur'an).

www.ingramcontent.com/pod-product-compliance
Lightning Source LLC
Chambersburg PA
CBHW070836160426
43192CB00012B/2204